A Useful Fiction

for Matthew Rhys

PATRICK HANNAN

A Useful Fiction
Adventures in British Democracy

seren

Seren is the book imprint of
Poetry Wales Press Ltd
Nolton Street, Bridgend, Wales
www.seren-books.com

ISBN 978-1-85411-495-2

A CIP record for this title is available from
the British Library

The publisher works with the financial assistance
of the Welsh Books Council

Cover design: Andy Dark
www.andydark.co.uk

Printed by Bell & Bain Ltd, Glasgow

Contents

Acknowledgements

In the course of researching and writing this book many people have been very generous with their time in helping me attempt to unravel the nature of Britain and contemporary Britishness in a rapidly changing political landscape. There is no correlation between the illumination they offered and the number of times they are mentioned in the text. Without exception I learned a great deal from them and I hope their wisdom and expertise is properly reflected in the book. Any number of times, finding me wandering in a fog of incomprehension, they pointed me in the right direction. In all cases they did so for nothing more rewarding than a cup of tea and, quite often, even provided the tea themselves. Those I would particularly like to thank are John Curtice, Mark Douglas-Home, Brian Feeney, Bob Franklin, Peter Hain, Phil Harding, Robert Hazell, Neil Kinnock, Pat Loughrey, Paul Murphy, John McCormick, Alan Taylor and Brian Taylor.

The peerless and indispensable Penny Fishlock once again purged the text of innumerable errors of fact, style, grammar, spelling and punctuation. As always I was in awe of her rigour in dealing with the written word. Any mistakes and idiocies that remain are entirely my own.

My wife, Menna, has somehow found the time to read the work in progress and provide both encouragement and analysis. She has also been extremely tolerant of the fact that a lot of writing takes place, not at a desk, but when the preoccupied author is supposedly engaged in some other activity, conversation for example, so that daily life becomes littered with incomplete thoughts and unfinished sentences. She knows a great deal about the territory I have tried to cover and my work has been much improved by her insight. Not only would this have been a much poorer book without her, there might not have been a book at all.

Introduction

WHEN IT COMES TO BEING British everyone is an outsider. Now more than ever. There's always been an uneasy relationship between the component parts of the United Kingdom, a political construction that over the centuries has been adjusted to meet the needs of changing times. Rivalries have persisted within its walls when you might have expected them to have been erased simply by the passing of the centuries during which we've all lived in the same house, even if not all the original occupants are still in residence. But to think that is to fail to understand the tensions of cohabitation. The Scots, the Welsh and the Irish have maintained their sense of otherness in particular, perhaps, because of the sheer weight of the English numbers ranged against them, Englishness being a form of national identity which until recently lacked much by way of a sense of self doubt. Power was overwhelmingly concentrated in England, most of the population lived there, most important decisions were made in London and so British and English inevitably became interchangeable adjectives.

That state of affairs has been overturned, and it's happened during what has been, in historical terms, a matter of a moment or two. When Britain joined the European Union (then called the Common Market) in 1973 it meant removing one of the foundation stones that had until then defined Britishness: there was no longer a sovereign parliament at Westminster that exercised total authority over the people of Great Britain and Northern Ireland. That was the first and most important change in the nature of the United Kingdom, the biggest shift of power, you can argue, in its entire history. In due course that gave added weight to another argument over the exercise of authority. If parliamentary sovereignty could be transferred outside the country in this manner, why couldn't the same thing be done within Britain itself?

Not much more than a quarter of a century later it happened, in fact if not in theory, with the establishment of administrations in Edinburgh and Cardiff and, eventually, the restoration of devolution in Northern Ireland. These two matters, we can see now, were not independent of each other, but two parts of a single process by which power has been relocated both outside the borders of the UK and within them. What the final consequences will be is impossible to say but it's difficult to believe we have reached the end of that particular road. One change begets another and the distinctive political character that's emerged in the devolved countries, no one-party dominance for example, may eventually be reflected at Westminster where the key question of devising some kind of parliament for England remains unresolved. It seems to me that the group least alert to the nature of the governmental revolution that's taking place are the great British majority, the English people themselves.

That is one of the themes I explore in this book, the kind of changes that are indeed altering the nature of Britishness, but not, as some traditionalists fear, eliminating it. It's easy enough to see what's going on and to understand that a rearrangement of systems and relationships within the UK and within Europe does not necessarily mean the whole enterprise is doomed to collapse. Independence, a live issue in Scotland, is only one of a number of possible destinations, as is home rule for England.

What is more difficult to establish is what it means to be British, to discover the common values and institutions that join British people to each other and separate them from the rest of the world. Some people reject the term itself. In Scotland, for example, four out of five describe themselves as Scottish rather than British. Experts declare that in Scotland Britishness is dead. Sinn Fein politicians, although in government with Unionists in Northern Ireland, refuse to take their seats in a British parliament and resent the continued presence of British troops. In Northern Ireland you now have an official choice of being British or Irish or both. There are plenty of people in Wales, not all of them nationalists, who admit the bureaucratic imposition of a British nationality but will not agree that the description applies to them in any other sense. If you ask politicians what characterises Britishness you're likely to get a sermon on tolerance and a sense of fair play, almost invariably virtues we ascribe to ourselves rather than collect from dispassionate observers.

Politically Britain is becoming increasingly diverse, with the authority of the Westminster parliament diluted and diminished both by a rearrangement of power inside and outside the country and by a growing suspicion of the public service credentials of an increasingly professionalised political class. Many elected representatives are seen by their constituents as a species of middle manager on the make; some of them deserve to be viewed thus.

The Royal Family remains what it has long been: a bulwark of discrimination and privilege set against the modern world. The Queen's resolute silence (with one or two uncharacteristic lapses) over more than half a century has probably saved the monarchy itself from serious damage. Now that we know so much about her heirs and successors it's at least questionable whether the whole circus can long survive her death, at least in its present form. Prince Charles, the mystical environmentalist who drives an Aston Martin, might yet have to get on his bike, like his cousins on the European mainland.

Religion, which has divided Britain and provided the occasion for much violence for well over five hundred years, now largely unites the country in communal indifference combined with hostility to people, particularly those who are identifiably foreign, who profess a faith of some kind.

Even finding out what sort of place Britain is and what kind of people live in it becomes increasingly difficult as what are known as the national media, in a carefully judged mix of real life and fiction, devote most of their space to cataloguing the activities of the establishment figures, celebrities and *bêtes noires* milling around in their own back yard. As far as they are concerned non-metropolitan activity takes place for the most part in another country. Meanwhile the people who live in that country have fewer ways of discovering about their own lives as the local and national press faces collapse and regional broadcasting, in particular on ITV which was established specifically to serve the differing communities of Britain, fades away like the white dot on an old television set.

The result is that in some places a form of identity that can be more readily understood, a team to cheer for, gets picked out of the uncertainties of Britishness and in the process Britain itself becomes different. That is what's happened in the establishment of elected governments of different kinds in Scotland, Wales and Northern Ireland. One inevitable consequence is a culture of dispute between the politicians of those countries and those in Westminster, something that will become an increasingly significant element in British public life. One reason for that is that even those who originally thought devolution was a terrible idea can't now ignore its reality and so have become part of the process of reinforcing it. Those who were enthusiasts all along want to take it further. Occasionally someone says those new institutions should' be abolished but no one seriously believes such an offer would now find many takers. It would be seen simply as an insult.

I've followed the constitutional adventures of the various countries of the United Kingdom since the nineteen-seventies and I've been astonished by the speed at which the landscape has changed. During those years I've reported on these matters as they have affected Wales in particular, where I was for a long time convinced that a sceptical public would never buy the devolution idea. In 1997 I was in fact within a few thousand referendum votes of being right, but soon enough the waters closed over the arguments that had divided the country almost exactly in half. Now the debate is not about whether you should have a devolved political system but how you should run it. It is in such ways that Britain springs surprises on us all. And because one constitutional answer inevitably raises further questions, it will certainly do so again.

Put Out More Flags

IF YOU WANT TO FIND OUT what Britishness is there are some obvious places to go for an answer. Top of the list, perhaps, is the British Council, the United Kingdom's leading cultural messenger abroad. If they don't know, who does? And who better to consult there than the chairman, Neil Kinnock, a man who over many years has been on a long journey around questions of national identity within Britain and outside it; forty years of travelling from denim-clad, red-haired, endlessly loquacious, Welsh scourge of the establishment to an unexpected terminus as the neatly-suited, bald-headed, ex-Eurocrat, the Rt. Hon. Lord Kinnock of Bedwellty. So I went to the council's offices in a street which, on the borders of the Mall, Whitehall and Trafalgar Square, is at what is more or less the centre of gravity of establishment Britain. In Kinnock's office on the sixth floor you felt you could almost lean out and touch the Houses of Parliament.

As we drank tea I asked him: "What does the British Council say Britishness is?"

His answer was unexpectedly succinct: "It never does."

I suppose it might have done so once, though, particularly three quarters of a century ago when it was founded and Britain, at the centre of a vast empire, could boast as much as it liked about its cultural superiority. Now we have to be much more tentative; self-deprecation is the national trait that's been cultivated most assiduously as power has given way to influence. We know we're good but pretend we're not as we put our cultural cards face up on the table and allow others to play the hand for us. In the modern world you have to tread very carefully when you are discussing national virtues, marketing them, really. A little earlier a senior official had talked to me about what he called the British brand and, I assume thinking of Iraq, the danger of it being devalued.

That was reflected in what Kinnock said next. "I'm trying to get the council to describe in intriguing, evocative terms what it really is, what it stands for, what it seeks to do. There's no better definition than the one that's existed for most of our seventy-odd years, which is to secure greater understanding of the United Kingdom in the world."

And, as a man who's always liked to put a cherry on top of his rhetorical cake, he continued: "You could add, to secure a better understanding of the world in the United Kingdom. But it's in that order. The problem then arises, what is it about the United Kingdom that we want to be better understood in the world? And on a good day we would say, tolerance, accommodation, generosity, creativity, the best words that you can apply to Britain to try and make sure that the reputation abroad for arrogance, calumny, perfidy, are at least offset if not obscured by the genuinely good news."

But that wasn't the answer I was looking for. It was more of a statement of the difficulty of identifying what it is to be British. Tolerance, generosity and creativity are all reassuring words but it's difficult to think of a single country in the world that wouldn't try to lay claim, however unconvincingly, to those great virtues.

"I mean," I suggested, "even Robert Mugabe might say, 'Oh, yes, in Zimbabwe we stand for freedom and tolerance.'"

Kinnock started to laugh and agree and then corrected himself: "No, maybe not Mugabe."

Almost every politician other than Mugabe, though, especially a few hundred yards away in Downing Street. Gordon Brown has nagged away at this question for years and he talks in very similar terms to those employed by Neil Kinnock. Well, wouldn't you have a lot to say about Britishness, people suggest, if you were a Scotsman representing a Scottish constituency, wanting to establish himself as Prime Minister of a United Kingdom remodelled by devolution? But there's more to it than that and one element in Brown's attachment to the virtues of Britishness is the romantic way in which that formidable intellectual states his case.

For example, in his Fabian Society lecture early in 2006 he picked out commitment to liberty, responsibility and fairness. And he quoted, as if it were a clincher, a poll that showed that "as many as ninety per cent of British people thought that fairness or fair play were very important or fairly important in defining Britishness."

But what did he expect people to say when confronted by such a question? That the British believed themselves characterised mainly by self-interest and a hatred of foreigners. As Roy Jenkins once pointed out, a statement isn't worth making if you can't imagine the opposite being said.

At the Labour party conference in the autumn of 2007 Brown was positively fighting-them-on-the beaches Churchillian when he said: "There is no weakness in Britain today that cannot be overcome by the strengths of the British people." Later he added: "We all know that in our society we have problems to solve, real needs to meet but don't let anyone tell us – the British people – that this country of ours, which has over the centuries given so much to the world, has ever been broken by anyone or anything."

He has spoken frequently of a golden thread running through British history from 1215 and Magna Carta to the present day. "Even before America made it its own," he said in that Fabian lecture, "I think Britain can lay claim to the idea of liberty. Out of the necessity of finding a way to live together in a multinational state came the practice of toleration and then of liberty."

Curiously enough, a government publication, *Life in the United Kingdom*, the Home Office's indispensable guide for people seeking to become British citizens, doesn't present Magna Carta in quite such a rosy light. It says: "Nineteenth-century historians and states-men presented it as a charter of liberties for all. But in fact it had little in it for ordinary people, even though centuries later a myth grew up that made it sound like a modern charter of human rights." Thus the guide gives useful if unintentional advice on the need to be wary of British politicians when they bang on about what they claim are the time-honoured principles that have created the great nation that is the United Kingdom today.

Gordon Brown has returned to this central question time and again in big speeches. Among other things he has celebrated Britain's part in ending the slave trade, although without examining the country's enthusiastic participation in it for many years previously. In something of a post-modern, perhaps even supernatural, approach to history Labour politicians have adopted the interesting practice of popping back in time to put right various transgressions. As London marked the anniversary of the abolition of the slave trade, the Mayor of London, Ken Livingstone, wept openly as he recounted the cruelties inflicted on the victims. Tony Blair more or less apologised over the Irish famine. Everybody's at it. Forty years after the event Liverpool Council said sorry to the people of North Wales for the drowning of Capel Celyn in the nineteen-sixties to provide their city with a reservoir, although they did not propose *un*drowning it. In the summer of 2007 a Danish minister went to Dublin to apologise for the Viking invasion of Ireland twelve hundred years previously. I wasn't there myself, the message seems to be, but if I had been I wouldn't have allowed these terrible things to happen. There's no better alibi than to have been born hundreds of years after any event for which you might otherwise be blamed.

But this kind of time travelling could turn out to be more important than misty-eyed politicians realised when they caught those first excursions to the shameful past. It can also be a contemporary weapon. In Scotland, for example, increasing numbers of people maintain that the Act of Union, which in 1707 constitutionally joined that country with England, was in effect a fraud perpetrated on an unwilling and deceived Scottish nation. So it is used to reinforce the argument for independence, an independence which, its supporters say, was dishonestly snatched away. In Ireland the past has been the permanent engine of conflict.

Gordon Brown also stepped back into history for other purposes, in particular to produce evidence of virtuous Britain, according to him the country that more or less invented liberty, tolerance and freedom. So in a speech in October 2007 he felt able to assert: "The commitment in Britain to basic freedoms of worship, assembly, speech and press began to emerge in the sixteenth and seventeenth centuries alongside a rejection of religious persecution."

That account conveniently ignored the fact that the sixteenth and seventeenth centuries were in Britain a period of stupendous religious intolerance. Even Brown had to admit: "This did not happen all at once, or without setbacks and struggle. The flames of religious intolerance burned across this land too. But never as strongly as in continental Europe."

So that's all right then. On mainland Europe, as usual, they were worse than us. That doesn't erase the fact that there is a not-so-golden thread of discrimination and persecution that disfigured Britain for centuries internally and in the various lands that made up the British Empire. After all, Catholic emancipation arrived only in 1829, some time after the abolition of the slave trade. No Jew was allowed to sit in Parliament until 1858. Even today such traditional attitudes remain embedded in the constitution in minor but significant ways.

What we have to remember is that Gordon Brown is a politician, and politics, even more than history, is a matter of argument rather than a process of attempting to establish definitive truths. So his conclusions can be powered as much by string-pulling rhetoric as they are by critical analysis. Once again, for example, there's more than an echo of updated Churchill in this: "I believe that because these islands – and our maritime and trading traditions – have made us remarkably outward-looking and open, this country has fostered a vigorously adaptable society and has given rise to a culture both creative and inventive. But an open and adapting society also needs to be rooted and Britain's roots are on the most solid foundation of all – a passion for liberty anchored in a sense of duty and an intrinsic commitment to tolerance and fair play."

Neil Kinnock also told me he thought Gordon Brown's first major public exploration of this subject had been, as it happened, in the British Council annual lecture he gave in July 2004. And the then Chancellor used forms he was to return to in succeeding years saying, for example, that "…Britain could legitimately make claim to be the first country in the world to reject the arbitrary rule of monarch; that Britain was the first to make a virtue of tolerance and liberty…" and so, you will have noticed, on.

As he was gathering ideas on this theme, Brown asked Kinnock to suggest a few sources he might profitably look at. As you might expect, Kinnock pointed him towards the modest collection of essays that form Aneurin Bevan's only book, *In Place of Fear*, a work by R.H. Tawney, the Christian socialist historian, and an essay by George Orwell, *The Lion and the Unicorn*. Of these only Orwell figured in the completed lecture, and then only in passing, perhaps because, in its mixture of light and shade, it was to some extent in conflict with the bright sunlight of Brown's picture of modern Britain. It was published in 1940 but if you read it now you get a sense of nationality that was confident all right, but which remains particularly persuasive because of its clear-sighted description of the blemishes as well as the strengths in the British character. And perhaps Brown would have been well advised to pay a little more attention to some of its analysis.

For example: "In England all the boasting and flag-wagging, the 'Rule Britannia' stuff is done by small minorities. The patriotism of the common people is not vocal or even conscious. They do not retain among their historical memories the name of a single military victory. English literature, like other literatures, is full of battle-poems, but it is worth noticing that the ones that have won for themselves a kind of popularity are always a tale of disasters and retreats.... The most stirring battle poem in the English language is about a brigade of cavalry which charged in the wrong direction."

Orwell catches exactly the self-deprecation that is such a familiar characteristic of British public postures, even if it might not represent exactly the private thoughts of many British people. And if a sense of superiority is largely unspoken, the inferiority of other nations is often taken for granted, especially, Orwell wrote, by the working class.

"Even when they are obliged to live abroad for years they refuse to accustom themselves to foreign food or to learn foreign languages. Nearly every Englishman of working class origin considers it effeminate to pronounce a foreign word correctly. During the war of 1914-18 the English working class were in contact with foreigners to an extent that is rarely possible. The sole result was that they brought back a hatred of all Europeans, except the Germans, whose courage they admired. In four years on French soil they did not even acquire a liking of wine. The insularity of the English, their refusal to take foreigners seriously, is a folly that has to be paid for very heavily from time to time. But it plays a part in the English mystique and the intellectuals who have tried to break it down have generally done more harm than good."

It is perhaps not difficult to see that passage, and its last sentence in particular, as a message sent across almost seventy years directly into the Downing Street letter box. In twenty-first century Britain, after all, no schoolchild is obliged to study a foreign language beyond the age of fourteen. Many people go abroad simply to seek out a version of their own country set in a warmer climate, at the Dog and Duck in Marbella, perhaps. And in 2001, when he was Foreign Secretary, another clever Scotsman, Robin Cook, began a speech with the words: "Tonight I want to celebrate Britishness." Part of his message was to proclaim that chicken tikka masala was "...a true British national dish.... It is a perfect illustration of the way Britain absorbs and adapts external influences. Chicken tikka is an Indian dish. The masala sauce was added to satisfy the desire of British people to have their meat served in gravy."

As an example of multiculturalism I suppose this kind of thing is harmless enough, especially if you don't mind the tartrazine that often adds an enticing luminosity to the masala sauce. But it remains a depressing example of how something presented as an appreciation of another country's way of doing things turns out instead to be a demonstration of contempt for it. It's only any good if you've poured Britishness all over it, the culinary equivalent of a dollop of common sense. Politicians who say this sort of thing aren't really celebrating the adaptability of the British people but patronising their lack of adventure.

You might accuse Orwell of doing much the same thing, but for all his doubts about the character of the British people – "their world-famous hypocrisy – their double-faced attitude towards empire, for instance..." is one of his strictures – what he clearly admires is the robust common sense of the ordinary man and woman he sometimes describes in terms that might have been written in the contemporary world.

"The liberty of the individual is still believed in, almost as in the nineteenth century. But this has nothing to do with economic liberty, the right to exploit others for profit. It is the liberty to have a home of your own, to do what you like in your spare time, to choose your own amusements instead of having them chosen for you from above. The most hateful of all names in the English ear is Nosey Parker. It is obvious, of course, that even this purely private liberty is a lost cause. Like all other modern people, the English are in the process of being numbered, labelled, conscripted, 'co-ordinated'. But the pull of their impulses is in the other direction, and the kind of regimentation that can be imposed on them will be modified in consequence. No party rallies, no Youth Movements, no coloured shirts, no Jew-baiting or 'spontaneous' demonstrations. No Gestapo either, in all probability."

Did anyone say the war on terrorism? Did anyone mention identity cards? Orwell's words about wartime Britain echo across the decades and the arguments are resumed afresh in uncannily familiar terms, as in his earlier reference to "the flag-wagging, the Rule Britannia stuff". Gordon Brown would specifically like more of this, as he made clear in the 2006 Fabian lecture in which he spoke of the Union Jack: "...the flag should be a symbol of unity, part of a modern expression of patriotism... we should assert that the union flag is, by definition, a flag for tolerance and inclusion." And in his first weeks as Prime Minister he changed the rule that said the union flag could be flown from public buildings only on a small number of days each year. More than that, he was keen that people should adopt the practice of flying it at their own homes.

His model was clear enough. This is what they do in America, a country for which he has great admiration, in particular the way in which the Stars and Stripes is used as a symbol of the drawing together of people of almost endless diversity. In 2006 he asked: "...what is the British equivalent of the US 4th of July, or even the French 14th of July for that matter? What I mean is, what is our equivalent for a national celebration of who we are and what we stand for? And what is our equivalent of the national symbolism of a flag in every garden?"

It's a question that really contains its own answer. If displays of patriotism aren't spontaneous then they are worthless. And you don't have to be George Orwell to recognise that drawing attention to yourself by sticking a Union Jack on a pole outside your house is to invite neighbours to talk of calling in the men in white coats. In the British scheme of things anyone waving a flag is, in general, to be avoided. They can be weapons as much as expressions of national pride, a fact underlined by the menace with which the flag of St. George is flourished by football supporters looking for trouble. In some parts of the United Kingdom the Union Jack is seen as a symbol of English triumphalism. In Northern Ireland the colours painted on pavements – the red white and blue of Britain, the green white and orange of the Irish tricolour – advertise the allegiances of districts and towns. As for a national day? Well, there is one which has long been enthusiastically celebrated without any prompting from governments. That's November 5th, Bonfire Night, which commemorates the defeat of a Catholic plot to murder a Protestant king. Somehow I don't think this is the sort of thing Gordon Brown had in mind.

Up at the British Council talk of flag flying produced groans from the chairman. What did he think of the idea? "I think what most outward-looking modern Americans think. Not much." Not least, I suspect, because, to use a favourite word of his hero Aneurin Bevan, he finds the whole business 'vulgar'. Ostentatious displays of patriotism simply don't seem to fit in with his view of what it is to be British. But that doesn't mean there aren't methods of making the same point that are more in tune with the national ethos. It was something in his mind, he said, at the time when the Labour Party was abandoning one symbol for another – the red flag for the red rose.

"I started in the late nineteen-eighties and right through to the 1992 election, having a subtle representation of the flags of the constituent countries of the United Kingdom and the Union Jack. It came about partly because the National Front were using the Union Jack but secondly I was talking to Jim Callaghan. We were talking about the red rose. He thought it was a great idea and he said symbols were very important. 'Of course,' he said, 'until the mid 1950s you would never see a Labour Party election platform without a Union Jack on it – usually spread over a table, like a tablecloth. In the fifties it just disappeared.' So it was restored to documents and manifesto covers, never emblazoned but always there."

You can argue that Gordon Brown is doing very much the same thing, if in a less subtle, shadowy way, perhaps because the issue has become more urgent. "Part of Gordon's motivation is the same thing. There is nothing essentially reactionary and certainly nothing that belongs to reactionary, racist, regressive elements in our society about the Union Jack. So if we want to lay claim to it we'd better bloody well use it."

It's a point Gordon Brown has made directly: the way in which Labour's unease over the flag, the left's deep suspicion of anything that looked like British nationalism, actually created an opportunity for the growth of a menacing version of that nationalism, rather than its suppression. In 2006 he said: "…when people on the centre-left recoiled from national symbols, the BNP tried to steal the Union Jack. Instead of the BNP using it as a symbol of racial division, the flag should be a symbol of unity, part of a modern expression of patriotism. So we should respond to the BNP by saying the union flag is a flag for Britain, not for the BNP; all the United Kingdom should honour it, not ignore it. We should assert that the union flag is, by definition, a flag for tolerance and inclusion."

No one denies that the BNP has some appeal, in particular to people who feel socially and economically left behind, most obviously in the older industrial areas where change and decay have left so many deprived and bewildered. In these circumstances it's natural enough to cast around for someone to blame and tempting too, perhaps, to fall for the BNP's explanation that non-Britishness in its many aspects is at the root of the problem. The BNP doesn't

overtly say non-white but that is the permanent subtext of its propaganda. What is more disturbing perhaps is that the BNP articulates
a feeling of generalised discontent not reflected in the numbers who
vote for the party, less than three quarters of one per cent at the
2005 general election. But in modern Britain, where foreigners of
one sort or another are often portrayed as the source of many of the
country's social and economic difficulties, it might be that the BNP
has more influence than the simple numbers would indicate.

In these circumstances the more Gordon Brown preaches
about those coveted national characteristics, the regard for liberty
and tolerance he argues is in effect part of the British DNA, the
more you wonder what exactly is going on. The very absolutism of
his language suggests more than a little desperation. Yes, most of us
would probably like to think we're the sort of people he describes
living in the kind of country he portrays, but looking around, it's
often difficult to see it. What seems possible is that in this argument
the BNP is only one aspect of a great range of terrors we are told
are threatening to erase the kind of Britain he so wants to preserve.
We are now so uncertain about key questions of nationality, so
alarmed at the way in which the processes of globalisation have
disrupted our understanding of our own lives, that we fear that
someone might break in during the night and steal our Britishness
from us. Among the burglars lining up to jemmy open the window
are Islamic fundamentalists, asylum seekers, demented American
neo-cons, multi-national corporations, Polish plumbers, Scottish
nationalists, just about the entire cast of the European Union,
especially the leaders at any given time of Germany and France,
and unscrupulous members of our own government who, in pursuit
of self-advancement, are willing to sell us out to any gang of
foreigners with a talent for flattery. You can find politicians and
newspapers willing to tell you some or all of this any day of the
week. The outside world is a threat, we are constantly told, and we
must have nothing to do with it. Confronted by the fierce convic-
tions of others, centuries of prejudice and the malign influence of
Megabank and Globecom, up to their necks in ruinous financial
schemes, we look for a new sense of exclusive national identity on
which to hang our hats.

One way for some people to achieve that might be for them to
withdraw entirely from the whole business of Britishness. It's
perhaps an outcome Brown fears as much as anything. In a hostile

world, his theme is, we on these islands are all in this together. In *The Lion and the Unicorn* George Orwell more often than not used the word England to stand for Britain. He was well aware of what he was doing and explained: "It is quite true that the so-called races of Britain feel themselves to be very different from one another. A Scotsman, for instance, does not thank you if you call him an Englishman. You can see the hesitation we feel on this point by the fact that we call these islands by no less than six different names, England, Britain, Great Britain, the British Isles, the United Kingdom and, in very exalted moments, Albion. Even the differences between north and south Britain look large in our own eyes. But somehow these differences fade away the moment that any two Britons are confronted by a European."

In the twenty-first century the races of Britain are not 'so-called' any more. The Scots, the Welsh, the Irish and the English are officially separate nationalities and anyone who disputes that risks being squeezed through the legal mangle by the Equality and Human Rights Commission, a state of affairs Orwell might have put to satirical use. England means England and not Britain. The separate identities of the constituent countries have been defined by Act of Parliament. Those countries think increasingly of how this condition might be further turned to their advantage, financially perhaps, or through the assumption of the moral superiority of being able to disown those aspects of Britishness they don't care for, like foreign wars. In England politicians grumble and wonder how to change the system of government to repair what they see as a settlement that's put them at a disadvantage. In the summer of 2007, a deal was finally done in Wales that shared power between Plaid Cymru and Labour; the SNP had formed a government in Scotland and the Democratic Unionists and Sinn Fein were together in the Northern Ireland administration. A text message went from one part of the BBC to another: "The nats are now in power in all three Celtic countries." It was a sign of a significant change in the nature of Britain, an indication that it is not actually a country but a state of mind and one that is perhaps at the beginning of the process of change. Independence for Scotland might not be just around the corner but it's no longer considered a joke. And the more the Scots talk about it the more notice people take of them, a lesson that won't be wasted on other parts of the United Kingdom.

All of which illustrates the elusive nature of Britishness, how its intricate mechanism is shaped by circumstance and history, how it has always meant different things in different places and at different times. It is often eccentric, unexpected and inconvenient. Far from being a steady beacon of enlightenment, as the Brownian version has it, its intensity can be turned up and down according to circumstances, like the flame on a gas cooker. Understanding such things, much more than congratulating ourselves on a dubious version of the past, may determine whether or not it lasts in a recognisable form. More important, if it doesn't would it actually matter?

Us and Them

KING LEAR IS ONE OF THE most powerful plays in the English language. It deals with many of the great themes – among them madness, family, love, ingratitude, cruelty, betrayal and the existence of God. Who would have thought that it was also about devolution? Well all right, not in the sense the word is used in the modern world, but nevertheless as an exploration of the political nature of what we have now come to call Britain. It's probable that the play was first performed on Boxing Day, 1606, in the presence of King James I and its message, obscure now, was clear enough then: that a monarch intent on dividing up his kingdom would surely bring chaos. Only a madman would do it. It's unlikely that Shakespeare would, unprompted, have embarked on such a blunt warning to his king. Instead it seems more plausible that this was something that, in turbulent times, James himself wished to make clear to his court.

You don't need to search too hard for parallels. The cataclysm that in the play descended on England was the consequence of Lear having no male heir. He therefore proposed to divide his kingdom between his three daughters. James had come to the throne when, with the death of Elizabeth I, the Tudor dynasty had come to an end. As James VI, he was already King of Scotland, the son of Mary Queen of Scots who had been executed by Elizabeth. The union was a dynastic rather than a constitutional one. Scotland remained a separate kingdom. It's significant, too, that in the play one of Lear's daughters, Goneril, marries the Duke of Albany, Albany being another name for Scotland, while her sister, Regan, marries the Duke of Cornwall, whose title is generally taken to make him the representative of west Britain, including Wales. And it's worth remembering too that at this time Wales had been constitutionally united with England for fewer than seventy years.

In the circumstances it's easy to understand why James, only a year after an attempt by Catholics to assassinate him in the Gunpowder Plot, should seek various means of emphasising the new relationship that had been established between England and Scotland, in particular the need to head off the dangers of factionalism and civil war. It might have come about by one of those accidents of inheritance, but this was a crucial time in the political process that was eventually to unite the disparate parts of the British Isles into a single British entity. Indeed, when James came to the throne the very idea of that description was enough to shock an MP called Tobie Matthew who in 1604 wrote to the poet John Donne: "Touching the Union, divers projects have been sent to the House. The name of Brittaine was absolutely refused."* It was to take another couple of hundred years and, inevitably, it didn't last very long. Britain has never really been anything other than a work in progress. What its various parts have in common is of course a shared history but it's a history of antagonism more than it is of unity. The past is never over, and today as much as ever it reaches down to furnish fresh arguments.

One summer a few years ago, for example, I was interviewing a Northern Ireland politician, a Catholic, about some issue concerned with one of the Orange parades, events at Drumcree perhaps. I picked my way carefully through the arguments, eventually saying: "Well, I suppose that's the sort of thing that happens when you're dealing with three hundred years of history."

The sound of outrage came from the other end of the line.

"More like a thousand."

I'd been thinking of 1690 and the Battle of the Boyne, the occasion being celebrated by the parades. I had forgotten, as a stranger might, that in Irish terms three hundred years is pretty much the day before yesterday. My interviewee no doubt had in mind the twelfth century and the invasion of Ireland, never previously conquered, by forces sent by Henry II. This rebuke for my lack of perspective was another reminder that, even in a small country like (to be pedantic) Great Britain and Northern Ireland, it's frequently the case that people in one part of what is officially the same state are culturally at sea with those from another part of it.

But it isn't only Ireland. History isn't simply a record of what

---

* Quoted in John Stubbs, *Donne, the Reformed Soul*, Penguin 2006

happened long ago but an argument that never ends, a weapon that can be shaped to the particular purposes of the day. The more distant an event, the easier it is to maintain that it isn't really what it has generally been supposed to be. What this means, among other things, is that in Scotland and Wales historical change can be exhumed and handed over to the political pathologists for a fresh post mortem. So it is in modern Scotland that, if you talk about the Act of Union, it's quite likely that you'll get Burns quoted at you:

We are bought and sold for English gold –
What a parcel of rogues in a nation.

The idea summed up in those two lines, that Scotland was deceived and betrayed into union with England by a mixture of bribery and threats, sold out by a Scottish parliament that had no voice for ordinary people, is understandably popular among nationalists. That version of the events of 1707 certainly doesn't go unchallenged. Some historians argue that, far from betraying Scotland, many Unionists were acting out of principle, in what they believed to be the country's interests. But naturally enough that interpretation doesn't have the same appeal in today's context when you're arguing there are ancient wrongs to be righted through the twenty-first century ballot box.

In contrast, if you were to ask the man or woman in the Welsh street about the acts that joined their country to England you would almost certainly get a look of incomprehension. In Wales the country's own history is a modern industry. Until the nineteen seventies there were scarcely any books on the subject and it was taught in schools only in the most perfunctory manner. The impetus for an investigation of its significance came from young historians who used the events of the past as a way of commenting on the present. In particular they unearthed the stories of the industrial working class in the nineteenth and twentieth centuries. Most of those who wrote these accounts came from the political left and, although some of them were nationalists, their message in general was about class and economic power rather than portraying Wales as the helpless victim of some kind of English colonial oppression. As you might expect, though, that hasn't prevented other people from doing so because, if your message is about national freedom then you have to have some kind of tyranny, real or imagined, from which to break free, whether it's capitalist exploitation or foreign rule or a mixture of both.

In Wales in the last half century or so the most obvious sign of dissent from the British project has been over cultural matters, in particular over the Welsh language. This is the only specifically Welsh cause that has brought people out on to the streets and even taken them to prison, if only briefly in most cases. It's been handled with great skill and persuasive diplomacy by most of its advocates. Its particular character, its general politeness, the lack of serious violence except for a few isolated incidents, might be considered to reflect the rather tentative way in which Welsh identity often asserts itself. It is characteristically Welsh, too, in the way in which some of those who were most active and did their time in gaol also maintained an almost genteel respectability and soon enough moved smoothly into comfortable places at the upper end of Welsh public life.

The reasons for the decline of the Welsh language are not straightforward and some clearly lie at the door of the Welsh themselves, in particular an understandable appreciation of the fact that being able to speak English had any number of material advantages. So it was common to hear someone brought up in the nineteen twenties say that, while their parents spoke Welsh to each other, the language was deliberately not passed down into the next generation. Conveniently, though, the English can be blamed for that as well since this was clearly a consequence of cultural and economic imperialism, yet another example of their contempt for the individuality and traditions of other people. More than that, it was all part of a consistent plan carried out over something like five hundred years, ever since the day that King Henry VIII decided to abolish the Welsh language entirely.

Not that the king put it as bluntly as that. Far from being a modern invention, spin doctors were clearly at work even in the sixteenth century and so the process of uniting England and Wales was, in the acts concerned, presented as an indication of the monarch's great love for Wales and its people. And after all, even if there's no record of his mentioning it, Henry was, somewhat distantly, of Welsh descent.

The language of measure was distinctly conciliatory. "His Highness therefore, of a singular zeal, love and favour that he beareth towards the subjects of his said Dominion of Wales..."

("Yes, yes, get on with it," you can hear a sceptical twenty-first century audience shouting) "minding and intending to reduce them to perfect order notice and knowledge of the laws of this his realm and utterly to extirp all and singular the sinister usages and customs differing from the same...". And those sinister usages and customs on the extirpation list included most notably the Welsh language. Perhaps not exactly that, because while it was the case that it was obligatory for certain office holders to be able to speak English, there could hardly have been a rule saying they couldn't speak Welsh as well.

In any case, despite what you might call a 'sinister' modern interpretation being put on sixteenth-century attitudes, the Welsh language was far from being destroyed. If Henry VIII really intended to wipe it out he was to be confounded. Instead Wales was entering a period when, among other portentous events, the Bible was first translated into Welsh, one of the most important literary and social developments in the whole history of the language. More than that, it was to be another three hundred and fifty years before the number of people who didn't speak Welsh in Wales outnumbered those who did, that's to say quite late in an era of industrialisation that was to change so much throughout Britain.

In any case, the king's singular zeal, love and all the rest of it had a rather more radical purpose than making public officials speak English. His idea, a strategic necessity, was to abolish Wales. And to abolish England, come to that. For well over a century Wales had been disadvantaged by penal laws introduced in the wake of the rebellion against the crown by Owain Glyndŵr at the beginning of the fifteenth century. (Interestingly enough Glyndŵr, a rather dubious figure who might well have been rather keener on his own interests rather than the independence of Wales, is someone else who's crept out from the shadows of history to be claimed as a hero of more than one political party. Even, sometimes, as an early Liberal Democrat.) The deal was that, under the Acts of Union of 1536 and 1543 (act of union being a somewhat misleading term since the Welsh got it whether they wanted it or not, having no parliament to give or withhold authority) in effect the two entities known as England and Wales effectively ceased to exist and became instead England-and-Wales. While it's a very dangerous business to start attributing attitudes to people who lived hundreds of years ago it's certainly not ridiculous to think that those Welsh who were actually aware of what was going on might have considered this to be quite a decent offer, one in any case they couldn't refuse. There was something in it for both sides, after all. The Welsh got what might in modern terms be called full citizenship while Henry headed off disaffection in the west that might have been turned to their advantage by his various Catholic enemies. This was the moment when the split with Rome dramatically changed the course of English history and marked the beginning of what was, in effect, a long civil war between Catholics and Protestants, something that even now is not quite over.

From today's perspective perhaps the most striking thing about the strategy of joining England and Wales was that it didn't work. Not that Wales was or became a hotbed of turmoil and rebellion, but the one thing the Welsh didn't do was become English. Legally there was now no distinction between the two peoples but the difference between them remained clear. Much more than in the case of Scotland, much, much more than in the case of Ireland, there was no particular reason why the Welsh should not have taken their place in the overall scheme of things woven into the English system like, say, Lancashire, or perhaps Cornwall. But it didn't happen and in the twenty-first century, it's disconcerting to realise, the Irish, the Scots the Welsh and the English are officially racially separate. Discriminate against them at your peril. Be rude about the Welsh, like Anne Robinson for example, or even Tony Blair, and you get reported to the police. And the police, who don't think it's funny, travel around Britain collecting evidence trying to establish whether or not a crime has been committed.

It's the sheer persistence of Wales down the centuries, grumbling its way into our own lifetimes, that is the arresting phenomenon. It's not that many people go round complaining about 1536, not least because the vast majority of the population is happily unaware of the date or its significance. Unlike Scotland where, as I say, a solitary mention of 1707 can get them quoting Burns at you. And certainly unlike Ireland where any date from 1169 onwards might well provoke an argument.

None of this should be taken to suggest that the place we know as Britain is a seething mass of discontent based on wrongs that might or might not have been visited upon its various components centuries ago, even if it boils up now and again. But a shared history is only a part of the story. After all, it was only with the introduction of yet another act of union, that with Ireland in 1801, that the whole circus was put together in one United Kingdom. That lasted not much more than a century, until 1921 and the treaty that established the Irish Free State. Nor was that anything like the end of the matter because what were still in angry dispute were the six counties of Northern Ireland, the home of some of the most passionately British people in the entire universe. There were times when the rest of Britain, exasperated, might have turned its back on those people but in the end it was the Irish Republic that broke with its past and gave up its claim to the north. And it did so, it's generally agreed, not with any great sense of regret from the vast majority but with a sigh of relief, In consequence Northern Ireland bubbles on to whatever conclusion it might reach, if it ever reaches any kind of conclusion at all, a place as mysterious and alien to most of its fellow citizens in the rest of the UK as, say, the Amazon basin.

The particular case of Northern Ireland might be as good an illustration as any of the erratic course of the history of Britain and the difficulty of defining what it is to be British, even among people who share a long political heritage. The arrival of James I on the throne of England in 1603 and those warnings about division contained in *King Lear* marked a crucial stage in relations with Ireland. In 1609 the process of colonising Ulster with protestants from Scotland and England began and lit the touch paper on centuries of violent dispute. The city then known as Derry was renamed Londonderry and began a familiar argument about nomenclature that persists four hundred years later. It was another important change in the shifting set of allegiances that still characterises the idea of Britishness. It was and continues to be one of those useful fictions in which the language itself persists but what it describes is altered behind the constitutional façade. Or, as a senior figure in the BBC put it: "Isn't Britishness really a dexterous exercise in ambivalence?" You don't have to know much about the subject to recognise at once that it was an Irishman who said that.

True Brit

AT THE END OF THE nineteen-nineties, as the new constitutional arrangements for Scotland and Wales came into operation, a number of books appeared with obituary notices attached to the word Britain. In *The Day Britain Died*, for example, Andrew Marr was rueful but resigned and non-judgemental (just what you see him being on the telly) about the new order of things. In fact, he suggested, Britain might actually have died some considerable time before.

"Was it Indian independence? Suez? The Treaty of Rome? Or Maastricht? Was it when Margaret Thatcher agreed to the Single European Act? Or was it those other great events of her premiership, when the end of exchange controls, then privatisation, and the in the Major years, the World Wide Web and the signing of the Uruguay Round of the GATT Treaty, created today's global economy?... Or... was it the day when Scotland voted 'yes' to its own Parliament? Was it 1994, when the last volume car producer in Britain went into German ownership. It was, surely, all those dates and none of them."

In his account, *The Death of Britain?* with its last-chance-to-save question mark, the former Conservative Cabinet Minister, John Redwood, identified any number of threats including the creeping and apparently inexorable influence of the EU in British life, the threat to the monarchy (to be sidelined by the EU or Labour or both, according to Redwood), reform of the House of Lords, the modernisation of the House of Commons, devolution and proportional representation (another plot to advance the cause of European federalism). This was, he said, a country being torn up by its roots.

At the same time Peter Hitchens in *The Abolition of Britain* (reissued, perhaps significantly, in 2008) spent three hundred and fifty-one pages explaining why almost everything that altered between the death of Winston Churchill in 1965 and that of Princess Diana in 1997 had been to the detriment of Britain and Britishness, in particular because of the malign influence of the Labour Party.

Despite the funereal attitudes struck by these authors it is nevertheless difficult to see exactly what it is they are mourning. They write the obituary without convincing us of the greatness of the deceased. What Redwood and Hitchens in particular represent is something that is perhaps the most British characteristic of them all: the view that practically all change makes things worse and that, contrary to the lessons of history, if we're sufficiently resolute everything can stay very much the same as it's always been. There was a time when John Major thought it could do so. What else could he have meant when he said: "Fifty years on from now Britain will still be the country of long shadows on county grounds, warm beer, invincible green suburbs, dog lovers and – as George Orwell said – old maids cycling to Holy Communion through the morning mist."

Did he mean it, you wonder. He was talking to the Conservative Group for Europe at the time so he might simply have been trying to cheer them up rather than offer any kind of realistic prospectus. Perhaps it was possible to say such things without laughing in 1993, but now it's as dated as a sepia postcard. Many of the county cricket grounds have become stadiums where the shadows are cast by floodlights rather than the evening sun. The warm beer is cold lager, probably drunk at home as the pubs go out of business. Anyone who valued his life would hardly dare use the expression 'old maids', even in quotation, while clergy and church-goers are on the verge of being declared endangered species. If you look a little more closely at Major's idealised Britain and its references – the invincible green suburbs, the Anglican church, the county grounds – you realise that when Surrey-born John Major talked of Britain he actually meant the Home Counties. More than that, Major (born 1943) was talking about a kind of England he was too young to have experienced. He was dealing in the kind of posthumous references quite common when people cast about for something that represents British tradition to them, something they can admire. Very often they discover it just that little bit late.

It's revealing for instance that some newspapers, the *Sun* in particular, like to refer to British troops fighting in Iraq and

Afghanistan as 'our boys'. No one thinks there's anything wrong with that, but what it evokes in particular is an image of wartime Britain, a time when 'our boys' came from practically every street in the United Kingdom to be sent to around the world without the option. We were British then, all right. A few years after the war, for example, children were still chanting rhymes about Hitler.

> In nineteen forty-four
> Hitler went to war.
> He lost his pants
> In the middle of France
> In nineteen forty-four.

So reluctant were we to abandon this tradition that even the Fuhrer's death wasn't allowed to stand in the way of our communal derision.

> In nineteen forty-six
> Hitler chopped some sticks.
> He missed the block
> And cut his cock
> In nineteen forty-six.

A particularly ruthless disciplinarian at the local grammar school was nicknamed Tojo after the Japanese prime minister who had been hanged as a war criminal. We lined the streets to cheer as Field Marshal Montgomery passed through our valley, standing in the back of a jeep, instantly recognisable by his beret. We named our dog after him. It must be admitted that, in an even-handed way, we also sang of our hostility to Winston Churchill, but that was because of the argument that persisted over his role in putting down the riots by miners in Tonypandy more than thirty-five years previously. He was good at war, though, and there was no doubt about our patriotism. Long after it was all over we were convinced, like William Brown, that every stranger in town was a German spy; we were passionately behind Biggles in his prolonged struggle, book after book, with the German officer, Erich von Stalhein; reading the comics we admired the defiance and courage of our soldiers in the face of the sneering cruelty of German prison guards: "For you, Englischer pig-dog, ze war is over."

Well into the nineteen-fifties a lot of radio comedy depended on services humour. *Much-Binding-in-the-Marsh* ran until 1954, and it can perhaps be counted authentically British that a series that was first broadcast while the war was still on was based on the general incompetence of people running an RAF base. Some of the humour of *The Goon Show*, which began in 1951, was based on the apparently innocent punchlines of dirty jokes ("It's your turn in the barrel..." etc.) heard during war service by the programme's creators.

Young men who'd been in the forces were demobbed and resumed civilian life. Others left to do their National Service and to fight different wars, in Korea and Malaya among other places. One or two might show you awesome knives they'd brought home as souvenirs. At least one had smuggled a pistol out of the army and fired it in his small back garden as we looked on in wonder. One day, rooting through old photographs with some relatives, a reliable source of entertainment on a rainy afternoon, I turned over a picture of a young man wearing a forage cap. "Who's that?" I asked. There was a long silence.

Later I was told: "That was Dor's fiancé. He was killed in the war." It was just another of the ways in which, for much of the twentieth century, people's lives were so frequently touched by war and the language and hierarchy of military life were part of our common experience. We knew about it even if it was hardly ever discussed by those who'd done the fighting. To British people the Second World War, perhaps like no other, created a sense of unity that generally, if not entirely, crossed place, class and politics. Nowadays, I suppose, most people would be unable to distinguish between a brigadier and a traffic warden. Even all those one-time majors and lieutenant-colonels who were the loyal backbone of so many Conservative associations have gone to their last great reunion.

When did this come to an end? One clear punctuation mark was the Suez crisis, that pseudo-imperial adventure in which Britain, joined by France and Israel, responded to the nationalisa-tion of the canal by attempting to invade Egypt. There was no national unity on this matter. Labour opposed the action and had much the better of the political argument. And when President Eisenhower intervened decisively to end the whole affair it was an unmistakeable illustration of the way in which Britain's authority in the world had diminished. Most people already knew it perhaps, but now they had been made to face it. From then on it's difficult to think of a military action abroad that has aroused any real sense of national purpose. Except perhaps the Falklands, in which government and opposition were in official harmony even if there were many voices raised against the justice and wisdom of the strategy. That in time of war, however inflated a word war is to describe the Falklands campaign, a member of the public could go on television and rattle the Prime Minister over the sinking of the *Belgrano*, officially an enemy ship, showed you how much the world had changed. And when Mrs. Thatcher stood in Downing Street and urged the British people to rejoice at the news of the recapture of South Georgia (a place as obscure and undesirable to the average voter then as it is now) she seemed to be out of tune with the times.

After the Falklands the public mood seems to have become hostile to almost any engagement of British troops abroad. They are seen as instruments of (often dishonest) political ambitions in Iraq, Afghanistan or the Balkans. The forces themselves have become, in the eyes of the press at least, the unwilling victims of official incompetence and the vanity of people like George Bush and Tony Blair who postured haplessly on the world stage. In another astonishing break with tradition, generals explain to the media how the army is under intolerable strain, a strain imposed by politicians who are more or less entirely ignorant of how the military world functions. It is in these circumstances that British armed forces become 'our boys' once more, but this time brave people who need protecting from their own government.

For most people in Britain the army, the navy and the air force are remote institutions. The last national servicemen were called up in 1960, so the vast majority of people in the country have no experience of service life. Nor are they very much aware of it as they go about their daily business since it's now quite exceptional to see a military uniform being worn on the streets of Britain. That state of affairs came about in part because of the need for service personnel to avoid becoming targets for the IRA and, today, other terrorist groups. But that's by no means the whole story. In 2008, men and women serving at RAF Wittering were banned by their commanding officer from wearing their uniforms in the nearby town of Peterborough where they were abused by the local civilian population because of their involvement in Iraq and Afghanistan. In the same town even a group of Sea Cadets were accused of being murderers. A hotel in Surrey refused a room to an army corporal who, when asked for identification, showed his military pass.

What exactly provokes such incidents is difficult to determine. Perhaps it stems from an understandable distaste for the whole business of war, particularly when there are serious doubts about the legality of some of the conflicts in which Britain has recently been involved, never mind their military and political logic. We can't possibly defeat the Taliban, we're told by experts, so why bother to try? Perhaps, too, it arises from a fear of unknown enemies in distant countries who, if provoked, will visit their revenge on us personally. It all adds up to a powerful sense that many people have come to believe that it might somehow be possible to disengage from the most threatening aspects of the modern world, from the huge, unanswerable questions of war and peace. More than that, to turn their backs on many other less attractive aspects of modern Britain, to avert their gaze from the many things they cannot change and concentrate instead on the domestic challenges of day-to-day living. It's already reflected in an altered political system by which everyone in Britain, whether they know it yet or not, seems certain to be affected.

*

One of the persistent difficulties of investigating the idea of a British national identity is the problem of discovering institutions or attitudes that reveal the unique nature of what it is to be British. Some times the answer seems to lie in trivial matters. While there appears to be nothing in Magna Carta about the number of times people should have their bins emptied, a visitor from abroad leafing through the newspapers could be forgiven for thinking it was a central tenet of British freedom. A normally docile public, he would read, had been driven to furious protest by a decision by some councils to collect rubbish only once every two weeks instead of once a week. Leafy suburbs had been reduced to rat-infested squalor, binmen had been attacked by angry residents, Oxford dons had threatened to go to gaol in protest while local authorities used spy cameras to see that innocent taxpayers were putting the right rubbish in the right bins and leaving them in exactly the right place. "MARCH OF THE DUSTBIN STASI", the *Daily Mail*'s lead story shrieked on November 1, 2008. "Half of councils use anti-terror powers to train cameras on people putting rubbish out on the wrong day." It's difficult to think of any serious human rights issue that arouses such passion.

Perhaps more than any other, the controversy that provokes the expression 'Only in Britain...' is that of the group known as the metric martyrs. These are mainly people who run market stalls selling fruit and vegetables and who insist on using imperial weights. They have a big following in traditionalist papers like the *Daily Telegraph* which treats the pound, the yard, the pint and other such measures as a bulwark against arbitrary change imposed by a bunch of constipated European bureaucrats whose chief purpose in life is to dismantle the British history of which they are insanely jealous. It would be foolish to suggest that this view doesn't have a substantial constituency, but it ignores the most important aspect of the story: the triumph of Britain against an EU plot designed to take us yet another step or two on the road to a United States of Europe. The truth is that the European Commission long ago gave up (almost certainly in despair) any attempt to impose metrication on the country.

In September 2007, Günter Verheugen, the Commissioner for Enterprise and Industry, announced: "Neither the European Commission nor any faceless Eurocrat has or ever will be responsible for banning the great British pint, the mile, and weights and measures in pounds and ounces." And in case you thought that Germans like Mr. Verheugen don't do irony he went on: "...we have no proposed legislation endangering Britain's right to retain pints of milk and beer, miles on road signs and dual indications of weights and measures from now until Kingdom come."

Instead of holding street parties to celebrate another great victory over Johnny Foreigner, however, the complex nature of Britishness further revealed itself in the failure of the government to get on with passing the necessary legislation that would have prevented those market traders getting into trouble. Local authority officials, topped in the demonology of the British press only by health and safety busybodies, saw an offence being committed and went round prosecuting people until the government asked them, on the sledgehammer and nut principle, to desist.

This may seem an essentially trivial issue, which of course it is, except that it reflects as well as anything the uneasy feeling that

British people often have that any change is simply a ruse to further rob them of their Britishness. That might suggest their sense of identity is a fragile thing but it also reveals another important national characteristic. As one observer explained: "Catholic countries signed up to every detail of the European regulations and ignored the lot of them, while the Protestant UK worried about the shape of bananas."

You know what he means, but the term Protestant is now almost entirely a cultural and historical description rather than carrying very much by way of religious significance in most of the United Kingdom (except, as usual, in Northern Ireland). What appears to be the case in contemporary Britain is that while most people don't believe, they would nevertheless like it to be believed that they believe, despite the fact that there is now no reason to say that Britain is a Christian country, still less a Protestant one. Figures published in 2008 showed that fewer than seven per cent of people were churchgoers and twenty-nine per cent of those were over sixty-five years old. Forecasts suggested that in another forty years or so there would be well under a million people going to church in the whole of Britain. Those trends, if maintained, meant that by 2050 there would be fewer than ninety thousand Anglicans in the country but ten times as many Hindus and more than two and a half million Muslims. The figures may turn out to be inaccurate to some degree but you don't have to be a statistician or a social scientist to see for yourself the unmistakeable reality of disappearing chapels, decaying churches, dwindling congregations and, in the case of the Anglican Church, an institution bitterly divided over matters of gender and sexual orientation. This preoccupation makes the Church the object of public derision by some of those who take any notice of it at all, summed up in the *Sun* headline of some years ago: "Pulpit poofs can stay". It doesn't help that the Archbishop of Canterbury, Rowan Williams, is cleverer than most of his secular critics. It means he's inclined to test them with ideas they can't understand, something that makes them even crosser. There was outrage, for example, when he suggested that there might be a way in which aspects of the Muslim system of Sharia Law could work within the British legal system. He didn't mean what the papers and politicians said he meant but Williams is not only an intellectual but looks like one and so is clearly a dangerous figure in the robustly un-cerebral British tradition of argument.

As the publicly-funded broadcaster in a nominally Christian state, the BBC continues some minor ritual observances with daily services ("Meanwhile on Long Wave...") and the sore thumb element of 'Thought for the Day' sticking out of the *Today* programme. But even in these circumstances people find it possible to turn their backs on one of the obvious consequences of this state of affairs. The junior government minister, Phil Woolas, must have read the figures because in October 2008 he said he believed that within fifty years the Church of England would be disestablished. The reason for that, he said, would be further reform of the House of Lords and an acknowledgment that Britain was now a multicultural society. His forecast brought a chilly response from the Ministry of Justice which outlined the present position of the Church and added: "The government remains committed to this position and values the establishment of the Church of England."

Woolas (the phrase 'gaffe-prone' now firmly attached to his name by the press) had offended by saying something that was perfectly obvious. The Church of England is an anachronism in itself, but its place at the heart of the British constitution, in particular the presence of its bishops in the House of Lords, making it part of the legislative system, is a contradiction of what modern democracies claim to represent.

Scotland, Wales and Northern Ireland have different arrangements for their national churches. The Church of Scotland has no bishops; the Church in Wales was disestablished in 1920 and so ceased to be part of the Church of England. The way these things work, however, meant that an Archbishop from a disestablished Church, Rowan Williams, could move across from Wales to become the religious head of the established Church of England and so take one of those seats in the House of Lords. The only bishops who sit with him are those from English dioceses, which means that, even in an era of devolution, English clerics have a privileged, if minor, position within the governmental system of the United Kingdom. The Christian denominations around the UK are used to it and may not care very much, but how can such a position possibly be maintained, as Woolas pointed out, in a multicultural society? That's to say, institutional discrimination in favour of a small religious and geographical minority. It's a question of principle, which is probably why it is usually greeted with an embarrassed silence or a request for troublemakers to pipe down. It's treated as a minor matter but it's not. Instead it's a clear illustration of why religion continues to divide Britain, even when people don't believe in it.

★

Something similar might be said about the matter of class, which we are often assured is a rapidly disappearing aspect of British life. When he was prime minister John Major declared that his ambition was for Britain to become a classless society while at the same time yearning for the unchanging social order he admired so much but which, he must have known, had already changed. You can't have both, any more than you can have something called 'a more democratic monarchy' which was another aspiration of the nineteen-nineties. That is a club none of us can join, whatever our virtues, and the message that birth can be decisive, in however limited a way, creates a distinction that cannot be erased.

It might be argued that Mr. Major's own story somehow counters this argument. That a grammar school boy from a famously deprived background, including according to one of his biographers, a 'Dickensian' interlude of poverty, a one-time bank clerk who never went to university, that someone like him could become Prime Minister of the United Kingdom surely gives the lie to the idea that class any longer determines status in modern Britain. Something similar might have been said about Lloyd George seventy-five years previously, or, later, Ramsay MacDonald, but their careers illustrate how the traditional system adapts for a while and then reasserts itself. The truth is that, even if what's called the establishment has changed somewhat in character and personnel, there is still an establishment.

That fact was powerfully chronicled by the late Anthony Sampson in his book *Who Runs This Place?* published in 2004. He wrote then: "Today the circles of Britain's power-centres look very different from the patterns of forty years ago.... The Palace, the universities and the diplomats have drifted towards the edge. Many institutions – including parliament, the cabinet, trades unions and industry – look smaller. The prime minister, the Treasury and defence loom larger at the centre. The bankers are more dominant, overlapping with corporations and pension funds, while the nationalised industries have almost disappeared as separate entities. The media are more pervasive, seeping everywhere into the vacuum left by the shrinking of the old powers."

The key to the new establishment, Sampson went on, was money. "The new elite is held together by their desire for personal enrichment, their acceptance of capitalism and the need for the profit-motive, while the resistance to money-values is much weaker – and former anti-capitalists have been the least inclined to criticise them, once in power."

Sampson drew a distinction between the old British political elite that kept its distance from what it disparagingly called 'new money' and the present establishment. "Today the elite looks much more unified, as a small number of familiar names keep reappearing in different disguises – whether as tycoons, trustees or patrons of public funds. Visiting Americans are surprised that most people they want to see can be found at a few clubs, dinner parties or gatherings, without ever leaving a handful of postal districts in central London."

At the same time, however, the move of power from one establishment to another has been accompanied by a process which has apparently blurred the old distinctions. Everyone is on first name terms with everyone else, few men wear ties, accents are modulated so that, for example, Tony Blair, although educated at a leading Scottish public school and Oxford, adopted a manner of speaking in conversation that owed a great deal to estuarial English. David Cameron, too, has liked to pretend that he's at ease with the language of the *hoi polloi*, (as he would have been taught at Eton) by using expressions such as: "I'm fessin' up to this," an embarrassing bid for, well, street cred. So much has modern British life been taken over by this false matiness that, according to researchers at Macquarie University in Sydney, even the Queen's accent has changed during her reign. She has stopped sounding like Celia Johnson on helium and shifted her vowel sounds closer to those of her subjects. She has, for example, stopped saying 'had' as if it rhymed with bed and instead, like most of us, started rhyming it with bad. It's difficult to see this change as a giant step towards an egalitarian society, but it's interesting that the demotic shift has reached so far up the social scale. As far as marking any serious change goes, though, it is illusory. While the managing director or the Prime Minister goes round in his shirtsleeves and signs his memos Mark or Tim or whatever, or says, "Call me Tony", the truth is that the structures of authority are the same as they always were.

You will discover that when you try to defy them. It's just that they are no longer visible as the pips and stripes of rank.

Of course it's true, as Anthony Sampson described, that the nature of the establishment, of the elite, is today less closely linked to old ideas of class and more to money, in particular to 'the desire for personal enrichment' a collective ambition that came to an unhappy junction in the financial calamities of 2008. Mixed with that is the pursuit of celebrity so that rich and powerful people seek the company of singers, actors, comedians, best-selling writers and others, particularly those who, like themselves, are wealthy. Politicians do it as well because it gives them a populist image and, they hope, a little stardust will rub off on them, but the dangers were well illustrated when Tony Blair invited various rock stars to Downing Street at the beginning of his premiership. They drank his champagne but soon enough were explaining to anyone who'd listen that the Prime Minister had on the whole turned out to be pretty useless. Even so, it can't be seen as anything less than refreshing that Mick Jagger and Tom Jones, who would once have been considered too disreputable to be entertained in the drawing rooms of polite society, now go about town as Sir Mick and Sir Tom. The celebrated (and rich) comedian and actor Ricky Gervais told the *Guardian* in 2006 that comedy was about aspiration and added: "Until Basil Fawlty, comedy was about class and now it's celebrity. Before, people wanted to be part of the aristocracy. Now they want to be famous."

While some might have doubts about the details of this analysis it can nevertheless be taken to indicate a move in the right direction. If you are good at things – comedy, sport, singing, getting rich – then you are welcome in the magic circles of power and influence. It doesn't matter who your parents were or where you went to school. What's vital is tangible evidence of success. If one word sums it up it's something popularised by Tony Blair: meritocracy. Blair didn't dream up this term, but he used it often as indicating an improved social order, one in which people rose and were rewarded according to their merits. But did he know, or did he care, that the man who invented the description thought this state of affairs was anything but desirable?

It was coined by Michael Young (later Lord Young of Dartington) for his 1958 book, *The Rise of the Meritocracy*, and it wasn't intended as recommending an appropriate goal for any government but rather as an awful warning. In 2001, when the word gained its new currency, he wrote that the book was in fact a satire which predicted disaster and revolution if people's progress in society depended on a narrow assessment of what constituted merit. In particular he was writing about merit as defined by the educational system.

"Ability of a particular kind, which used to be distributed between the classes more or less at random, has become much more highly concentrated by the engine of education. A social revolution has been accomplished by harnessing schools and universities to the task of sieving people according to education's narrow band of values. With an amazing battery of certificates and degrees at its disposal, education has put its seal of approval on a minority, and its seal of disapproval on the many who fail to shine from the time they are relegated to the bottom streams at the age of seven or before."

So this is a system that only appears to be more justly based because it apparently depends on people's abilities rather than accidents of birth. But accidents of birth still influence ability and what someone can make of it; the nature of a person's family, what kind of parents they have, their economic circumstances, where the family lives and many other random factors determine the kind of education someone gets and, more often than not, their eventual place in society. It is not enough, Young says, indeed it's positively dangerous, to make so much depend on what is essentially the ability to pass exams.

A similar point is made by Ferdinand Mount in his book *Mind the Gap* in which he says: "...we cannot help noticing that the old class system has been reconstituted into a more or less meritocratic upper tier and a lower tier which is defined principally by its failure to qualify for the upper tier." Mount himself is an interesting example of the persistence of the old kind of class distinctions. What qualifications has he got to write such a book, he asks rhetorically. "I was educated at independent schools, I live in a very nice house on a conservation area, I have a languid upper class voice and a semi-dormant baronetcy."

That last phrase, 'semi-dormant baronetcy' is exquisite in its sinuous journey through one of those comically British matters of status. Mount, *Sir* Ferdinand Mount in fact, is indeed a baronet (the lowest level of hereditary title), but he prefers not to be known as such. Or as it explains helpfully in *Who's Who*: "3rd Bt....but does not use the title." That doesn't stop him being a baronet nor will it eventually prevent his son becoming one. Nor can he get rid of it. Semi-dormant looks like a construction used by someone trapped embarrassingly in the peculiar world of the British honours system. But then, Mount was for some time head of Margaret Thatcher's policy unit at 10 Downing Street and in this matter he shows rather more sensitivity than his old boss's son, Sir Mark Thatcher, Bt.

There were plenty of Blair-style meritocrats in Downing Street and elsewhere in the government in Mrs. Thatcher's time. Indeed, as the exam-passing daughter of a Grantham grocer she was very much one herself. But sometimes even that journey isn't always sufficient to secure a proper position in the hierarchy of power. John Prescott served as Deputy Prime Minister from 1997 to 2007, but throughout that time one of his chief roles was to represent, in a cardboard cut-out way, the idea that in New Labour's modern Britain, an old-fashioned working-class trade unionist could also play a leading role in a government of polished talents.

So important was it that he could carry out this representative function that Prescott remained in office when others might have found themselves back in the bus queue; for not being a very good minister, perhaps, or for having an affair, on official premises, with his diary secretary. He might even have got into trouble for hitting a man who threw an egg at him from close range during the 2001 election campaign. But Tony Blair put on his indulgent dad voice and said: "John is John", suggesting that Yob of State was part of his deputy's role. In fact he might have made the better point that, at a time when security considerations have increasingly kept senior politicians and the public well apart, Prescott was independent and brave enough to walk through a crowded street in North Wales. Hit suddenly from close range it's not surprising he retaliated. In the modern world, indeed, his attacker was very lucky not to get shot.

For all his untouchable national treasure status, however, Prescott felt himself a victim of the elaborate considerations of class which, just as you believe you've understood them, leap out from a doorway and surprise you with another egg in the face. He later complained that, in all his years as Deputy Prime Minister, he and his wife had never been invited to a state dinner at Chequers. He thought the blame belonged to Cherie Blair who, he implied in a television documentary, was a snob. But Cherie Blair was a working-class woman from Liverpool who, like Prescott, had achieved a significant position in life through her own talent and efforts. You begin to realise that even in what is advertised as a new social order some people are more meritocratic than others.

It's easy to get dazzled by words and not think too much about what they really mean. Meritocracy has a nice ring to it. So does classless. But they are politicians' words of vague aspiration rather than a programme for reform. Even as the nature of class in Britain shifts and reorganises itself it's still an important part of the British identity. Understanding that it exists unites the country; the reality continues to divide it. Nor can it be argued that reliance on a meritocracy necessarily brings improvements. Most of those responsible for the banking crisis that swept over Britain in 2008 were from that allegedly classless sector of society. Most notably, perhaps, Sir Fred Goodwin (Paisley Grammar School and Glasgow University), who went into retirement at the age of fifty staggering under the weight of his vast pension, leaving behind him the wreckage of the Royal Bank of Scotland of which he had been chief executive. However many exams Sir Fred had passed they didn't keep him out of one of the greatest disasters in British financial history.

★

Politicians often like to demonstrate their classless, ordinary-blokeishness through an ostentatious display of their sport-loving credentials. It's not new. Many years ago I rang the then Newport Labour MP, Roy Hughes (later Lord Islwyn), to ask how he spent his weekends. On Saturday afternoons, he said, he usually went to see Newport County play football. Was he a fan? "Oh, no. It's just that they announce that I'm there and it helps in the constituency." Nor is this kind of calculation anything unusual. Alastair Campbell's *Downing Street Diaries* are educational in this regard as they are in many others. Indeed, the chief pleasure in reading them is for the way in which Campbell unintentionally reveals aspects of his character he might have preferred to keep hidden. At one point he records a visit to Wembley to watch a football match between England and Germany. "I have never really supported England, and for political reasons I found myself rooting for Germany, though, as I was sitting next to one of J.M.'s [John Major's] bodyguards, even though he was a Scot, I pretended to be backing England."

When you read this and recall that Campbell is a bagpipe-playing Burnley supporter of Scottish parentage you realise at once how complicated is the relationship between sport and Britishness. And, as in Campbell's case, it often depends on the circumstances of the day. What it doesn't do, however, is fit in with the assumption that British people are particularly distinguished by their passion for, as the official line has it, freedom and tolerance. Anything but, indeed.

In fact, for anyone who doesn't take much of an interest in these things it's startling to be alerted to the apparently pointless antagonism that is often brought to football, otherwise known as 'the beautiful game'. You look twice when you read that the chairman of Celtic Football Club, the former cabinet minister, Dr. John Reid, in September 2008 complained to Rangers, his club's great rivals, about their fans' singing at a match between the sides. Perhaps not everyone knows that Celtic are a Catholic side and Rangers Protestant. The song Rangers' supporters sang went: "The famine's over, why don't you go home?" Yes, really. More than a century and a half after the famine that caused a million deaths in Ireland they're still singing gleefully about it at Ibrox. In a similar way in the eighties, Chelsea fans taunted Cardiff with chants of "Aberfan, Aberfan, Aberfan...". What Swiftian satirist could have imagined that the deaths of 116 children could so quickly become the subject of a derisive football chant?

The problem is that this sort of thing has been going on for so long the authorities seem to have given up hope of changing it. When the European football governing body, UEFA, investigated the singing of an inflammatory song called 'Billy Boys', which has its origins in gang warfare between Protestants and Catholics in Glasgow, it was considered to be buried too deep in the football culture of the city to be stopped now. UEFA shrugged: "Supporters have been singing the song 'The Billy Boys' for years during national and international matches without either the Scottish football or governmental authorities being able to intervene. The result is that this song is now somehow tolerated."

I suppose people who don't go to football matches don't have any idea what's going on, but this isn't something confined to historic aggravation in Glasgow. London fans seem to specialise in racist abuse. Black players are regular targets but anti-semitism is also common. In fan-speak Tottenham Hotspur are known as 'the Yids' because many of the team's supporters come from Jewish areas of London. So they are greeted with chants of: "Spurs are on their way to Belsen. Hitler's going to gas them again", and, accompanied by Nazi salutes and hissing gas noises, "I'd rather be a Pikey than a Jew." In January 2008, close to the fiftieth anniversary of the Munich air disaster in which seven Manchester United players were killed, the club were asked to abandon plans for a minute's silence because fans of their opponents, Manchester City, would behave badly. At an earlier game Manchester City supporters had been heard to sing: "We're all going to the golden jubilee", to the tune of 'Yellow Submarine'.

Having dealt with racial taunts with such obvious success the Football Association announced in 2007 that English football would be banning homophobic abuse aimed at specific players, "**** **** is a rent boy" being about the mildest of them. The crowds are still chanting. In 2006, the Swansea City player Lee Trundle received death threats after celebrating a game at the Millennium Stadium in Cardiff by putting on a T-shirt which showed a Swansea City player urinating on a Cardiff City shirt.

I suppose this is what they mean by popular culture, but although football represents some of the less attractive aspects of the British character it seems to be a game that has now moved beyond nationality. At one time Gordon Brown was said to be pursuing a strategy that would introduce a policy of British players for British clubs, an idea about as likely to succeed as his other reality-defying slogan: 'British jobs for British workers'. Many football clubs are owned by non-British billionaires, managed by non-British coaches and field teams full of non-British players; sometimes without any British players at all. The game's chief contribution to a sense of national identity comes from the continuing comedy provided by the vast gap between the aspiration and misplaced self-confidence of the England team and the reality of its embarrassing defeats. It is an enduring source of pleasure to those who are not English and some consolation for the cycle of hope and shattered dreams that regularly afflicts the people of Scotland, Wales and Northern Ireland and their national teams. And those lesser countries of the Union are firm in their view that they would rather lose to San Marino reserves twice a week than form part of a United Kingdom football side.

So far rugby has avoided much of the hooliganism that's been such a feature of football in the United Kingdom. Rival groups of fans mix warmly enough in the stands at the Millennium Stadium and then on Westgate Street, Cardiff, for example, as they enjoy other important aspects of their sport like being sick in the street and urinating in doorways. Yet in Wales in particular the passion behind the national rugby side, the weight of expectation, often doomed to anticlimax and disappointment, can rattle your teeth. To some extent it's whipped up by the media, in particular the BBC and the *Western Mail*, not least because there are not enough identifiably Welsh events to get excited about. The important thing is that this is a sport in which Wales can make some kind of claim to world status, a view that seems to be largely unaffected by actual results.

It looks ominous, though, that rugby has become recognisably more like football as it has plunged into the money culture, admittedly on a much smaller scale. Millionaires control some of the clubs; players are brought in from overseas; managers are sacked for failure; cheque books in hand, the management of the Welsh Rugby Union comb the world for a unicorn: the great coach who can make it all come right. On and off the field rugby has always been a physical, boozy culture, yet so far it hasn't been disfigured by the unpleasantness, violence, ill-feeling and incendiary rivalry that have so often exploded in football. Why this should be is difficult to say. Perhaps it's because some of the more relaxed attitudes of amateurism persist sufficiently to temper the financial impatience for success of a professional game.

Will it last or will it turn nastier? The precedents aren't good but one indication that such a mood can exist was demonstrated in Dublin in February 2007. The six nations match between Ireland and England was played at Croke Park, a place of incalculable significance in the long and troubled relationship between the two countries. Croke Park, a stadium that holds 80,000 people, was expensively rebuilt from the nineteen-nineties onwards. It belongs to the Gaelic Athletic Association, an organisation of a rigidly Irish nationalist character which strictly bans the playing of 'foreign games' (by which it really means English games) on its grounds. As a schoolboy, the Irish writer, Benedict Kiely, was suspended from the GAA when he was seen by a local committee man playing "a foreign game [football] with Protestant boys on a Protestant field."

During a Gaelic Football match between Dublin and

Tipperary at Croke Park in November 1920, British soldiers started moving through the crowd in a search for the killers of twelve British spies in Dublin. The troops opened fire and fourteen people were killed, including Michael Hogan, the Tipperary captain. That was another day that became known as Bloody Sunday and even in history-burdened Ireland there can be few more sensitive arenas. In such a place Ireland versus England could have been part of a long war continued by other means.

So when the GAA relaxed its rules and allowed the match to take place at the ground there was a sense of nervousness and anticipation. Who could say what might happen when an English team ran out at a shrine of Irish nationalism, a place where the Black and Tans had gunned down innocent spectators? When they lined up for the 'God Save the Queen', who could forecast what the response might be? It was in its way a quite remarkable one: the anthem was heard in respectful silence. A lot more respectful than it is in Cardiff where it's invariably accompanied by booing and jeers. What a curious world it is when the Irish turn out to be less anti-English than the Welsh.

Perhaps it shows that, sometimes, sport can be a civilising influence. Or perhaps it is another thing that blurs the boundaries of life outside the stadium. After all, Irish rugby teams have, entirely uncontroversially, ignored the border, mixing players from both the Republic and Northern Ireland. And those players are invariably part of the team that represents the British Isles abroad, a team known for a long time as the British Lions until, in 2001, someone noticed... oops, that's not right... and changed the name to the British *and Irish* Lions.

Sports like rugby can suggest contradictory things about the nature of Britain, but there is one activity that reveals it with great accuracy and which, in the early twenty-first century, reflects the style and preoccupations of society as a whole and the way in which those attributes are changing. The sport is cricket, which proverbially ('It's not cricket') is supposed to encapsulate the famous British sense of fair play. The country took it to colonial territories around the world and, in a triumph of continuity, still plays it against those same nations, loss of empire being appropriately reflected in the way in which England (which in this case is Britain) usually lose the test matches concerned.

For a long time it was also a game that reflected British class divisions. It was only in 1962 that the distinction between Gentlemen (amateurs) and Players (professionals) was abolished, something that until then had been marked by one of those careful social gradations in which we once specialised. Amateurs were listed with their initials in front of their names, professionals with the initials following. On one occasion the correction had to be issued: "F.J. Titmus should read Titmus, F.J." Part of the class aspect of the game was the way in which the privileged amateur whose upbringing imbued him with indelible qualities of sportsmanship turned out to be the ruthless competitor who would stop at nothing in pursuit of victory. Most famously of all this attitude found expression in the person of Douglas Jardine (Winchester and Oxford) who captained England in the 'bodyline' series played in Australia in 1932-33.

Jardine developed a strategy of getting his fast bowlers to aim at the batsman's body, constantly threatening him with injury. It meant, Neville Cardus reported, "that none but the fittest could hope to survive", and was intended in particular to subdue the Australian's Donald Bradman, probably the greatest batsman ever. To underline the class element further, Jardine's most potent bowler was Harold Larwood, a Nottinghamshire collier. Larwood recalled later that when, at the age of seventeen, he played for his village First XI, he had bowled in sandshoes "because I didn't own a pair of boots. I sent down 20 overs during the match, even though I'd worked down the mine all the previous night."

It's easy to see cricket as a paradigm of British life and society, at its most revealing, I think, in the traditional county game in which, for long periods, nothing very much happened. Long stretches of distant ritual were occasionally interrupted by moments of furious activity, excitement even. There'd be sudden loud noise of bat on ball. 'Good shot', people would say in that respectful murmur of civilised appreciation reserved for largely deserted county grounds. Bored players would tour the outfield, keeping half an eye on the game in which they were supposed to be taking part, chatting to spectators who were wrapped in travelling rugs and pouring tea from thermos flasks, sometimes signing autographs for small boys. There'd be another, different noise and sudden applause. What's happened? Who's out? Who caught him? It would be a long time until the next bit of excitement and you'd missed it. No television replays, of course, so it was lost for ever. In any case,

hardly anyone really understands cricket, although more than
understand rugby, and most of it takes place too far away to be seen
properly with the untrained naked eye. It's little wonder that those
two enigmatic playwrights, Samuel Beckett and Harold Pinter, were
so devoted to the game.

Cricket drifting on through the summer was as much a social
event as it was a sport. At Sophia Gardens in Cardiff it was important to tour the ground, stopping to chat to acquaintances, in
particular the groups of regulars, retired men who never missed a
ball. Most days you could talk about the uselessness of the England
selectors who, as usual, were ignoring the great brilliance of any
number of Glamorgan players but, there we are, they wouldn't be
able to find their way to Wales anyway, we agreed. There was also
time to be spent assessing the various eccentrics who I suppose
were then to be found on every ground, including people with
scorebooks carefully recording every ball, every run, every wicket.
And inevitably, The Man Who Knows All About Cricket, a statisti-
cal obsessive in a game in which numbers and history are often
more important than the actual match taking place in front of you.
There was never any crowd trouble because, except on very special
occasions, there was never any crowd. Some people would drink
steadily through the day before falling quietly asleep in mid-after-
noon. When play ended they would stagger off home, scarlet with
sunburn.

At Glamorgan you might meet Wilf Wooler who had played
rugby for Wales at the age of nineteen, when still at school. Wooler
had captained Glamorgan for many years and had then become the
club secretary, a position that allowed him to pretend that the cricketing side of the club had nothing to do with him. If you sat with him
for half an hour he would run through the shortcomings of many of
the Glamorgan players, ("I reckon his wickets have cost us £700
each," he said of one superannuated hiring from a more glamorous
county) and, if you stayed for a while, any British politician to the
left of Oswald Mosley. He was a tireless opponent of anti-apartheid
campaigners who wanted to stop sporting contacts with South
Africa, advertising himself as a man entirely without prejudice ("I'd
play against pink-eyed pygmies if they wanted") while insisting that
black people had smaller brains than white people.

He was big, tough, combative and fearless. He liked to tell a
story about how he'd taunted a fast bowler into trying to hurt him

and succeeding in doing so. "Oh, it hurt," he said, laughing. Players crippled with injury were told to 'run it off'. He'd been a prisoner of the Japanese in Changi gaol in Singapore during the war, an experience which taught him, he explained, that communism didn't work. You had to be selfish to survive. At the end of the war he took up cricket again. When he told me about this in a television interview I was amazed.

I said: "You went through an experience that destroyed the lives of many men, physically and mentally, and you're telling me you just picked up your bat and went out to play for Glamorgan?"

"Oh, no," he replied. "I had to practice first."

I suppose Wilf (Rydal School and Cambridge) was a late flowering of the Jardine school of sport and, for all his obnoxious views on many subjects, he was a collector's item. He was cricket's equivalent of Detective Chief Inspector Gene Hunt in the television series *Life on Mars*: shocking but also compelling in the unconcealed incorrectness of his attitudes, a visitor from the past. It's a thread found in Sir Henry Newbolt's poem 'Vitaï Lampada' which carries the spirit of the cricket field through to the battlefields of the First World War.

> The river of death has brimmed his banks,
> And England's far, and Honour a name.
> But the voice of a schoolboy rallies the ranks,
> "Play up! Play up! And play the game!"

Who would recite such a verse now except as a piece of satire? In the same way cricket has come to reflect the society in which it's played. Who's got the time or the patience to sit through a four day game, particularly as the great players, too precious to risk at such a low level, are hardly seen on the county grounds any more? Test cricket can still produce gripping drama over an entire summer, as in the case of the Ashes series of 2005, but you can no longer watch it on television unless you pay lots of money to Rupert Murdoch. People complain and talk about sporting 'crown jewels' being sold off to the highest bidder, but it's difficult to say what's wrong with a system that only reflects the overwhelming commercial imperatives of much modern sport. Why should cricketers be singled out as a group to get paid less than other sportsmen? Is it because in the public subconscious it represents a last piece of territory over which

Britain (or England) wants to maintain proprietorial rights because, after all, it all began here, as early as the sixteenth century, or maybe even in Anglo Saxon times? (Hey, we thought of it first.)

It's all too late. It seems entirely appropriate that professional cricket is on the way to becoming much more accessible, much more entertaining and much shorter. And how delicious it is that such a change, overwhelming the hapless English administrators (the initials ECB, interestingly, are said to stand for England *and Wales* Cricket Board) should be driven by India which has become, in cricketing terms, the richest and most powerful nation in the world. It clearly won't be long before the normal form of a cricket match will be Twenty20 – each side batting for just twenty overs. A match takes a total of three hours and as often as not is played under floodlights. It's an entirely manageable and exciting sporting occasion to which people can allocate a sensible amount of their time.

The British thing is to pretend that this isn't the case, that everything can be squeezed in and all traditions can be maintained. How forlorn a hope this is was demonstrated clearly, and perhaps terminally, by the decision to send an England team to compete in an event staged in the West Indies in October 2008 by a Texan billionaire, Sir Allen Stanford. Twenty million dollars were offered, winner takes all. Terrified that their best players would be tempted by huge sums of money, from India in particular, into abandoning test cricket for the more lucrative form of the game, the ECB joined the circus, believing the other sides involved weren't much use. In any case the rules meant that England and a West Indies side had to get into the final of the tournament, the other games being played to string the whole circus out over a reasonable length of time. So, the theory was, the England stars could pick up a million dollars each for a few days' work and would, consequently, stay loyal to England. The newspapers were speculatively spending the loot for them when the final was staged on November 1. England were easily defeated by a West Indian XI and so left without any prize money at all. A few months later Sir Allen's status shifted from billionaire to 'billionaire' and the US Securities and Exchange Commission accused him of an $8 billion fraud. The British cricketing authorities said they were shocked and surprised – but the great cricket adventure was no more. It had been a sporting and financial disaster the only dividend of which was humiliation and derision.

You can't get more British than that. Or is it English?

Norman Blood

"I generally don't like England very much"
– Prince Harry, February 2008

IT'S NOT ENTIRELY IMPOSSIBLE to imagine that occasionally, on a wet Sunday afternoon perhaps, some of the more obscure members of the royal family settle down wistfully to look one more time at *Kind Hearts and Coronets*, one of the most brilliant creations of the post-war British film industry. Indeed there can be few works of cinema more British, the product of a time when the industry made a brief and forlorn effort to resist the cultural imperialism of Hollywood cinema. Even though it first appeared in 1949, its heartless comedy remains fresh and ingenious. It's the story of Louis Mazzini who takes an elaborate revenge for the death of his widowed mother, ostracized by her aristocratic family because of her marriage to an Italian opera singer. Louis' response is to set out to dispose of the eight people of the D'Ascoyne family who stand ahead of him in the line of succession to the dukedom of Chalfont, something he achieves chiefly through committing six murders.

Unusually, the fictional dukedom could pass through the female line, something that might give those distant heirs to the House of Windsor particular cause for reflection since this is how it works in our own royal family. Boys first, *naturally*, but in their absence, girls. That is why, for example, the princesses Beatrice and Eugenie, daughters of the Duke of York, are for the time being at numbers five and six respectively in the line of succession to the throne. Such a state of affairs might well provoke at least passing homicidal thoughts in someone less scrupulous than the Duke's ex-wife, Sarah. The further down the list you are, of course, the more murders you would have to commit to make your way to the top of the pile. So it's unlikely that any detailed schemes are forming in the brain of, say, Prince Wladimir of Yugoslavia who, in 2006, had ninety-nine people ahead of him in the queue. Nor, for that matter, is it probable that any similar ambition often troubled the thoughts of Lord Nicholas Windsor when he was twenty-fifth in line to the throne and, obviously, not at all once he had been excluded entirely as a result of his own actions.

By all accounts Lord Nicholas, who was born in 1970, is a perfectly decent man, although he might have a tendency to be what was once called highly strung. The only offence the newspapers found recorded against him was that, in his youth, he was once caught smoking marijuana in St. James's Park, an entirely appropriate place for a member of the royal family to relax with a joint, but nevertheless still against the law. His subsequent career, distinctly less louche, involved him in teaching disadvantaged children. Even though his qualifications aren't all that impressive he seems to be harmless enough and, by royal standards, not particularly unsuited to the job of being king if, by some chance, asteroids were to land simultaneously on Buckingham Palace, Windsor Castle, Clarence House and some of London's most expensive nightclubs. But it's never going to happen. Lord Nicholas is now expressly prohibited from ascending the British throne. Yet the reason for his change of status is, in the modern world, essentially trivial and of specific interest to no more than a handful of people who, like Lord Nicholas himself, are of little or no account in the wider scheme of things. But at the same time it reveals something absolutely fundamental about the nature of Britain and what a very peculiar thing it is to be British.

The explanation was reported excitedly – and inaccurately – in the *Daily Mail* in November 2006. In breathless tones an indifferent public was informed that Lord Nicholas, "the youngest son of the Duke and Duchess of Kent, has given up his place as 25th in line to the throne in order to marry… Princess Paola de Frankopan, the British-born daughter of a Croatian aristocrat." In the world of the *Daily Mail* the idea that someone should deliberately abandon his entirely theoretical prospects of succeeding to the British throne is somehow an impetuously romantic act. But then this story is essentially a classic Ruritanian comedy. *The Times* reported in September 2006 that there were serious doubts about whether the princess's family as entitled to call itself de Frankopan or, come to that, whether she was actually a princess at all. Her father, a

businessman called Louis Doimi di Delupis, was said to have
adopted the ancient Croatian name as recently as the year 2000 and
to have been denied membership of the Croatian Nobility
Association on the grounds that the de Frankopan family had died
out some time in the nineteenth century. The princess's brother,
Prince Peter, was unimpressed by footling arguments about matters
of authenticity. "The title is not a claim on anything," he said. "It is
just a reflection of the age of the family."

In the light of the history and present character of much of our
own aristocracy it would be unwise of anyone British to sneer at
how these matters are handled in Croatia. To do so would be to miss
the most important aspect of this affair. As far as Princess Paola was
concerned the problem was not her social status, noble or otherwise, but the fact that she was a Catholic, which meant that in order
to marry her Lord Nicholas would have to give up his claim to the
throne. Or would have had to do so if it hadn't been the case,
overlooked by the *Daily Mail*, that he himself had become a
Catholic five years previously and so had already taken the plunge
into becoming a kind of royal un-person.

Instead of bothering themselves about why this prohibition
existed and whether it had any contemporary significance, most
people probably preferred to go no deeper than *The Times* version
when it said: "Royal match that really is a fairytale", a headline the
neatly caught our ambiguous attitude to royalty as well as the
unresolved issues concerning the pedigree of the bride's parents,
Prince Louis and Princess Ingrid. What was not further explored
was the question of whether there was something not entirely
British about being a Catholic, something alien, so that even in what
poses as a multicultural society, a particular group, religiously
defined, was subject to one last statutory ban.

In the modern world we can assume that hardly anyone lies
awake at night worrying about the last gasp consequences of a
three-hundred-year-old act of parliament, the Act of Settlement,
that established definitively the Protestant succession. From time to
time a modest row breaks out when people denounce this way of
going on as offensive and absurd (the heir to the throne must be a
Protestant but can marry a Muslim or a Hindu or a Scientologist -
almost anyone, in fact, just as long as they are not Catholic) before
change is described by ministers as theoretically desirable but in
practice too complicated. In politics that means there aren't enough

votes in the matter to make it worth spending a great deal of time over.

You might think, if you didn't know politicians, that they would be anxious to attend to the matter of principle that appears to be involved here, that in a country in which there are modern laws against religious discrimination there should persist a dusty statute that enforces religious prejudice in a small but unmistakable way. More than that, this reaches the very top of the British constitutional and social structure, a little bit of poison in the very place where you might expect the most concern for the character of national life.

As it happens this is one topic that seems to have escaped the attention of the Prince of Wales, despite his habit of fretting publicly over various aspects of modern Britain. Yet he might perhaps have been expected to take a particular interest because this is one of the few subjects about which he has specialist knowledge. Indeed, he's even got a track record on the question of religion and the monarchy, having declared at one time that when eventually he became king he yearned to be regarded as the 'defender of faiths' rather than Defender of *the* Faith, the latter title referring to the Church of England, of which in due course he will become Supreme Governor. In the light of his personal history, an intervention by the Prince of Wales on any matter connected with marriage might turn out to be counterproductive, but he's never made an issue of exclusivity in religious matters. From time to time, for example, he has retreated to a monastery on a Greek mountain top to meditate on his next big idea, a practice that underlines his intense interest in spiritual life. And while it might be argued that the exclusion of Catholics is a political business rather than a religious one it is nevertheless the case that the prince has for many years scribbled away furiously to acquaint government ministers with his views on all kinds of controversial issues. Since, for example, he's been perfectly happy to rubbish publicly various aspects of the education system he surely wouldn't be deterred by the appropriateness or otherwise of his intervening in this sensitive territory. This is, after all, one of the reasons he apparently cherishes his reputation as a 'royal rebel', a status that, as with his various senior military ranks, has ceremonial rather than practical significance.

Like many of the great comic characters in history the chief entertainment value of the Prince of Wales lies in the fact that he

clearly hasn't got the faintest idea of the size of the gap between
what he would like to be and what he really is. He often seems very
like the persona created by the great comedian Tony Hancock,
someone whose abilities always left him short of his aspirations in,
for instance, intellectual matters, and who subsided into a state of
truculent pique at each failure. The idea of the prince being a royal
rebel is a difficult one to sustain, given the wealth, privilege and
deference which surrounds him and which he has shown no sign of
wishing to diminish. Anyone who has met him, however briefly,
understands at once that there are two classes of people in the
world: the royal family and everyone else, everyone else being
subordinate in a way that is, simultaneously, both unstated and
absolutely clear. He might like to kid himself that because not everyone agrees with him he must be a bit of a rebel. It doesn't seem to
cross his mind that he might actually just be wrong. Perhaps Prince
Charles is the only person in the world who doesn't realise that
those people who pay respectful attention to his ideas and his
campaigns do so because of who he is and not because of what he
knows. It is absolutely impossible to take him as seriously as he
takes himself.

It's easy enough to laugh at the prince and tempting to do so;
this is a man, after all, who loves the past so much that he's never
got over *The Goon Show*. But it would be careless to dismiss entirely
the royal rebel label he sports so proudly. Of course he is not a rebel
in the sense that he is someone of a radical bent who wants to sweep
away the ideas and conventions that confine the freedom of those
who will one day be his subjects. But he *is* a rebel in the opposite
sense of the word: his objective is as far as possible to put the world
back the way it once was, or the way he thinks it once was, which is
not the same thing. And in this he is by no means a lonely oddball
dabbling in metaphysical ideas about the nature of the world, but
part of a large, eager crowd.

In all the contradictions, eccentricities, prejudices, flaws and
delusions that characterise both his personality and his place within
the structure of the United Kingdom, he is to a large extent the
embodiment of what it is to be British. In particular his Britishness
lies in his fear of change, his indifference to knowledge, his distrust
of science, his addiction to the past, his adherence to class and his
elevation of the mystical above the rational. In these matters and
others he mirrors many of the attitudes of what's known as Middle

England (the Celtic nations having a slightly different centre of gravity), that are so persistently articulated in the pages of much of the British press.

So, for example, he often favours superstition over objective knowledge, something that leads him to put at least as much emphasis on any kind of mystical, atavistic explanation of the nature of the world as he does on the outcome of scientific inquiry. This means that when it comes to medicine he talks up what are called complementary therapies, arguing that many of them "...are rooted in ancient traditions that intuitively understood the need to maintain balance and harmony with our minds, bodies and the natural world. Much of this knowledge, often based on oral traditions, is sadly being lost yet orthodox medicine has so much to learn from it. It is tragic, it seems to me – and indeed to many people who have studied this whole area – that in the ceaseless rush to 'modernise'... many beneficial approaches... have been cast aside...".

The thrust of this argument (or you might say 'argument') lies not so much in its content, which is clearly limited, but in its punctuation. The Prince of Wales is a master of sarcastic quotation marks. 'Modernise' is an expression of scorn, as is his view of 'experts' in education, another typographical nudge of disbelief. He uses the same technique to undermine his critics, sprinkling inverted commas over their descriptions of him as 'old-fashioned' or 'irrelevant'. The prince is a supporter of homeopathy (as is his mother, who is reported never to travel abroad without her case of sixty homeopathic remedies) even though the best scientific evidence suggests that as a treatment it is almost entirely useless and, sometimes, positively harmful. When doctors and scientists, including a Nobel prize winner, the president of the Academy of Medical Sciences, and six fellows of the Royal Society, argued that the health service should stop wasting money on it, a spokesman for the prince's Foundation for Integrated Health dismissed them as 'clinical barons'.

In these circumstances a natural reaction is to consider that Prince Charles is out of touch with the modern British society (or 'out of touch' as he would no doubt put it) but in one sense the exact opposite is the case. He represents the pervasive belief that everyone in authority, politicians in particular, but scientists, industrialists, company directors, civil servants, policemen and any number of other groups, is engaged in a systematic campaign of deception against the public in the interests of their particular administrative or commercial objectives. Phone masts and power lines are scrambling our brains, new vaccines are making our children ill, genetically modified crops ('Frankenstein foods', as the popular press calls them) will destroy our immune systems and turn the countryside into a biological desert. In these matters and others, we're told, governments ignore evidence and public concern for reasons which are never entirely clear, but are generally assumed to involve personal greed and the financial interests of mighty multinational corporations. In the face of such odds, you might argue, who better to defend the interests of the ordinary British man and woman in the street than someone who doesn't gain his authority from deals or votes but by virtue of being who and what he is: a prince.

So it is possible to argue that the Prince of Wales, far from being a remote and alien figure, actually represents Britishness in a particularly vivid manner. Not only does he share the prejudices and suspicions of a large section of the public, he gives them a new legitimacy through his elevated position in the world. And, of course, along with the authority bestowed by the very fact of being royal, he belongs to the people in another, perhaps even more important way. That's because of the cult of celebrity which means that, for instance, a singer or a film star – Madonna, perhaps, or Tom Cruise – can get a hearing for pronouncement which, coming from another source, would immediately be dismissed as totally barmy. When the prince screws up his face in anguish and worries away about the state of the world, he might be Bono or Bob Geldof or someone else who has translated his fame into becoming a surrogate conscience for an admiring public.

It's most peculiar, but when you look at it you can see that, of all unexpected things, Charles is actually a kind of one-man Britain walking (or, more often, being driven) among us. He's not a royal rebel at all but rather something equally paradoxical, a royal common man or, to adapt a famous phrase, the people's prince. Is he doing it on purpose, you wonder? It seems unlikely, but I suppose it's just possible that bred into the royal family DNA is a self-preservation mechanism that allows its members to tune in to popular opinion and adjust their own behaviour accordingly. And given all those deposed relatives around the place, from Greece and elsewhere, there have been plenty of practical examples to reinforce the need to behave in this way. Yet when it comes to indications of hereditary sensitivity, the House of Windsor seems to point in a different direction; in particular in the lives of the Prince of Wales's father, brothers, sister and aunt, none of whom has been noted for caring what the public thinks about anything very much.

But there's even more to it than that. Members of the royal family are now public property in a way that would have been unthinkable not long ago, certainly not before 1969 when the famous television documentary, *The Royal Family*, twitched aside the net curtains for a moment and sensationally revealed them as people who knew about things like washing up. Now it's possible to see that the system of monarchy perhaps depends as much on popular approval as it does on the principle of heredity.

No one knows that better than the Prince of Wales himself who for a time carried the label of one of the most hated characters in the language of the tabloid press: the love rat. It happened when his estranged (later ex- and, after that, late, ex-) wife, a much more astute manipulator of the media than him and his advisers, trounced him in the battle for the people's affection. His crime was to fail to love someone who was adored by practically everyone else in the country, just as Heather Mills was later brutally demonised by the red tops for the failure of her relationship with another national treasure, Sir Paul McCartney. Just as significantly, though, the prince's experience also illustrated how a public figure is not judged directly on the basis of ascertainable facts but instead through the filter of television and the popular press; in other words by the standards of the tireless public relations construction of image as distinct from the rough-edged, inconclusive business of daily existence. Soon enough the two things become blurred.

The result was that Prince Charles and Princess Diana came to play leading parts as our representatives in real life versions of two preoccupations of the British public – soap opera and daytime infidelity TV. The prince's Jerry Springer moment came when he went on ITV to confess to his pal Jonathan Dimbleby that, yes, he had committed adultery. After that it was impossible not to think that the hand of some kind of national executive producer was guiding the schedules of real life as, the following year, Princess Diana put on a performance of dramatic brilliance to flay her husband and his mistress, the then Mrs. Parker Bowles. And it was a particular triumph in the language of television because her appearance was made not only on the establishment broadcaster, the BBC, but on *Panorama*, of all staid, old-fashioned programmes, which had never seen anything like it. She got an audience as half as big again as the prince – more than 22 million. That meant that she was a bigger star than he was and, therefore, was bound to be in the right, the acclaimed winner of Royal Idol.

Every day the tabloid press writes about the characters in television soap operas without making much distinction between reality and the fantasy world of the studio set. Lust, greed, violence, drink, drugs and death stalk their pages, sometimes descending on the characters invented by scriptwriters, sometimes on the people who play those characters. Quite often you have to be very alert to spot the difference. So it was in the story of Diana and Charles as one public drama followed another until, finally, in the manner of a producer confronted with falling ratings, fate put on a spectacular car crash and wrote the star out of the show.

But even then the question arose: was this real? Had it actually taken place? For a while millions refused to believe it. Surely the next episode would have someone stepping out of the shower to reveal that the whole thing had been a dream. And if that didn't occur there were still plenty of twists left in the plot. In modern Britain nothing just *happens*. A narrative of explanation, preferably guilt, has to be discovered. For such reasons there seemed to be plenty of takers for the theory that the car crash in the Alma tunnel was part of an elaborate conspiracy, and quite a few for the idea that it had been arranged on the instructions of someone at the very heart of the British establishment.

There's something very winning in the idea that the elderly Duke of Edinburgh, appalled by the threat to Britain posed by the possibility that his former daughter-in-law was about to marry the Muslim whose baby he believed she was carrying, ordered the security services to kill her. After all, this is no more than the plot of dozens of thrillers in which the last person you suspect eliminates those who threaten to expose some devastating secret and thus thwart his master plan. There's not much point in trying to insist that these are simply stories in works of fiction. This is a world in which it has become increasingly difficult to separate real life from the confections of novelists and screen writers.

So, for example, millions of people who bought *The Da Vinci Code* became persuaded that, because it contained just enough facts

and garbled learning, the truth about Jesus Christ, his marriage to
Mary Magdalene, and the birth of their son (sorry, Son) had been
concealed by secret societies down the centuries. And when the
author, Dan Brown, insisted that, no, it was simply a work of fiction,
devotees of the book assumed that he was just winking at them. The
more he said it wasn't true the more they thought it was.

In the case of the Duke of Edinburgh the absence of any
evidence to support the proposition that he ordered Diana's death
was taken by some to be a conclusive endorsement of its truth.
Obviously only the most powerful people in the country could
organise a cover-up with such efficiency. As for the details of the
assassination itself, it looked like a haphazard set of reactions to a
series of unplanned events the course of which could not have been
predicted by anyone. Far from undermining the plot theory,
though, that either demonstrated how fiendishly clever the intelligence services are or, alternatively, bore out their reputation for
incompetence. Either way, their fingerprints were all over it.

Although in the modern world this sort of thing is given great
momentum by the free exchange of conspiracy theories across the
internet, it's by no means new. After all, there are plenty of takers
for the idea that the Duke of Clarence, the son of the then Prince of
Wales, was in fact Jack the Ripper. Then again, what role did the
Duke of Windsor play in the arrival in Scotland in 1941 of Hitler's
deputy, Rudolph Hess? Had he come to negotiate a peace which
would have put the duke, who had been forced to abdicate five
years earlier, back on the throne? Or perhaps install him as some
kind of president or prime minister? If there's no truth in this why
is it that some of the official papers relating to the duke in this
period remain firmly sealed? But then again, perhaps Hess's contact
was actually the Duke of Windsor's brother, the Duke of Kent.
Which might explain why, in1942, the Duke of Kent was killed in a
crash involving a flying boat carrying him from Scotland to Iceland.
After all, the weather was fine and there was no sign of mechani-
cal... and so on and on. In any case, was the man who parachuted
into Scotland really Rudolph Hess? Or was it some kind of double
who fooled almost everyone through the long years he spent in
Spandau, except for Hugh Thomas, a doctor from Merthyr Tydfil,
who spotted at once the absence of the scars that would have been
on the real Hess's body? "The torso cannot lie," Thomas
pronounced definitively.

In reality, though, the only truth we can get out of this sort of thing is an illustration of how easy it is to construct an elaborate narrative out of any available group of facts, rumours, misunderstandings and gossip; plus a burning desire for things to be other than they really are. And if you say it often enough it comes to sound more true than the truth, especially when everyone else involved denies it or is silent, denial and silence being, as we know, the conditions that unerringly identify the guilty. No event that disturbs the public imagination is exempt from this kind of treatment. The persistence of the idea that the Kennedys had Marilyn Monroe murdered is the exact American equivalent of the Diana story (royalty have inconvenient woman rubbed out), but at the same time that car crash in Paris and the tumult that followed has a unique character as a British story, in particular in the way it reveals important aspects of what constitutes Britishness.

In the popular imagination Mohamed Al Fayed has managed to combine two roles that recur constantly in Britain's ambiguous attitudes to outsiders. At one and the same time he has managed to be both the comic foreigner and the malevolent alien. He is mocked for his imperfect command of English, which is always good for a laugh in a country notorious for its lack of interest in foreign languages. But he is also considered to be a rather shady character whose dubious business practices run entirely counter to the probity that, we are often assured, distinguishes Britain from the less fastidious commercial regimes that persist in many other parts of the world.

For a long time Al Fayed's dearest wish was to become a British citizen but this he was rejected at every turn. He could own Harrods, the country's most significant department store, complete with royal warrants, in the retail lives of the establishment; he could buy a castle in Scotland; he could take over a football club; he could walk with the Queen at the Royal Windsor Horse Show; he could give millions to British charities; he could even revive (unsuccessfully) that monument of old-fashioned Britishness, *Punch* magazine; he could live in Britain undisturbed. The one thing he couldn't have was the one thing he wanted above anything else: a British passport. The problem was, it was made clear by the authorities, that he was not someone of good character.

You don't have to admire Mohamed Al Fayed to think he might have had something of a rough deal. After all, the list of businessmen, foreign-born or home-grown, who lie about their origins or their wealth would fill its own reference book. It's difficult to argue, for example, that Al Fayed is a more desperate character than, say, Robert Maxwell. Nor has he been to gaol, unlike Harold Wilson's pal Joe Kagan, Lord Kagan, the inventor of the Gannex mack. Even Tom Bower, in his unauthorised biography, a demolition job running to almost 500 pages, concedes that some aspects of the government's behaviour towards Al Fayed looked spiteful, that it could be seen as some kind of vendetta. "Even some of their enemies conceded that the Fayeds, after thirty years' residence, were entitled to British nationality." In other countries the authorities take a more pragmatic view. After Al Fayed had restored the Ritz Hotel in Paris, the French government, far from shunning him, made him a member of its most important order of chivalry, the Légion d'Honneur.

His revenge was spectacular, in particular because his answer to accusations of dishonesty and, let's face it, some kind of vulgar *un-Britishness*, was to reveal that, if he was being accused of being corrupt and venal he was only following the example of leading figures in British public life. In particular he was instrumental in exposing the fact that there were politicians who were perfectly willing to place themselves at the disposal of wealthy people and ask questions in parliament or perform other services in return for sums of cash delivered, so the Harrods' owner said, in brown envelopes. He had been told that British MPs plied for hire, like taxis; far from being the malicious invention of a disappointed man this turned out in some cases be no less than the truth. And the Ritz Hotel in Paris was a dangerous place to pass the time. It was to play a part in ruining the careers of two politicians who stayed there, the Conservative MP Neil Hamilton, who lost his seat and went bankrupt, and the Cabinet Minister, Jonathan Aitken. Hamilton has regularly protested his innocence but was forced to carve out a new career in the less glamorous parts of showbiz. In1999 Aitken was sent to gaol for perjury.

In such a world it was perhaps to be expected that many people would at least half-believe that the Duke of Edinburgh, who has long starred in the Carry-On version of the British story as another comic foreigner, might have sent some trained killers to save his adopted country from... well, from what exactly it's difficult to say, but something terrible involving Muslims. This is all self-evidently a mountain of piffle, sustained only by Al Fayed's ability to spend huge sums of money on expensive lawyers who would happily create a two-year court case out of whose turn it is to make the tea. But this extravagance perhaps gives us one reason at least to be grateful to him. His pursuit of the establishment through the courts revealed the inequalities of British (or in his case non-British) citizens under the law. Because he had millions of pounds to waste in this way he could make authorities jump through hoops, investigating his allegations over and over again and staging the most expensive inquest in history. It cost taxpayers at least six million pounds – and perhaps as much as ten million – to conduct this elaborate farce. Anyone who had been the subject of a genuine injustice could not have had his case examined in such exhaustive detail if he didn't also have vast wealth available to pursue it. Al Fayed's activities echoed as appropriately as possible the words of an Irish judge, Sir James Mathew, more than a century before. "In England justice is open to all – like the Ritz Hotel."

However preposterous the theories might have been, in the broad sweep of public life you can see why people might be prepared to believe such things. They had already made clear their displeasure at the Prince of Wales's behaviour with Mrs. Parker Bowles, not least because the whole atmosphere of the times made it unthinkable that he could choose someone older, less fashionable, less photogenic, less glamorous and less openly in need of affection than Diana. And in its turn that revealed in particular what was to be underlined a thousand times over after the Mercedes crashed into the tunnel wall: that the country had decided to dispense with many of the traditional virtues that were supposed to characterise Britishness and to put others in their place.

Out went stoicism, determination, the stiff upper lip and a refusal to blub, whatever the provocation. For at least a hundred and fifty years the royal family (with a couple of notable exceptions) had set a particular example in this regard, resolution in the face of adversity, reticence and understatement. It might have been untrue but it was how people liked to think of themselves, something summed up in particular by the remark attributed to Queen Elizabeth when German bombs fell on Buckingham Palace during the war. "Now," she is reputed to have said, "we can look the East End in the face." Sixty years later her grandson and his disgruntled aristocratic bride were appearing on television to talk about their adulteries and seek from an astonished public some kind of absolution for their transgressions.

It was another of those changes that were knocking away the props from what had long sustained the structural identity of Britishness. In the same way many of the great questions that once dominated political debate have disappeared from the agenda, in particular the central struggle between capitalism and socialism. Religious arguments, even the experience of what it is to belong even nominally to a particular religious tradition, ceased to have relevance to the everyday lives of the vast majority of people. Richard Dawkins lectures us on why we shouldn't believe, but we don't believe anyway so his advice is largely redundant. As for those Dawkins opposes, it's difficult to escape the conclusion that, far from concerning themselves with central questions of belief and the way in which they should shape the lives of their congregations, Christian churches have become almost completely preoccupied by disputes about the sexual practices of the clergy.

At the emotional height of the torrid dispute between Prince Charles and Princess Diana, grumbling could be heard around the country, encouraged in particular by a moralising press which wouldn't have anything very much to publish if people stopped committing adultery, but which nevertheless condemns it with the zeal of a nineteenth-century Nonconformist preacher. Charles was no good, the argument ran, not fit to be king. Chuck him out and make Prince William the heir to throne. Circumstances defused that one, but if reproachful pictures of Diana had gone on appearing day after day in virtually every newspaper and magazine around the world, who knows how much momentum such a campaign might have built up. The people's view does matter in the end, something that was thunderously demonstrated when the public mood forced the Queen to return to London and mourn with them. Protocol said the Royal Standard should not fly at half mast above Buckingham Palace. But protocol is nothing more than what you did last time and the flag was lowered.

So it is that the voters continue to be reconciled with the anachronism that is the monarchy and the eccentric principles that support it. In theory the hereditary principle is paramount. When it comes to kings and queens you get what you get. If you passed over one heir in order to install someone else who looked like a better bet, the system would crack and break. In the same way abdication, even for an ageing monarch who's done her time, looks more or less impossible. It separates the role from the person and thus undermines much of its mystique.

But the rule is not absolute. An unsuitable king, an unsatisfactory heir, can be disqualified, even if it's for an offence as minor in the contemporary world as marrying a Catholic. That was the consequence of what became known as the Glorious Revolution which, in 1688, saw the Protestants William and Mary invited to replace, as joint monarchs, the Catholic James II. Power was irrevocably shifted from the Crown to Parliament, in theory from monarchs to the people. And that was the principle – no Catholics – that thirteen years later was carved into the constitution by the Act of Settlement and which remains an inescapable law to the present day.

In the modern world I suppose this can be glossed as a kind of twitch on the leash for the Prince of Wales, a constitutional reminder that the system isn't quite as straightforward as the unwary might consider it to be. Perhaps, in Tennyson's words, the idea that there is a bit more to all this than the imperatives of history:

Kind hearts are more than coronets,
And simple faith than Norman blood.

At the same time there's no escaping the fact that the bar on Catholics, just like the system that maintains a hereditary monarchy as an important element of a notionally democratic state, is at best an anomaly and at worst an offence against the principles of religious and cultural tolerance and political equality to which we are all urged to subscribe. Who cares? Nobody much it seems. Not that glamorous couple, Lord Nicholas Windsor and Princess (or perhaps 'Princess') Paola, released from even having to think how many murders might stand between them and the throne. In the end perhaps it's no more absurd than many of the other quirks and oddities that characterise the way in which the country is run. But yet it somehow continues to matter in the traditionalist world that some newspapers like to keep on life support. When the Queen's grandson, Peter Phillips, got married in the summer of 2008 you could almost see the editorial brows being mopped in relief when his fiancée, the Canadian Autumn Kelly, decided, almost at the altar steps, that she would renounce her Catholic faith. The result was that Mr. Phillips retained his place – at that time eleventh – in line to the throne. Which left you thinking: who wouldn't be willing to give their services to a plot that would lead to Britain being reigned over by King Peter and Queen Autumn, a confection straight from the pages of the kind of celebrity magazine to which the royal couple sold pictures of their wedding.

What becomes clear from such events is that monarchy is institutionalised unfairness, a monument to class distinction, but, paradoxically, it is at its most vulnerable when it tries to pretend otherwise. When faced with the awkward questions raised by this state of affairs politicians, like most of the rest of society, prefer to look away. Which, of course, is very British, as you might expect in a land where everyone is theoretically equal but some people are officially more British than others.

*

Even if you consider that this represents an eye-wateringly odd state of affairs in the twenty-first century, hardly anyone believes it is important or sensitive enough to go trouble of getting it all sorted out. Quite the reverse, indeed. Among the national newspapers the *Guardian* is alone in thinking it's worth making a fuss but, towards the end of 2008, it announced, entirely unexpectedly, that the government had been converted to the campaign it had pursued for the previous eight years.

On September 25, the paper's lead story was headed: "End of the Anglican Crown". It went on. "Downing Street has drawn up plans to end the 300-year-old exclusion of Catholics from the throne. The requirement that the succession automatically pass to a male would also be reformed, making it possible for a firstborn daughter of Prince William to become his heir."

The experienced reader's first reaction in these circumstances is: 'Hey, not so fast', and only a day later it became clear that this was not what's called a done deal. At first it was presented as a triumph for the *Guardian's* campaign but the language said otherwise. On September 26 the paper reported: "Constitutional experts and minority parties yesterday rallied behind proposals to repeal the 300-year bar to Catholics succeeding to the throne and end male precedence in the royal succession."

What had been "plans drawn up in Downing Street" had overnight become "proposals" which had "gone to Downing Street" where they didn't seem to be quite as decided as the newspaper. A Downing Street spokesman said: "To bring about changes to the law on succession would be a complex undertaking involving the amendment or repeal of a number of items of required legislation as well as requiring the consent of legislatures of member nations of the Commonwealth... we are of course aware of the concerns felt by many and we are always ready to consider the arguments in this complex area."

Being ready to "consider the arguments in this complex area" is not quite the same as having a specific plan to make any changes. But just in case, opponents of the idea, who immediately detected a plot to get rid of the monarchy altogether, lined up their forces. Soon enough A.N. Wilson was telling readers of the *Daily Mail* – across two pages: "As if Labour haven't wreaked enough damage to the British identity, they are now, in their death throes, trying to destroy the monarchy. It is precisely because we are now multicultural that to change this law would be so very divisive. At present many religious people – Jews, Muslims and Catholics among them – are pleased to live in a country in which faith is enshrined in the constitution. They can see that our Head of State is in fact a deeply religious woman, and they would rather be ruled over by a seriously religious Protestant than by a heedless secularist.

"New Labour has been a constitutional disaster. It went ahead with devolution for Wales and Scotland, and it looks perilously as if the end of that road will be something which the majority of the Scots and Welsh do not want – namely the break-up of the Union." And on and on he went, turning an attempt to address a piece of institutionalised discrimination into a betrayal of British history. "We British are incredibly lucky, not just because we have a good Queen but because we have a constitutional monarchy, which has been a bulwark against the political storms of the European land mass. Why did this country not go Communist, as Russia and Spain had done, or Fascist, as Italy, Germany – and then eventually Spain – were to do? The answer to that is very largely because we had a monarchy which was embedded in the constitution but had been shaped by the wisdom of the ages. By abolishing the hereditary principle in Parliament, New Labour went a long way to abolishing it in the monarchy as well."

Really? is the only word that comes to mind, but it's unwise to take newspaper columnists too literally. Wilson was only one of a number leaping to the defence of the status quo.* They have to write something and they have to write it with absolute certainty; passion first, facts second, doubt nowhere. Nevertheless it's as well to recognise the professional skills that allow them to articulate with great clarity the opinions of many of the people who read them, people who like to have their view of life reinforced rather than challenged. At the same time, though, it appears that the Queen herself and her advisers take a rather more subtle and pragmatic view of changing Britain.

In general we don't know what the Queen thinks about most questions of the day, although sometimes you think you can guess from the expression on her face. So we have to be cautious when told that, for example, she took a dim view of the introduction of devolution. Whether she did or she didn't, she and her staff are shrewd enough to make the necessary adjustments. She has made a point, for example, of opening the new sessions of the Scottish Parliament and the Welsh Assembly, as well as being present for other important occasions. She's joined by the Duke of Edinburgh and, particularly in Cardiff, by the Prince of Wales who struggles through those bits of the Welsh language he learnt long ago as a student in Aberystwyth. It's difficult to see how the royal family could be more explicit about their core message: whatever the distribution of decision-making and the details of institutions under the crown, this remains firmly a British enterprise.

Prince Charles himself was often criticised for being less than attentive to Wales. His heart, people felt, was in Scotland where he was often photographed wandering about in a kilt. In particular, while he had many homes around Britain, he didn't have one in Wales. Because of the need to emphasise the essential unity of Britain under the monarchy, advisers came to the conclusion that

---

* When in March 2009 Gordon Brown revealed that he had been in discussions with Buckingham Palace about making changes to the laws of succession there was the usual traditionalist hysteria. In a rather confused attack on the ideas involved the historian Andrew Roberts wrote in the *Daily Telegraph* that the Act of Settlement was one of the key pieces of legislation that has defined what Britain was and still is. "For a Prime Minister who claims to care deeply about the concept of Britishness, the Act should be sacrosanct, rather than sacrificed in a gross bout of politically correct gimmickry."

he should get one, *pronto*. This was house buying as politics. Now he has a modest residence, Llwynywermod in Carmarthenshire, and, in deference to the increasingly egalitarian mood of the times, anyone can rent out part of his coach house as a holiday home ("Premier self catering cottage in Wales – part of the courtyard range") when he's not around, which is quite often.

In Scotland Alex Salmond has made it clear that an independent Scotland run by the SNP would cherish the Queen. She would remain monarch of that country too (which she is already, of course, being Elizabeth I of Scotland, as well as Elizabeth II of England). In 2007 he told the *Daily Telegraph*: "Don't people associate the United Kingdom with the Union of the Crowns? If you have a monarch, a common head of state of independent countries, it underlines and stresses the social union between the two."

Significantly, when Salmond took office as First Minister and so became a minister of the crown, he wasn't asked to make the journey to London. Instead the Queen took a helicopter to Scotland, met Salmond at Holyrood for forty minutes or so, and then took the helicopter home again. A neat piece of royal diplomacy.

Which makes you think about the political insight of those who defend her position so furiously over the matter, for example, of the prohibition of Catholics. In his *Daily Mail* article, A.N. Wilson concluded: "...let us hope to God that the Queen, who somewhat to her shame allowed the disgraceful wreckage of the Lords without even questioning what was happening – will at last put her foot down. Enough is enough."

Somehow you get the feeling that the Queen is rather smarter than that.

---

* When Prince Harry went to serve with his army unit in Afghanistan, the media transformed him overnight from drunken wastrel into Prince Hal. Even the fact that he explained on camera that, on the whole he preferred Afghanistan, where large numbers of people would have been delighted to shoot him, to the United Kingdom, passed without much by way of critical comment. Having said he didn't like England all that much he added: ...you know, it's nice to be away from all the press and the papers." Good old Harry, the tone was, as most of the papers carefully left out his last, barbed comment on their work: "...and all the general shite that they write."

Where Have All The Voters Gone?

ONE OF THE MOST revealing stories in modern political life is that of the man who began his activism as a campaigner and agitator, went on to reach the highest levels of government and then, quite suddenly one day, was left shaking his dusty head in disbelief among the debris as his career collapsed around him. In the morning he had not one but two Cabinet jobs. In the afternoon he was on the train home.

Peter Hain had perhaps the best start possible for a young man planning a career in politics. Before he was out of his teens his name was known around the world. Even better, he was hated by large numbers of people. That's to say hated for the right reasons by the right people: in his view members of a reactionary establishment who stood shoulder to shoulder with tyranny while pretending to be defenders of freedom and equality.

Hain came to Britain in 1966, at the age of 16. He arrived from South Africa with his parents who were prominent opponents of apartheid. Both had spent time in gaol for their activities and were subject to restrictive banning orders. He was an outsider. Perhaps he was always to remain one, despite his eventual position at the heart of British public life. At the same time it might have been a quality that allowed him to see through some of the assumptions and evasions that people in his new country often took for granted. Perhaps, too, it gave him the nerve, while scarcely more than a boy, to confront those evasions in a particularly dramatic manner.

Given his history it was probably inevitable that Hain should become involved in one of the most spectacular campaigns mounted in Britain against the South African regime: stopping the country's sports teams touring the UK. In 1967, soon after he arrived, one case in particular pushed the sporting issue much higher up the political agenda. In 1967 the Worcestershire and England all-rounder Basil D'Oliveira was omitted from the England party that was to tour South Africa that winter. D'Oliveira was a coloured South African who wasn't allowed to play with white men in his own country. In England he'd made a successful career in the game and, while for much of that season there might have been cricketing reasons to leave him out of the tour, there seemed little doubt that the people who ran English cricket had decided it was important to avoid embarrassing the South African government. The fact that D'Oliveira scored a big century in a test match shortly before the touring party was named strongly suggested they were thinking of matters other than cricket. Even they couldn't keep up the sporting judgement facade, however, when another player dropped out and D'Oliveira clearly had the strongest claim to be included in his place. What it was really all about was swiftly revealed as soon as his belated selection was announced. The South African Prime Minister, B.J. Vorster, treated the decision as provocative and cancelled the tour.

Acquiescence in a naked piece of racism of this kind was very much what you might have expected from the cricketing establishment at that time. And at Lords, where they made such decisions, they didn't see any reason why the response should stop a South African side coming to Britain two years later. Nor did other authorities raise any objections to a South African international rugby team touring in 1969. In the circumstances it was hardly surprising that, despite his youth, Hain should become an enthusiastic opponent of these fixtures. In the process he was to discover some uncomfortable truths about the nature of British society and in particular the flexibility of some of its political allegiances.

"I think that what shocked me was, having come out of a bitter struggle against racism and apartheid, to find that many of the same attitudes were prevalent in Britain and you could almost see them capable of being reincarnated here."

He might have expected that among the committee men at Lords in their panama hats and bacon and egg ties, or the big men at Twickenham in their camel coats, people once described as 'old farts' even by one of their most successful players, Will Carling. While they breathed, imperial values would never die. They made no secret of their views nor had any desire to change them, particularly in the light of argument. Hain's surprise originated elsewhere. It came from people you would expect to have sympathy with the oppressed because of their own particular experience of life, the history of their communities and, in many cases, their persistent boasting about the importance of international solidarity. Not a bit of it, as he discovered.

Years later, long established as a Labour MP in South Wales, he told me about his shock. "In communities like this the reaction of working-class people who would never vote anything but Labour was virulent. There was actually a common viciousness that transcended English-Welsh rivalry or Scottish-English rivalry. The reaction in Wales to our rugby demonstrations, despite Wales's radical tradition politically, was vicious."

Like everyone else, like the British as described by Gordon Brown, the Welsh are keen to advertise their fundamental decency but sometimes the reality indicates an entirely different character. One of the worst incidents during that 1969 rugby tour took place at St. Helen's in Swansea, a famous rugby-mad ground in the middle of rugby-mad territory. Opponents of the game invaded the pitch to be challenged by local rugby enthusiasts, described by some observers as vigilantes. Two hundred demonstrators and ten policemen were injured. Years later Hain became the MP for Neath, only a few miles away from Swansea. Down at the local rugby club he became aware that such battles were now part of sporting folklore. They were recalled with an emotion that could easily be mistaken for pride. In the bar, members would tease him and would claim they'd been among those who'd carried him off the pitch during the demonstration. He didn't contradict those reminiscences, even though he hadn't actually been in Swansea on that day. After all, this is an area and a sport in which legend is more important than the prosaic truth.

To a South African liberal who knew what it was like to have the secret police searching his family home, this was baffling. It was an education in the duality of British society, the ease with which people could proclaim the importance of principle but avoid the consequences whenever they might be inconvenienced by it. Labour politicians who send their children to private schools are often accused of a similar sort of hypocrisy.

"People argued passionately and sincerely that sport had to go on regardless because sport was about bringing people together. But the South African team didn't bring people together. It couldn't have been more of an expression of a divided nation because only whites could be selected – by law."

In the end this whole campaign turned out to be a crucial element in Hain's life and career. Not because of the admirers it brought him, although there were plenty of those, but because of the enemies he made. An important part of a radical's credentials lies in the quality and ferocity of the people who denounce him. He inevitably got his share, especially among those who resented the idea of some alien figure coming along, spoiling the rugby and cricket, and telling British people how to conduct their lives.

"There was a lot of it, especially in the pages of the *Daily Telegraph*. They said you, you've got no right, especially when you're a student on a grant. We're subsidising demonstrations by this foreigner. When I got a first class degree a friend wrote to the *Daily Telegraph* and said its readers would be glad to learn that, despite concerns about him, Peter Hain got a first class honours degree. That provoked a torrent of letters saying that it just showed how university standards were falling."

Later he was to be declared South Africa's 'Public Enemy No.1', a title for which there was considerable competition. He was sent a letter bomb that didn't go off and he was framed, apparently by the South African security services, for a bank robbery in Putney. He was put on trial and acquitted. All this time he was a Young Liberal, which surprised some people, but the Young Liberals had a substantial reputation for idealistic troublemaking and it was a party in which it might have been rather easier for a young and energetic man of an independent disposition to become a biggish cheese. In 1977, anyway, he switched to Labour and a rather more conventional career was under way.

In September 2008, almost forty years after the events that first brought him to public notice, I went to see Peter Hain at his house in Neath. It was a curious meeting and, to be honest, it felt as though I'd somehow stepped into a bereavement. The last time I'd been there, to talk about some of the matters dealt with in this book, my appointment had been squeezed into a busy schedule by his diary secretary. As my time came to an end the next meeting was assembling, a group of officials from his constituency party was at the door. As I drove up on this next visit, early on a Thursday after-noon, he was just getting out of a car with his daughter-in-law and a small granddaughter. The atmosphere of high pressure politics was conspicuously absent.

The reason for that was his peremptory departure from office in the preceding January. The previous summer his attempt to become deputy leader of the Labour Party had ended in failure. Then, months after that event, it emerged that more than £100,000 in donations to his campaign had not been declared to the proper authorities. When the discrepancy came to light it was Hain himself who reported it but, after a period of uncertainty, the Electoral Commission referred the case to the police. He had no alternative but to resign from his two Cabinet jobs, as both Secretary of State for Work and Pensions and as Secretary of State for Wales. He was stepping down, he said, to clear his name.

I should say at once that I don't know of anyone who thinks that Peter Hain is dishonest. In the modern world, however, innocence is not enough. Some kind of offence, some breach of the rules, seemed to have been committed and, under the regulations introduced by Hain's own colleagues in an effort to clean up the system, it looked as though the candidate had to take the ultimate responsibility. It might have been a mistake, an oversight, someone else's fault or simply a consequence of Hain himself being "too busy", as he'd told the press, but those were reasons for the failure rather than an excuse for it. Once the whole business was referred to the police he was, as one journalist put it, toast.

It would be a mistake to think that this affair was simply about some failure of low level accountancy. Instead it was symbolic of an atmosphere of decay in a system in which a significant preoccupation had become an argument about how parties and politicians were funded rather than what they believed in. Hain's attempt to become Labour's deputy leader fitted neatly into the argument about this particular aspect of public policy.

One of the central problems was that, as well as the £103,000 that somehow hadn't been declared, another £83,000, about which the authorities had been notified, had also been spent by the Hain campaign. It took your breath away. Almost two hundred thousand pounds lavished on an attempt to become *what*? Deputy Leader of the Labour Party? This was a job that had been held for the previous ten years by John Prescott whose largely inadvertent contribution to political comedy had been rather more compelling than his ministerial achievements. But at least Prescott was also

Deputy Prime Minister, which gave him some theoretical clout. Those laurels were not on offer this time. And who comprised the constituency being wooed by Hain and five other hopefuls? The membership of the Labour Party who, you would have hoped, were clued-up enough about the candidates to make up their minds without being bombarded with pamphlets, newspaper advertisements, direct mail shots and all the other expensive accoutrements of modern electioneering.

This looked excessive to say the least, particularly in a party which still has enough Roundheads in it for such extravagance not to pass without some residual feelings of guilt. Perhaps that evaporating tradition also accounted for some of the hostility to Hain's bid from the more old-fashioned elements in the party as well as those newspapers who like to portray him as vain and ambitious. Well, I haven't met a politician yet who isn't vain and ambitious in some way, but what seems to provoke some of Hain's critics is that they see something studied in his appearance, something calculated in the way in which he presents himself. It's captured in particular by the regular newspaper references (and jokes from Labour colleagues) about what they call his perma tan. They probably do it all the more because he's very touchy about the idea and denies it crossly instead of laughing it off. "What me, from South Africa? Using a sun lamp?" he says tetchily. I was once rebuked by someone close to him for reporting, entirely truthfully, that in the Welsh Office he had been known as 'His Orangeness', the kind of playground joke that is particularly relished in the British civil service. For all his talents, humour doesn't seem to be his natural territory.

He's clever, disciplined, hard-working, good-natured, generous with his time, devoted to his family and expert in those interpersonal skills that are indispensable in a modern politician. Despite all that, though, you sometimes detect a coolness towards him that goes beyond the normal internal rivalries of politics. At Westminster there doesn't seem to be the kind of group of supporters, *Hainistas* perhaps, that often gathers around ambitious and talented politicians, people who would hope to hitch a ride with him on a successful political journey. One of the difficulties might lie in the fact that even now he remains something of an outsider, in particular he can't be instantly identified within the class system that still colours social attitudes in Britain. Somehow you can't quite place him. He sees the point, although he believes it's something that works to his advantage.

"Everybody born in Britain is affected by the class system. You may deny it but you are. Less so than in the past but shaped by it and trapped by it. I wasn't born into the British class system – it was classless within the white community in South Africa. Here they can't pigeonhole you. I think British society is changing but I am still struck by how much of the old class apparatus is still there among the decision makers."

A coolness towards Peter Hain among a fair proportion of his colleagues seemed to be demonstrated by the fact that, despite his long and expensive campaign, he came only fifth out of six in the first ballot for the deputy leadership. That was a rejection any seasoned politician would shrug off readily enough, however wounding he might privately think it. But his real problem arose from the most intractable of all political conditions – bad luck. His difficulties struck at a time when public respect for politicians was close to an all-time low, which is saying something, a state of affairs compounded by the fact that the politicians themselves failed to realise what the fuss was about. They didn't understand that simply avoiding wrongdoing, not breaking the rules, wasn't enough to save them from opprobrium, not least because they operated under arrangements which they themselves had devised.

The most sensational of the allegations was what became known as the Cash for Honours scandal, the allegation that rich people who gave large sums of money to the Labour Party were subsequently awarded peerages. Well of course they were. Even the most unworldly of businessmen might have been able to work that out for himself and pay up (or not) accordingly. You only had to be bright enough to read the honours list to draw the appropriate conclusion. The important question was whether this was some kind of deal or whether it was an unspoken convention, operated as enthusiastically by the Conservatives as by Labour. You didn't even need a nod or a wink. The idea that some party functionary was going round saying: "Give us lots of money and you can go to the House of Lords," seemed bizarre. Maybe it did happen, but if so it would have been less a symptom of a corrupt system and more a monument to stupidity.

While no charges were brought against those under suspicion in the Cash for Honours affair there was a sense in which reputations were seriously damaged by implication. Not least because of the theatrical way in which the police sometimes conducted the investigation. At six thirty one morning, for example they turned up at the home of Ruth Turner, a political adviser in Downing Street, and arrested her. No one outside the Metropolitan Police could think of a good reason for behaving in this way towards someone who had already been interviewed twice. Except, perhaps, to underline the seriousness of their investigation and the zeal with which they were conducting it. They arrested Lord Levy, Tony Blair's chief-fund raiser, not once, but twice. Leaks about the course of the investigation, and the apparent discovery of damaging evidence, poured out of somewhere. Not from us, said the lads from the Met, but if not from them, from whom? Another mystery.

In the world of twenty-four hour news coverage even the least attentive viewers might have been persuaded to think there was something in all of this. Even the fact that no one was prosecuted didn't necessarily mean everyone was innocent. You might indeed think that that was what they were intended to think, that there was a murky underworld of political life in which hardly anyone could be trusted.*

The decision by the Crown Prosecution Service that no one should be charged with any offence was widely considered to fall some way short of acquittal. It meant not proven perhaps, in the ambiguous Scottish way. And even when everyone was off the hook, including the Prime Minister Tony Blair, interviewed on three occasions by Inspector Knacker, the politicians failed to draw the obvious conclusion. If there were no House of Lords people couldn't pay to go there, or even *appear* to pay to go there. If a small but meaningful role in the legislative system is to be obtained through the direct patronage of politicians perhaps there should be reform anyway, corruption or no corruption. And if people are in some way contributing in the hope of honours that carry no constitutional privilege – knighthoods, for example: well, more fool them.

The reason for the widespread scepticism about this affair and its conclusion was that there was plenty of evidence that the political parties, even if not actively dishonest, were prepared to use any wheeze just on the right side of legality that would allow them to taken handsome donations from the rich. The rules insisted that

---

*In a display of political even-handedness in November 2008, the Metropolitan Police laid on a similar public performance when they arrested the Conservative MP, Damian Green, over his use of leaked Home Office documents.

they must declare gifts, but not loans. So gifts became loans and were thus kept secret, until the inevitable day they weren't secret any more. Those who'd made the new arrangements looked guilty even if, according to the strict letter of the law, they weren't. Secret loans to the Conservatives for the 2005 general election amounted to £16 million; to the Labour Party, £14 million.

There are a number of very significant consequences of this kind of behaviour and the many other examples that have become public over a long period. One is that political parties are revealed to have become dependent on the goodwill and, presumably, self-interest of a few very wealthy individuals. Perhaps they give the money entirely philanthropically but it is another example of the way in which political influence and access is increasingly exercised by very small numbers of people. Nor do such people enjoy having their dealings made public. The consequence for the Labour Party in particular was that big donors largely disappeared and the party once again became more dependent on the unions for finance, the very situation that had persuaded New Labour to try and find other backers in the first place.

That's one of the reasons why it's very difficult for the parties to come to an agreement on a transparent system of funding. If you cap an individual donation at, say, £50,000, that would become the maximum amount an entire trade union could contribute and so a financial disaster for Labour. One result has been a scheme to combine a limit on donations with greatly increased state funding of the parties – between £20 and £25 million a year was proposed in a report from Sir Hayden Phillips, a former senior civil servant. But does that mean, an alert voter might ask, that because the political parties cannot be trusted to be honest about money the taxpayer must finance them instead?

Another consequence was that once such matters had been exposed, whether or not the people involved were technically guilty of any offence, it reinforced the idea that practically everyone in British public life was routinely dishonest in some way, in particular individual politicians who were accused of enjoying a lavish lifestyle at the taxpayer's expense. Allowances paid entirely legitimately, and about which there had never previously been any controversy, were produced as evidence of unscrupulous greed. And even if they were innocent they still contrived to look shifty. Then the notorious 'John Lewis list' was published, details of some of the accessories the taxpayer would fund for MPs' second homes, accommodation for which they could claim up to £20,000 a year to meet mortgage payments. Were the authorities willing to cough up for a bit of gardening or some window cleaning? Yes they were. Could MPs spend £1,000 on a new bed or £10,000 on a new kitchen and pass the bill on to the Commons authorities? Yes they could. Could they claim £499 a month for food without producing receipts? Yes, that was OK. Could they use their staffing allowance to employ their wives and children in their parliamentary offices? Sure, no problem. In the vast majority of cases there was absolutely nothing devious about this, no breach of the rules. But it looked bad: after all, it was the MPs themselves who'd devised those rules in the first place.

But in one specific way the system was dishonest, or at the very least less than transparent, illustrating a growing distance between professional politicians and the people they represent. Many MPs, ministers prominent among them, couldn't see that not breaking the rules was not enough, that it didn't mean there was no sharp practice involved. The system of allowances (a word with neat overtones of legitimacy) was in many ways a sham devised to keep the public in the dark about the money MPs received and why they received it. That was because, although there was a case for MPs getting more money, all parties were terrified at the way in which the public would react to a substantial pay rise. The answer was to make the expenses regime more generous instead, a practice that looks very much like a piece of institutionalised deceit which, ultimately, was bound to cast doubt on the character of all politicians in the eyes of the people who elected them. The political class was further discredited.

The problem has worked its way into the devolved institutions as well. The Scottish First Minister, Henry McLeish, resigned in 2001 over sub-letting an office in his Westminster constituency, an offence put down to poor administration, from which he had gained no financial benefit. In 2008, another Scottish Labour Leader, Wendy Alexander, resigned over an irregular donation to her leadership campaign the previous year. At the end of 2008 claiming for an iPod on expenses threatened the position of Nick Bourne, the Conservative leader in the Welsh Assembly. Mr. Bourne, who said he used the iPod to learn Welsh, was perfectly entitled to claim for it, the expenditure was properly authorised and no rule had been broken. His crime was, at worst, a lack of sensitivity, a failure to put himself in the shoes of the average spectator who looked at this public largesse with disbelief. The fact that Bourne also got the assembly authorities to cough up for a trouser press was, if anything, more embarrassing. It's difficult to think of an accessory that is less in keeping with the image so earnestly cultivated by modern politicians. He'd have been better off caught smoking dope.

These are mostly honest people caught in a complicated system, often compounded by the sanctimony of other politicians and the media. Of course there are crooks in politics as there are in every other walk of life. One or two of them even go to gaol from time to time, but all the evidence suggests that for the most part they are people who are genuinely anxious to improve society and are willing to work hard to do so. Even so it seems to be in the nature of things that they will be accused of some form of hypocrisy. I think a sceptical public usually harbours suspicions of a bloke who has to boast publicly about his own virtues in order to get elected. When I was a child it was common to hear people say that, on his way from London to his constituency, Aneurin Bevan would move from a first class compartment to one in third class and change from a smart suit into a shabby one as he prepared to appear before the people of Ebbw Vale. Another version of this story was that he would arrive in Newport in a limousine before being transferred to an Austin Seven which would then chug its way slowly up the valley. I suppose this attitude arose partly from a traditional suspicion of the motives and methods of anyone who was seen to rise in society, as well as the tribal antagonism between the inhabitants of one South Wales mining valley and those of another.

The difference is that fifty years ago, despite Bevan's reputation as a champagne socialist, he belonged unmistakably to the people who sent him to parliament. That kind of connection has been shattered by the professionalisation of politics in the last quarter of the twentieth century. Being an MP has for the most part become a kind of trade, a full-time occupation. Not all that long ago, if they wanted to telephone someone outside the Palace of Westminster, Members of Parliament had to reverse the charges. They sat in corridors dictating letters to the secretary whose services they probably shared with two or three others. Many of them had other jobs, there were any number of lawyers, for instance, whose professional lives were largely undisturbed by the late hours of the House of Commons. Conservatives in particular decorated the boards of various companies. Many didn't get to the Commons until they were middle-aged and so were perhaps less consumed with ambition for office than their modern counterparts, today's thrusting youths on the make.

Now they are provided with all the trappings of moderately successful executives, well-equipped offices, secretaries, researchers, computers and all the rest of it. They get decent if not lavish salaries and, if they can keep the voters onside for long enough, generous pensions. Their workload has increased, especially because there are many more important duties to attend to in the mornings, in particular the select committees that have proliferated since 1979. As a consequence the working day in the Commons has been changed in a way that makes conditions of employment a little more like those in the real world outside. Members are attentive to their constituencies. Surgeries on Friday evenings or Saturday mornings are an almost religious observance. On weekends, too, they are often to be found at concerts, sports events, religious festivals and other pressing engagements. Many more women have entered Parliament in the last couple of decades, something that has had an impact on the atmosphere and style of political life. The men seem to be less drunk than they were in the days when I spent a lot of time at Westminster and, as far as it's possible to tell, less lecherous.

This might seem to be a welcome kind of change, a civilising of the lives of our legislators, but the way in which their lives have been altered is perhaps part of a more sinister adjustment of the nature of British life that's been described by the political writer Peter Oborne. In his view MPs have, in the last three decades, become part of a narrow group of immense influence, the (capital letters needed) Political Class.

"It encompasses lobbyists, party functionaries, advisers and spin doctors, many journalists and increasing numbers of independent civil servants. All mainstream politicians of the three main parties belong to it. Gordon Brown is a member, so is the Tory leader David Cameron."

The consequence of the emergence of this class, according to Oborne, is that the real division now is not between Tory and Labour but between "a narrow, self-serving and... increasingly corrupt political class and the mass of ordinary voters."

It's easy to recognise at least some of what Oborne is on about. In the post-industrial world politics has become a significant employer offering an enticing career for bright young people. Researchers and advisers, all paid for out of public money, throng the corridors of Westminster and the devolved administrations. More and more they set the tone of political debate and in time some of them will rise to succeed the people they now serve; they are going through a kind of apprenticeship that means political life tends increasingly to become the preserve of people who know no other life but politics. That applies to all parties, but in particular to Labour where, even in areas long dominated by the party, rank and file activists, the people who sit on committees, stuff envelopes and make the tea, have faded away.

In part that's an inevitable result of the social change that's swept over Britain. The industries that were the reason for the existence of the Labour Party are much diminished and amalgamated. Once upon a time unions like those of the railwaymen, the engineering workers, the miners or the steelworkers had seats in parliament more or less in their gift. Now few of them send representatives to meetings of local parties. That was a change noted in a pamphlet written by Peter Hain in his enforced sabbatical from ministerial duties early in 2008. When he had been chosen as the Labour candidate for Neath in 1990, he wrote, the last pit in the constituency had just closed.

"The NUM and other trade unions were well represented on the Neath Labour General Committee, if not the dominant influence; they also provided a route into the workplace for me to meet voters. Today, however, trade unions retain affiliations but sadly send few representatives to party meetings and too few are Labour activists."

There's no reason to think that what's happened in Neath isn't reflected in most of the other parts of Britain where society was formed by heavy industry and a common experience of it. Now, as Hain wrote, the way in which people relate to each other has also been fundamentally changed.

"As a new candidate and then MP I used weekends to visit rugby clubs in all the former mining villages in the valleys around the town of Neath where I was quickly able to meet huge numbers of constituents. At my local one, Resolven Rugby Club, there would typically be 80 people in the bar after 9pm on a Saturday night. But that bar, like many others, is now empty on Saturday evenings unless there is a function. People's lifestyles have irreversibly changed, and everyone lives more private lives, like everywhere else in Britain. Cultural and political influences come more through television than the workplace or the local club."

What's particularly ominous about this kind of social change is the way in which it has developed into a widespread political agnosticism, particularly among the young. Hain reported: "Typically young people encountered on the doorstep 'don't know' or 'don't care' or 'won't vote'. In traditional Labour areas in Wales where the older vote can be rock solid, the younger people are less likely to vote Labour or to vote at all. In the 2007 assembly elections fully 80 per cent of registered 18-34-year-olds did not vote; half of the 18-24-year-olds knew nothing about the assembly."

That kind of indifference is a reflection of attitudes throughout the UK. At around sixty per cent, turnout at general elections in 2001 and 2005 was something like ten per cent down on the elections of the nineties, in fact seventeen per cent lower than in 1992. The figure for the Scottish Parliament election in 2007 was just under 52 per cent and for the National Assembly for Wales 43.7 per cent.

Hain is understandably depressed by this state of affairs but it is an inevitable consequence of the way in which political debate has been devalued and political activism has been removed from many people's lives. Why should they bother? Why should they vote? Where is the argument and what is it about? It might be significant that one of the most interesting British elections of recent times was the contest between Boris Johnson and Ken Livingstone for Mayor of London. There were two colourful and unmistakable characters – Old Etonian Boris, pretending to be a playboy buffoon, against old leftie Ken, a prominent and controversial figure for thirty years who'd forced New Labour first to disown him and then to forgive him and take him back into the party. There were easily grasped practical issues involving matters like transport and the environment about which Londoners had strong opinions. Voters could readily understand how their lives might be greatly influenced by their behaviour at the ballot box. Even under those circumstances, though, the turnout was only forty-five per cent. It suggested that in modern politics even when you put on a good show you still can't sell enough tickets.

What that London election also demonstrated was the fragmentation of power within the United Kingdom under the various forms of devolution introduced since 1997. Margaret Thatcher had taken away London's political and administrative identity when she abolished the Greater London Council, an act prompted specifically by Ken Livingstone's regime as the council's leader. Creating a new form of government for the city was an important recognition of the fact that it couldn't be run effectively without a strong authority. The novelty was inventing a job for a directly-elected mayor, something that meant London residents could be in no doubt about who was in charge and at whom they should throw flowers or rotten veg. And where there wasn't direct power, there was influence. Boris Johnson didn't have the authority to sack the Commissioner of the Metropolitan Police but when he told Sir Ian Blair a change of leadership was necessary, Blair had no alternative but to resign. The Home Secretary, nominally in charge of such things, could only stand and watch. It's another way in which the nature of government in the United Kingdom has been significantly altered.

At the same time the creation of separate centres of governmental power has inevitably imposed new strains on the constitution. The reality of Johnson's part in the departure of the police commissioner is one example. There are many other arguments between devolved governments and Westminster, disputes that are likely to become more frequent and more intense, particularly over money where Westminster has retained almost total control. But even more sensitive is the form of the democratic wrestling match that's broken out between different sets of legislators. Relationships between Members of the Scottish Parliament and Scottish MPs are described bluntly by some observers as dreadful. Or they were when the new dispensation got under way, with MPs, their monopoly as political leaders undermined by the opening of a rival business, openly deriding the new legislature in Edinburgh. That now appears to have cooled off to some extent, but it's inescapable that, once you elect a group of people, they will quickly be drawn into a campaign for more power. If you're in Edinburgh or Cardiff, where is the only place that power can come from? Westminster. And what happens to MPs if their powers, duties and status are consequently reduced? There will have to be fewer of them. That has already happened in Scotland, but the reduction following devolution simply got rid of the excess numbers of Scottish MPs, taking them to the UK average ratio of MPs to population. There's already a case for saying that Scotland has got too many people in parliament and, whatever happens, their numbers will have to be cut further. Since there's little that animates politicians more than the spectre of the dole queue they have a keen interest (apart from SNP members, naturally) in resisting any more authority drifting off to Holyrood. In Northern Ireland the number of MPs was raised from 12 to 17 after direct rule was imposed in 1972. Given the fact that the devolution settlement in the province has more than once coughed and spluttered like an old car it might be a bit premature – and insensitive – to revisit those figures just yet.

In Wales there is a different problem of unnerving complexity. It arises essentially from the search for what has become known as 'a proper parliament', by which Welsh politicians mean a similar parliament to the one established in Scotland, although the SNP argue that that isn't a proper parliament either. As a tentative step in this direction a new system, hitherto entirely unknown to the British constitution, was introduced by the Government of Wales Act 2006. To put it in the simplest possible way, this allows the National Assembly for Wales to seek parliamentary approval which would allow them to pass laws, known in this context as 'measures', implemented under something called a Legislative Competence Order, in broadly defined areas.

The political problem arises because one of the stages of this process involves Welsh Members of Parliament scrutinising the assembly's plans. Not only that, but those MPs, members of the Commons Select Committee on Welsh Affairs, have to approve the idea before it can proceed. As anyone might have foreseen, this creates a problem, but it's impossible to say with any certainty whether the problem is real or imagined. The point is that if it looks like a row then it is a row. So members of the Welsh Assembly accuse MPs of being obstructive and exceeding their authority. The implication is that up at Westminster they should stop interfering and just get on with giving the assembly whatever powers it asks for. The answer from the MPs, entirely reasonably, is that they have been given a role in this cobbled together legislative process and they're jolly well going to exercise it. To do any less would be a breach of the duties laid upon them.

The subtext of this argument is that Welsh Labour MPs in particular are accused of wanting to sabotage the new devolution arrangements, operated by other Labour politicians in Wales, because they always opposed the whole idea, not least because it has diminished their importance in the scheme of things. Plaid Cymru, the Conservatives and the Liberal Democrats go round suggesting there's a metropolitan conspiracy to withhold power; that's to say it's an argument that goes beyond traditional party rivalries. At the same time, the 'proper parliament' lobby is quite happy to be able to claim that the MPs are wrecking the whole system since they can then declare it unworkable. If that's the case, they can argue, the only course is to move on to the next stage, already incorporated in an act of parliament, and trigger a referendum on creating a Scottish-style parliament with some legislative powers. Discontent with the obstructionism of Westminster, they calculate, might help to carry them to victory.

The importance of these changes doesn't lie in the dizzying detail of a pseudo-legislative system which has more stages than you can count and any number of points at which a proposal can fail. They include a veto effectively held by the Secretary of State for Wales, something that from the very beginning provoked hypothetical arguments about hypothetical interventions by a hypothetical secretary of state representing a hypothetical government. That is how many political activists spend their lives and, while most of the rest of the population are oblivious to what such people are on about, it creates a new political agenda on which the voters will one day have to pass judgement.

Such disputes between Wales and London might also indicate a growing a feeling in which Parliament seems less relevant to people's lives throughout the United Kingdom. There's a sense that it doesn't really matter any more, that the great decisions aren't made there. Maybe they're taken on a sofa in Downing Street or at a meeting in Brussels, but the idea grows that MPs are increasingly ciphers in the business of government. Yes, sometimes there'll be an outbreak of principle, on identity cards perhaps, or the detention of suspected terrorists, or university fees, but the machinery of government keeps turning, unhindered by minor obstructions. Perhaps it is the case, as Peter Oborne argues, that "...the House of Commons is no longer really a cockpit where great conflicts of vision are fought out across the chamber. It has converted itself instead into a professional group, like the Bar Council or the British Medical Association."

I'm not so sure that's right. Anyone who's spent much time at

Westminster can testify that it's a pretty dull assembly for the most part. It fills up for half an hour on a Wednesday for Prime Minister's Questions, a piece of noisy showbiz rather than a serious contribution to the business of holding government to account. But at other times in the week people continue to make dull speeches to three or four other people waiting to make their own, equally dull, speeches. This has always been the case and up till now no-one has thought it was a sign of democracy coming to an end. The increased significance of committees and the altered hours of business have affected its character, but the real problem at Westminster for much of the last thirty years has sprung from the huge majorities enjoyed by both Labour and Conservative governments. In those circumstances, with very few exceptions, the administration has been able to expect to get its business through and the significance of the individual MP has been much reduced.

Even so, and despite the majorities, when it came to a vote on the invasion of Iraq the Commons became a dramatic and important forum once more. And it's not so long since those hung parliaments of the seventies kept everyone up at night as every division was decided by a vote or two. Every individual MP mattered then, as they did later when the Conservatives fought each other so ruinously over the Maastricht Treaty. It could happen again. Perhaps it will.

At the same time, taking account of all the shifts of structure and practice, it's possible to see how Parliament at Westminster, the embodiment of Britishness after all, has taken on a different character and an altered place in the lives of the population. It's partly to do with a change of focus in places like Scotland and Wales. It's also affected by the domination of professional politicians who, however industrious they might be, and however popular, more often than not don't share the experiences of most of their constituents and, in increasing numbers, never have. They are more like teachers, say, or accountants. There is also the question of money and the way in which it has infected the political system so that even honest men and women are lowered in the eyes of the general public.

One of the consequences is that a particularly judgemental atmosphere has settled over British political life in which minor offences (and sometime no offences at all) become capital crimes and those who have committed them (or sometimes haven't committed them) are declared unfit for public office. This is a world in which there is no so such thing as probation or a suspended sentence or even a few hours' community service: the only available punishment is the noose at the end of the political rope. If it weren't for the lynch mob element in this process British people might be inclined to congratulate themselves on the dazzling purity of their political system and the thoroughness with which it is policed. The hang 'em high posse is led with clamorous vigour by a press whose dishonest methods, fact-adjusting techniques and enthusiasm for various forms of bribery seem to sit uneasily with the moral outrage in which they specialise.

The result is that in the newspapers various politicians are presented as people whose entire lives are given over to how they can get some material advantage for themselves while secretly plotting to undermine the traditional values of a country in which, thanks to unscrupulous methods, they have undeservedly achieved positions of authority. This attitude works its way into the public perception and, eventually, back into the political system itself.

So, for example, when in 2001 questions were raised about Peter Mandelson's actions over a passport application for a wealthy businessman, he was once more out of the Cabinet before most people had had time to turn to the sports pages. A panicking Downing Street seemed to feel it was better to lose a minister rather than defy the pursuing press. On January 23, two days before Mandelson's resignation, Alastair Campbell wrote in his diary: "TB [Tony Blair] was now irritated we were having to spend so much time on this, which he said had nothing to do with real people and real lives and yet would get millions of words devoted to it."

Of course Mandelson had form, as the police say, having resigned from the Cabinet once before over irregularities connected with his mortgage. But an official inquiry later established that he was entirely innocent in this second affair, something that intensified the theatrical nature of his entirely unexpected return to the Cabinet seven years later. He suddenly became a vital component in the desperate campaign to rescue the failing administration of his old enemy, Gordon Brown. It was yet another of those soap opera moments when the writers decide something has to be done to rescue a flagging storyline: the political equivalent of an airliner crashing on Emmerdale.

They got David Blunkett a couple of times too, another Cabinet Minister who had plenty of enemies within his own party and outside it. More accurately, I suppose, he got himself. Maybe he was arrogant or careless or both but he unquestionably paid the full price for his breaches of the rules. Quite right too, many people would say, and it's impossible to argue with that point of view if you're going to have transparency and honesty in government. Nevertheless there was a noticeable element of rejoicing at his downfall. This was something exemplified by *A Very Social Secretary*, a play broadcast on Channel 4 in October 2005 in which the satirical argument rested on the facts that Blunkett was (i) an unsophisticated provincial Englishman who had an affair with, and at least one child by, a sophisticated American woman, (ii) blind.

This was described by Channel 4 as being "wickedly funny".

Nobody is going to spend too much time feeling sorry for Mandelson and Blunkett because there is a widespread view that politicians getting a kicking is part of the natural order of things and the more senior the politician the bigger the kicking ought to be. But the problem arises from the fact that in politics personality and character have come to obscure the view of more important matters. It's partly the result of the 24-hour news agenda where every activity and announcement must *mean* something and usually mean something other than the obvious. So the actions of politicians come to be interpreted in the light of their media images: Blair superficial and devious, for example, Brown dour and incompetent, the latter character following swiftly on the long period in which he was widely portrayed as dour and competent and eventually replaced by him being slightly less dour and competent again only for that to be followed by more dourness and less competence. That's how he was presented to the public but, in his darkest days of the summer of 2008, when there were anti-Brown plots around every corner, I was told by someone who knew the government intimately that, in fact, he had been useless all along but at the Treasury his more able advisers had seen to it that he didn't get into trouble.

Although the Palace of Westminster is packed to the roof with character assassins rubbishing their colleagues, they like to talk sagely about the need to concentrate on policies rather than personalities. That's a bit naïve since personality is an essential component of political life: charm and plausibility are as much instruments of policy-making as are intelligence and industry. The problem is that in modern politics image has increasingly become the key factor in political choice.

It comes to something, after all, when hawk-eyed commentators can look at the announcement of a five-pence in the pound increase in income tax to be imposed three years hence on people earning more than £150,000 a year and discover in it the return of socialism. And when David Cameron announces that, if elected, his party won't after all be following the public spending policies laid down by Labour it is portrayed as a sensational return to traditional Conservative values.

For such reasons it sometimes looks as though politics has disappeared from much of political life. When I went to visit Peter Hain in the early autumn of 2008 it was for that reason I wondered, not for the first time, why people like him bother. After all, this was a man of 58 whose entire adult life had been devoted to political activity of one kind or another. It had been snatched away, perhaps temporarily, and he seemed bereft. He'd served as a minister from the arrival of Labour in government in 1997. He'd been a key figure in the narrowly-won devolution referendum in Wales; he'd been given tricky jobs to do – in Europe and dealing with miners' compensation; he'd been Leader of the Commons and, at a vital time during the peace process, Secretary of State for Northern Ireland. He'd managed to make the transition from Blair to Brown, which some thought he might not survive, with a bit of a promotion. He was a man of inexhaustible energy, among other things the author of at least thirteen books, including a novel. Now here he was, hanging around month after month, waiting for someone else to make the crucial decisions about his future, which they seemed in no particular hurry to do.

Naturally enough I asked him about it and all he could say, almost eight months on, was that he was waiting for some kind of decision to be made by someone. There really wasn't much more to be added but throughout our conversation on other matters there seemed to be an untypical wariness about him. I've known him quite well over the years but there's always something of a ditch that separates the uncommitted political journalist from the dedicated politician, however cordial the relationship. You speak different dialects of the same language. Perhaps, I thought later, he was worried that during our conversation he might carelessly say something that would come back to haunt him when the day arrived to start rebuilding his career. He'd had plenty of time to think about such things while the authorities got on with whatever they were getting on with. It's impossible to be a serious politician without being an optimist, without believing that you can win that election, secure that policy, persuade that critic, make your country a better place. So, who could tell? After all there was a reshuffle due around the corner and perhaps....

On the other hand political careers in modern Britain tend to be a form of mountaineering in which you start young and prepare to haul yourself up the tricky challenges of the north face of Westminster. You need stamina, skill and good fortune. Even then, when you're somewhere near the top and you think you know how to do it, you miss a foothold or a rope snaps and you go plunging into the ravine below. Your former companions look down briefly and resume their climb. More than ever it's a way of life which outsiders can only observe in baffled wonder.

Then, one Friday morning in December, getting on for another three months after that conversation, the Crown Prosecution Service released a verdict that made the whole affair even more astonishing. Peter Hain was entirely exonerated of any wrongdoing in connection with his campaign funds. The official line was that there was 'insufficient evidence' to justify charges but that phrase was clearly designed to imply that the CPS hadn't been wasting its time for the best part of a year. Not only was Hain entirely innocent but, although someone should have reported the donations, they couldn't say who that person might have been. An offence had definitely been committed. It was quite clear that all donations had to be declared within thirty days of being received, but, for the life of them, they didn't have a clue who the declarer should have been. It was as if, in the last chapter, Hercule Poirot had gathered all the suspects in the library and told them he didn't have the faintest idea whodunnit.

It had taken the best part of a year to come to this conclusion but perhaps the time wasn't entirely wasted because of the wider significance of these events. What they illustrated with great clarity was the fond belief of modern governments that they can legislate the world into rectitude and obedience only to find that they have simply legislated themselves into further trouble. Among the dozens of political campaigns going on in this period, Hain's was the only one reported to the police (at least in part because he shopped himself) but it had proved impossible to point the finger at any individual wrongdoer. (Later he was to be rebuked by the parliamentary authorities for the irregularities in his campaign fund but they took the view that losing his Cabinet jobs had been punishment enough.)

On television that morning you could see how Hain had been restored to his normal optimistic vigour, talking with enthusiastic appreciation about his past career and looking forward to resuming it in due course. Downing Street issued some warm words, but warm words are easy and don't amount to a contract of employment. Perhaps he would return to government in some role in the near future but a long dislocation of this kind caused substantial problems – not least that the world had moved on and members of a younger generation had taken their place around the Cabinet table. Would Peter Hain demonstrate once more Enoch Powell's view that all political careers end in failure? Or in the modern world, in farce?

London Calling

Do you mind if I'm terribly London and ask for a cappuccino?
– BBC executive visiting Cardiff

ANYONE WHO HAS WORKED in broadcasting in Britain for any length of time will have lost count of the number of occasions on which the BBC has discovered Manchester. It is a city which more than once has been the symbol of the determination of the corporation to burst free of the stifling bear hug of the South East of England. It has served to demonstrate that the organisation is not, in the usual phrase, 'London-centric'. In the nineteen-nineties, for example, various disposable departments like religion were despatched there without having any discernible effect on the metropolitan nature of the BBC. A similar move is due in 2011, once more to the accompaniment of shrieks of dismay from *refusenik* producers and presenters. This time, though, it looks as if it's more serious and more important.

Because it is a daily presence in most people's lives. The BBC has become probably the most significant British institution that's survived into the twenty-first century. Everyone knows what it is; it has a huge influence on cultural, social and political life throughout the United Kingdom; its errors of taste and judgement instantly become matters of national controversy; it is blamed for being too popular and, at the same time, not popular enough; its quality and independence are admired and recognised throughout the world; it has many vociferous critics whose criticisms are often accurate, but most of those who wish it serious harm are commercial rivals rather than people who have at heart the interests of the British population.

The move to Manchester illustrates vividly the fact that the BBC is a much more important component of national life than simply being a maker of television and radio programmes. Shifting fifteen hundred staff, as well as and output like sport and the whole of Radio Five Live to a new broadcasting centre on Salford Quays, will cost around £500 million. It's something no commercial broadcasting organisation would contemplate because it's not a commercial move, except perhaps in the sense that the BBC's long-term survival might depend at least in part on demonstrating a practical commitment to the whole of the United Kingdom. It's what its royal charter says it must do; provide, in the sonorous words of the BBC Trust, "a range of perspectives and richness of coverage that reflects the diversity of the nations and regions of the UK." When the Salford Quays project was agreed in 2007 the Director General, Mark Thomson, said it would "shift the BBC's centre of gravity away from London, bringing a range of creative benefits to us and, I hope, helping us to better reflect and represent the whole of the UK."

Well, maybe. But how much real influence this "multimedia broadcast and production centre" will have when it eventually transfers from London will ultimately depend on how much authority lies there. Where you make programmes is important, but not as important as where you decide what programmes are made. It is, though, a significant move, but in this context it's worth remembering it isn't just the BBC but the whole of Britain that is London-centric. It's only the BBC that's trying to do anything about it. Understanding that, coming to terms with it and making changes as a result is crucial in a country that in a few years has undergone a revolution in the way in which it is governed, something that has shifted and diffused significant sources of power. Above all other British institutions, perhaps, an important part of the story of the modern BBC is in how it reflects that change.

Like most people and organisations throughout the UK it made a slow start. The former Director General, John Birt, records in his memoirs that in 1998, after the devolution referendum but before the Scottish Parliament had come into being, a proposal was made from the BBC in Glasgow that Scotland should opt out of the *Six O'Clock News* on BBC1 and instead produce an integrated international and local news programme made with a Scottish perspective. As one would expect from a big thinker like Birt, he instantly understood that this idea would inevitably lead to the effective destruction of the BBC as a significant British institution.

How did he get to that point so fast? Well, he reasoned, if they

gave in to Scotland, Wales and Northern Ireland would join in the
clamour. One news programme after another would fall. "Within a
few years there would be no UK-wide news on the BBC. I calculated that this domino effect would continue, with a momentum of
its own, until eventually the BBC itself was either turned into a
weak, federal institution – each part going its own way – or was
broken up, with an English Broadcasting Organisation headquar-
tered in London. The EBC would be a lesser force than the BBC –
with reduced revenues, and with its status as the world's most
successful cultural institution much diminished."

And so on down the slippery slope, with particularly dire
consequences for Scotland, Wales and Northern Ireland. However,
distinguished and influential figures were behind this demand for
what became known as the Scottish *Six*. A bold response was
needed. The only thing to do was to head for Downing Street and
Tony Blair. Birt outlined the impending disaster to an admirably
alert Prime Minister ("Blair was quick, as ever, to grasp the case.").
The arguments poured out. Scottish viewers deprived of the
breadth of UK-wide and international news... end of single,
common experience of UK news... encourage separatist tenden-
cies... if Scots one day chose independence... BBC, like everyone
else, would have to accept the consequences... BBC should follow
constitutional change... not lead it....

The decisive, Scottish-educated Blair responded with two
words: "Let's fight". He put Peter Mandelson on the case; Gordon
Brown wrote articles about the Union, but the BBC's Board of
Governors nevertheless looked for a time as if they might yield to
the Scottish argument. The Chairman, Christopher Bland, feared
that the entire Broadcasting Council for Scotland would resign if
they didn't get their way. Birt resisted the change, but Bland had at
least as shrewd a grasp of the issues as his D.G. "He chided me for
carrying out the wishes of the London politicians. I denied vigorously that we were dancing to their tune."

In the end Birt prevailed and later looked back on his achieve-
ment with considerable satisfaction. "This painful episode had an
ultimately benign outcome. In 1999, when devolution finally
became a reality in Scotland and Wales, no organisation was better
prepared to serve both the nations and the UK as a whole than the
BBC. Meanwhile the *British* [Birt's italics] Broadcasting
Corporation lived to fight another day."

Our hero was obviously rather pleased with himself, but despite his pleasure at the deployment of his tactical skills, separatists in Scotland might not have been all that disappointed with the outcome of the argument. While a Scottish *Six* might have been a desirable objective perhaps it was even better to have demonstrated so clearly that a centralised *British* Broadcasting Corporation, in cahoots with a British government, would never voluntarily let go of anything.

The Scots were getting used to this kind of thing. Twenty years previously, even a majority in favour of a Scottish Parliament wasn't enough to secure one because of the elaborate mechanism constructed by MPs at Westminster. In the light of this, and in the longer political term, John Birt might have been better advised to listen more closely to his Chairman and discover a way of meeting Scottish aspirations, in particular because they had support well beyond nationalist politics. A Scottish *Six* would have been a victory for public opinion even if something of an inconvenience for the BBC machine; no Scottish *Six*, like no Scottish parliament, created a handy grievance for years to come.

There was another problem with Birt's triumph. Ten years later it emerged clearly that his view of the BBC that "no organisation was better prepared to serve both the nations and the UK as a whole" was rather wide of the mark. In the summer of 2008, the corporation published a wounding report it had commissioned from the academic and political analyst, Professor Anthony King, who also had wide experience as a broadcaster on political affairs. The question he had to answer was essentially this: the political and governmental structure of the UK had been greatly altered by the arrival of devolved administrations. Had the BBC responded adequately to that change in its coverage of news and current affairs? The answer in King's report, politely expressed and with plenty of praise for the many strengths of the BBC, was, essentially, no. Good, he said politely, but not good enough.

Perhaps, by the way, there is nothing much more definitively British than the existence of a large state broadcasting organisation, by and large not pushed around by the state, that suspects itself of crimes, pays someone to investigate them and, when found guilty of the offence of which it has accused itself, punishes itself and promises to reform. It gives a new meaning to the expression show trial. This is one device by which the organisation keeps other people's police forces at bay. For example, while by its very nature the BBC is always a little bit behind the times, its sensitivity to the nuances of political change have been amply demonstrated by the way in which, as the years passed, Scotland, Wales and Northern Ireland were first described internally as regions, before becoming national regions and, finally, nations.

The faults explored by Anthony King are by no means confined to the BBC. The clear truth is that to the entire metropolitan media class the politics of the devolved nations is a subject almost entirely without interest. To some extent that attitude is perfectly understandable. How many more papers would the the *Sun* or the *Daily Mail* sell if they reported at any length (or, indeed, at all) the issues preoccupying Stormont or Holyrood or the Senedd? Pestering their readers with information which was neither entertaining nor apparently relevant to their lives would be a certain route to falling circulations. They know that their chief objective must be to grab people's attention and keep it for as long as possible. The idea some of these matters might be of great importance in the longer term is unpersuasive to an industry in which the longer term is next weekend. At the same time, though, this attitude sits uneasily with the resounding declarations of editors and proprietors and, above all, columnists, about the state of the United Kingdom and the risks to its stability posed, among other things, by the changing political character introduced by devolution.

Different considerations apply to the BBC. The existence of the licence fee means that the corporation has to be sensitive to the concerns of all those who pay it. In one way it does so through its own structures that serve Scotland, Wales and Northern Ireland. But that still leaves the questions of how the nature of those countries is explained to the rest of Britain and what significance their politics in particular might have for the whole of the UK. The difficulty is, though, that the BBC can't simply divorce itself from the news agenda that's mapped out in the rest of the media. One aspect of journalism often missed by people outside the trade is that while editors like to talk about novelty and exclusives their greatest fear is that they won't have what the competition has got. They want to be different but the same. When, for example, the search for Madeleine McCann went on for week after week and month after month, even when there was obviously nothing new left to say, viewers and listeners seeing the story continuing to dominate the news-stands would have found it peculiar, even suspicious, if there were nothing about it on the *Ten O'Clock News*. So night after night top television newsmen stood in the dark of Praia da Luz and told us... not very much. But eventually there came a time when the red top papers got bored even with the Madeleine McCann case. One day they simply packed up their tents and walked away in search of some new 'human interest'. The story was over.

A similar sort of process seemed to overwhelm much more than a passing concern with Northern Ireland. That was despite the fact that the conflict there had occupied endless hours of news footage for getting on for forty years. It had, through films and television drama, become an important component of British life well beyond the disputed territory itself. Year after year the newspapers had reported vividly on the terrible carnage inflicted by the province's two communities on each other and on the troops who had originally gone there in an attempt to keep them apart. Then one day in 2007, after ten years of negotiations had teetered on the brink of failure, it all seemed to be finished, in journalistic terms at least. Ian Paisley and Martin McGuiness were running a government together. That was all right then. Nothing more to report. Northern Ireland and its problems could return to the impenetrable quarrels and gloomy intractability of sectarian politics that had left the rest of the population of the United Kingdom in peaceful ignorance until the bombing and the shooting had broken out all those years previously. Media interest in the Irish question seemed to drop like a stone once the IRA had stopped blowing up people on mainland Britain, in particular in the South East of England. Now it could safely be ignored. Phew!

As we were to discover early in 2009, that might well have been a premature sigh of relief, but that's how journalism works, I'm afraid. Northern Ireland wasn't worth talking about in the years before the Troubles broke out, which is why the majority of the UK population was taken by surprise when they happened. Anthony King's report suggested that, because the present condition of the province lacked much of its previous drama and violence, we were in danger of reverting to the same condition of indifference and ignorance. He wrote about the lack of attention paid in what he called the BBC network's 'non-coverage' of the decline and fall of Ian Paisley as Northern Ireland's First Minister. Over the previous thirty years or so Paisley had become one of the most recognisable politicians in the Western political world. His intransigence and megaphone (lack of) diplomacy had been vital elements in keeping the inter-community warfare going during that period.* But it was also those same characteristics that gave such weight to his willingness, as an old man, to sit down with Sinn Fein and lead a government in Northern Ireland in the last stages of the peace process. If Paisley was willing to sign up to it, the message was, then surely the Protestant cause must have prevailed. As indeed it had some years before, although the idea took a long time to sink in. As one observer put it: "After the Good Friday agreement the war was over. The Provos had lost but the Unionists were too thick to see it and Sinn Fein too fly to admit it."

Dr. Paisley's time as First Minister was to be brief. Almost from the day he took office there was speculation that he would soon be pushed out. His age, his new intimacy with Martin McGuinness, which wasn't much appreciated by his DUP colleagues, the resignation from the government of his son and right-hand man, Ian Paisley Jr., after allegations over business dealings, all weakened his position. In Northern Ireland that last event in particular intensified speculation that Dr. Paisley couldn't last long.

In his report Professor King drew attention to the shortcomings of the BBC coverage of these events. "The BBC network," he wrote, "had little to say about any of these developments: not nothing, but very little. The question was, why should this be so in circumstances in which the fate of the DUP leader might be of great importance to the whole of the United Kingdom.

"He was joint architect of the DUP-Sinn Fein agreement that restored devolved government to Northern Ireland, and his personal relationship with the leaders of Northern Ireland republicanism had become, at the very least, stable and serviceable. No-one could know for sure to what extent the peaceful settlement in Northern Ireland depended on Dr. Paisley's personal presence and whether the settlement would survive under his successor. In the view of many in Northern Ireland, the peace settlement was considerably more fragile than it appeared to outsiders. They felt compelled to contemplate the possibility that, in the absence of Dr. Paisley, violence might flare up again."

---

* When Paisley eventually resigned as First Minister the tributes paid to his statesmanlike qualities by people like Gordon Brown underlined the fact that sometimes British political life is beyond satire.

Well it didn't, did it? BBC editors might be tempted to retort, but the lack of attention to the fate of Dr. Paisley is only one example of the way in which the newly-fragmented system of government in the United Kingdom might from time to time inflict some unexpected influence on the voters of Godalming, say, or Sheffield. The nature and extent of that influence isn't always immediately clear, but King gave another example: the distinct lack of network interest in the protracted political negotiations that took place in Wales in the aftermath of the national assembly elections in early May 2007.

It wasn't until July of that year that a government was eventually formed to run the Welsh administration. The final arrangement was a coalition between Labour, the biggest single party, and Plaid Cymru, which had the second largest number of seats. But during those long weeks of bargaining a number of other conclusions might have been reached. There might have been a Labour-Liberal Democrat government. Or there might have been what became called a 'rainbow coalition' in which power was shared between Plaid Cymru, the Conservatives and the Liberal Democrats, something of a sensation in a country in which Labour had for the best part of a century leant on power with the ease of a farmer on a gate. Among other things this whole affair illuminated important aspects of politics in Britain as a whole, including the state of the Labour Party as Gordon Brown took over, the rise of nationalism, and the resurgence of the Conservatives who have rebuilt themselves in Wales by adopting a *realpolitik* attachment to the opportunities provided by devolution. The business of coalition making, and the unlikely alliances that might have been formed, also gave an insight into the loosening of the bonds of party dogma in the modern political world.

Of this, Anthony King reported, the viewer and listener in the rest of the UK, was largely unaware: "...anyone who relied on the BBC's network bulletins for news of what was happening in Welsh politics between May and July 2007 would have been alerted quite fully to the beginning of the story and also, although far more briefly, to the end of the story but would have been provided with virtually no information about anything that happened in between."

Of course it's true you wouldn't have found much about it anywhere else in the UK national media, but the BBC is different. It is publicly rather than commercially accountable for what it does.

But it's one of the particularly valuable aspects of the King Report that it draws attention by implication to failure of any organisation at all, not just the BBC, to provide much that contributes to the understanding of one part of Britain by another.

Anyway, having found itself guilty the BBC set out on a programme of rehabilitation in the course of which the number of network news stories about Scotland, Wales and Northern Ireland seemed to take an upward curve. And when something applied solely to England – schools, perhaps, or the health service – the distinction was often made clear. Did we just imagine that newsreaders were inflecting the crucial words slightly differently, that they were now saying *Scotland* rather than just Scotland, or *England* rather than the more neutral England?

Coincidentally, a particularly appealing, although not especially important, story about Wales emerged at the time the King Report was published. In the circumstances you couldn't help feeling that there was more than a little relish in the way in which it was seized upon. When he announced the winner of the Welsh Book of the Year Award at a crowded dinner in Cardiff, the (soon to be ex-) Welsh Culture Minister, Rhodri Glyn Thomas, got it wrong. He was supposed to say that the prize had been won by the eminent poet Dannie Abse but instead called out the name of one of the runners-up, Tom Bullough, a virtually unknown author. The novelist Bullough, hard-up even by Welsh writer standards, was half way to the front and mentally spending the £10,000 prize when the minister corrected himself. It was a moment of anguished embarrassment that quickly found its way onto network television and radio. Over and over again. Short of holing up in one of those remote Greek monasteries favoured by the Prince of Wales it was impossible to miss it over the next day or so. "It shows," a BBC network news executive said to me a couple of weeks later, "that you need to be careful what you wish for." Was that glee I detected? Surely not.

The struggles of the BBC to grapple with the complexities of a country in the throes of significant political and administrative change represent more than the sclerotic nature of all large, centralised bureaucracies. They also illustrate vividly the central imbalance in the nature of Britain: not, as is sometimes popularly supposed, the tension between mighty England and the pipsqueak countries of the Celtic fringe, but that between the sophistication of the London intelligentsia and the backward provincialism of the other ninety per cent of the population of the entire United Kingdom. It's an attitude that has been encouraged at least in part by the growth of the international character of London, the city becoming in a sense almost beyond nationality, and the loss of a distinct identity in other parts of the United Kingdom as manufacturing industry in particular has declined. Political and media influence now belongs almost entirely in the capital.

The consequence in broadcasting is sometimes that the most unexpected programmes and presenters can be infected by the virus of thinking that events need a London gloss before they can be properly presented to the public. A few years ago I wrote a book called *When Arthur Met Maggie,* a substantial part of which dealt with the miners' strike of 1984-85. I talked about it on *Start the Week* on Radio 4. Among the things the presenter, Andrew Marr, said about it was this: "One of the interesting things about this book is that it's political history written as it were from a standpoint in Wales in the sense that quite a lot of your characters, including a key NCB – National Coal Board – official, are Welsh and you are telling the story of the times standing from Wales rather than standing from central London."

What I should have said, but didn't because I was too slow to do so, was that one of the reasons for that was that there were not many coal mines in central London. It was curious, to say the least, that such a question could be asked by Andrew Marr, who is Scottish, and, as it happened, was then engaged in writing a history of modern Britain. What was striking too, as I read those words again, was that it was necessary, in 2006, to gloss the initials NCB, which not many years previously would have been instantly recognisable throughout the country. But the question also reflected the fact that metropolitanism was no new phenomenon. For many years the coal board's headquarters was in Hobart House, in Belgravia, a few yards from the offices of the British Steel Corporation, despite a similar scarcity of steelworks in the London area. The NUM was also based in London until Arthur Scargill removed it to Barnsley, just in time to prepare for the virtual extinction of the industry, a process in which he was to play such a crucial role.

The useful identifiers of parts of the UK that served for so long as media shorthand have almost entirely disappeared: the South Wales valleys and coal, for example; Lancashire and textiles;

Glasgow and shipbuilding; Sheffield and steel; Dundee and jute, jam, the *Dandy* and the *Beano* and so on. One summer in the late sixties the town of Port Talbot was bursting with journalists for weeks on end because a strike at the steelworks threatened to halt a large part of the British motor industry. No such stranglehold could be exercised by any town in twenty-first century Britain so there's no longer any reason to go to the Port Talbots of this world, or even find out where they are. It's difficult to think now that political leaders like the Chamberlains of Birmingham, or Stanley Baldwin from a family of Midlands industrialists, will again have their power bases outside London. The result is that, seen from White City or Canary Wharf, the rest of Britain can easily become of little day-to-day account.

That may be why Jeremy Vine was able to appeal to *Newsnight* viewers not to switch off, despite the fact that the programme was about to devote a few minutes to some Welsh matter; or David Dimbleby, presenting *Question Time* from Cardiff, could say to a member of the audience: "I don't want to go into Welsh Assembly issues as it won't be understood outside Wales". Perhaps it was as a form of Communist-style re-education for Dimbleby that the BBC announced later that year that *Question Time* would in future be produced in Scotland, a decision that was said to have provoked the presenter to express 'dismay'. So shocked was he indeed that it was rumoured in the newspapers that he might even stop presenting the programme entirely. Curiously enough Dimbleby himself was not quoted directly about this matter, so perhaps the newspapers made it all up. Or perhaps not.

The whole business was described particularly hilariously in the *Daily Telegraph* which reported an unnamed (you bet) "senior BBC source" as saying: "In my view it is about as politically inept as it gets to move the most popular British political programme to Scotland which is riven with nationalist fervour." Following in Birtian footsteps the *Telegraph* went on to spell out the potential disaster that might be lurking around the corner. "If the Scots vote for independence the programme would have to be brought back or produced in a country which has cut off all links with Westminster."

And if not, of course, not. What the BBC announcement actually meant was that the office from which the *Question Time* programme was produced would, in due course, be located in Scotland. But since the programme is broadcast each week from different locations around the UK the practical effect of this change (apart from higher mileage claims) was difficult to discern. What it definitely didn't mean was that Dimbleby (70-year-old London broadcasting royalty, after all) would have to take up residence in (or even go to) Glasgow. Then again, if Scotland was trembling so close to the brink of independence that it was too unstable for it to be the headquarters of a little late-night BBC knockabout, why hadn't the *Daily Telegraph* told us about this before? And did the *Telegraph* have any idea of how peripatetic programmes like *Question Time* are made, in particular that they could be moved in and out of Scotland in the time it would take the SNP to get air in their bagpipes? You might also say that, in all these circumstances, the decision to move the programme was perhaps not quite the boon being advertised by the BBC.

But there we are. Metropolitan sophistication isn't invariably what it's cracked up to be and this is the level of debate that often passes for national journalism. The BBC spins, like every other organisation, and the newspapers spin the spin a little more thinly until the relevant facts, such as they are, entirely disappear from view. But it illustrates a problem deeper even than that of discovering a little about parts of the country in which you don't happen to live. It is the difficulty of understanding through journalism what the United Kingdom is really like.

Now and again substantial figures at the metropolitan centre seem to catch on to the idea that there's something going on out there on the fringes of British life, but at the same time they have difficulty in grasping quite what it is. A.N. Wilson, for example, is a writer of stupendous productivity. Books and articles and opinions pour out of him. He's fluent and very readable. Perhaps that's the problem. In *Our Times*, his survey of Britain from 1953 to the present day, he considers the downfall of Ron Davies, who had to leave the Cabinet and his position as Welsh Labour leader following his adventures on Clapham Common in 1998.

Wilson writes: "Most of his constituents continued to support him... but this was not enough to suppress the rise of his rival Rhodri Morgan, a Blairite placeman, to the position of Welsh First Minister." Apart from the elision of time in this description, it is also the exact opposite of what happened. Ron Davies was actually succeeded by Alun Michael, very much a Blairite placeman, who was squeezed into office by the Downing Street machine. Later he was pushed out again by a vote of the national assembly and replaced by Rhodri Morgan, despite Blair's desperate attempts over many years to keep Morgan from office. Blair's view of Rhodri was made clear when, on becoming Prime Minister, he had unexpectedly refused him the position of Parliamentary Under-Secretary of State at the Welsh Office, perhaps the lowest political office in the entire government apparatus. Wilson's account is so laughably inaccurate that inevitably you can't read the rest of the book without wondering what else he's got wrong. He writes, for example, that the Free Wales Army enjoyed blowing up railway bridges although no such incident ever occurred.

Even people who know Wales well don't always seem to understand what kind of place it is. Sir Simon Jenkins, a former editor of *The Times*, has a family home in Aberdovey which he visits frequently. Sir Simon knows Wales well but even so he once told me, in a slightly aggrieved tone, that when he had been struck down with peritonitis his wife had had to drive him at high speed to Bronglais Hospital in Aberystwyth. It was touch and go but, he suggested, it seemed a long journey to have his life saved (AA route: 30 miles; estimated travel time: 48 minutes). I asked him, and I hope I didn't sound sarcastic, if he thought there should perhaps be a team of surgeons on duty a little nearer Aberdovey, in Machynlleth say, ready to deal with emergencies of this kind. He didn't seem to see why not. Not for nothing is Sir Simon the apostle of localism.

It's widely accepted that the most important newspaper in Britain is the *Daily Mail*. The approval of its readership is the one most coveted by the political parties. Everyone in the trade agrees that it's a brilliant product, in particular because it reflects a version of Britain that reassures its readers, a group of people who are often taken to represent Middle England, something that is a version of society rather than a geographical definition. That's what newspapers do. If they disconcerted and contradicted their readers rather than reinforced their prejudices they wouldn't last very long. They don't do this by the use of any particular dishonesty but in creating a *Daily Mail* version of Britain through selection and emphasis. You can't do it any other way and to that extent all journalism is lies, or at least not the whole truth.

In this particular portrait of Britain a typical *Mail* story would be along the following lines: "Council workers sacked over jobless

Afghan mother of seven who got £1.2 million council house". At
first sight that looks like the winning entry in a literary competition
asking readers to invent a headline which represents, in the fewest
number of words, the paper's view of what was wrong with Britain.
In fact it really did appear, in October 2008, over a story that began:
"A council has sacked three officers after it was revealed an Afghan
family was living in a £1.2 million home paid for by the taxpayer.
Mother-of-seven Toorpakai Saiedi, 35, receives £170,000 a year in
benefits, a staggering £150,000 of that is paid to a private landlord
for the rent of a seven-bedroom house in West London."

What all this adds up to in popular newspaper terms is that
bungling council officials (jobsworths) in soft touch Britain are
paying a fortune to keep feckless (seven children) foreigners
(Afghans: aren't we fighting them or something?) in extravagant
comfort (seven-bedroom house) under a system (entirely legal but
clearly demented) in which even the beneficiaries can't believe their
luck. "Outside the house yesterday Mrs. Saiedi's son Jawad said:
'When I heard how much the council were paying I thought they
were mad'." The only thing missing in this account of contemporary life as described by the *Mail* was the newspaper's inability to
discover any involvement by the European Union, proverbially the
source of much of the idiocy in modern British life.

It pointed out in its account that no one was actually doing
anything illegal, but the tone of the piece and the prominence given
to it reflects the hatred of foreigners that pervades large sections of
the popular press. It represents the idea that there is some kind of
quintessential Britain (or, more likely, England) being stolen from
under our noses by unscrupulous immigrants, many of whom, it is
implied, are here illegally, or at least undeservedly, to take advantage
of our national lack of spine. Any nationality can be called into
service to reinforce the siege mentality peddled by many newspapers. With the expansion of the EU, Eastern Europeans became a
particular target, accused of bringing criminal gangs, drug traffick-
ing and prostitutes to Britain by the busload. For some reason the
Poles were high up on the list of offenders, accused of claiming
benefits to be sent back to support children living in Poland.

Only stupid, feeble Britain, the narrative runs, would put up
with this erosion of national identity. So one *Daily Mail* reporter
wrote of the shocking atmosphere in a Polish delicatessen in the
town where, she said, she couldn't make herself understood: "I feel

like a foreigner, but this is not Warsaw, Krakow or Gdansk. I am in Southampton." Only someone who'd never been in a Chinese restaurant could write such things, but there are no limits to which vigilant journalists will not go to expose the malevolent influence of any foreigner.

In September 2008 the *Mail* reported: "Households could be forced to share wheelie bins because of a shortage forced by soaring demand on the continent." A new law in Germany was to blame. "The shortage has increased fears that wheelie bins will be stolen and sold on the black market."

When in doubt blame the Germans, has long been one of the mottos of newsrooms in Britain, but what does that and all the other manifestations of rabid xenophobia tell us about Gordon Brown's idea of a country which is supposedly marked out by its fair-mindedness and tolerance? In the first place most newspapers don't do fair-mindedness and tolerance. Their pages are no place for the kind of weedy liberals who persist in the view that there might not always be simple answers to difficult questions. The newspapers set a tone for public debate and influence political parties perhaps even more than their readers. The endorsement of the *Daily Mail* and the *Sun* in particular are eagerly sought. If they consistently talk about Britain being 'swamped' by immigrants and dragged down by hordes of criminal spongers who sneak through our inadequately maintained borders then politicians announce that, while such a picture is exaggerated, they'll nevertheless do something about it.

Amid all the certainties of the popular press, though, there is a curious blurring of the boundaries between fact and fiction. It can be seen most clearly in the way in which it's often difficult to tell if newspaper stories about television soap operas refer to the real-life actors or the characters they portray. The attractions of writing big headlines and sensational-sounding stories about the soaps and 'reality' programmes like *Big Brother* are obvious. It's cheap, involves little effort and is almost entirely-risk free; it is make-believe journalism about make-believe people in make-believe communities but it can be made to look very like the real thing. The problem is when reality starts to get treated as if it had the same dramatic structures as the imaginary world of television, put together by a team of scriptwriters who will sooner or later offer a sensational denouement. Which is more or less what happened in the case of Madeleine McCann.

The abduction of three-year-old Madeleine in May 2007 had a great deal in common with the kind of storyline that might have been devised by a professional writer of thrillers. A little girl disappears without trace. There is a small cast of characters: her parents, both attractive, professional people (two doctors, indeed; would a writer have pushed it that far?), a group of their well-off, middle-class friends and the obligatory loner who is at first openly suspected by the police. It all takes place in a small resort in Portugal, a useful aspect of the story because foreign police can play their traditional role as bungling incompetents.

As the days went by and no evidence emerged, desperation seized any number of news desks. Reporters weren't being paid to hang around in Portugal to file stories saying that no-one knew anything. Not only did there have to be an explanation but it had to be one appropriate for the television age. So, variously, practically everyone was behaving suspiciously in one way or another. What was the significance of the church? Were there traces of DNA in a car hired long after the disappearance? What was the appropriate amount of grief and despair in these circumstances and was it on display here? Then Madeleine had been 'kidnapped to order'; she had been sighted in Morocco, Majorca, Malta, Amsterdam, the South of France, Brazil; twist after twist in which, at one time or another, it was implied that practically everyone concerned had some guilty secret.

In the end, though, it was the media themselves, in particular a number of newspapers, who were forced into a confession. Much of what they had published was rubbish. They admitted the 'utter falsity' of many of the things they had written, apologised for 'extremely serious but baseless' allegations and paid out large sums of money to numbers of those involved. The McCanns and their seven friends separately won cases against the Express newspaper group. The obligatory loner, Robert Murat, got apologies and damages from the the the *Sun*, the *Daily Express*, the *Daily Star*, the *Daily Mail*, the *Evening Standard*, the *Metro*, the *Daily Mirror*, the *Sunday Mirror*, the *News of the World*, *The Scotsman* and Sky TV.

It all cost the newspapers millions but, the question arose, did they care? Not much, it seemed. Media analysts thought that, on the whole, the newspapers might have considered it money well spent on promoting themselves. And did they worry about the humiliation of having to admit publicly that they had published endless fabrications? Would the fact that they'd got so much wrong about one of the biggest news stories of recent years destroy their credibility as a source of information? It didn't look like it. And did they agonise about the people they'd traduced, in particular the McCanns, haunted by the loss of their daughter? Get a life.

Such matters raise one of the most insistently important questions in public life. How do we know what we *think* we know? How do we discover what kind of country we live in? The answer is all the more difficult to come by because of the unspoken, if not particularly secret, agendas of some of the most important media companies. When *The Times* or the *Sun* or the *News of the World* or the *Sunday Times* complain about the unfair imposition of the licence fee and berates the BBC for its failings, it is anything but a dispassionate analysis. What it is instead is a reflection of the ambition of Rupert Murdoch's mighty News Corp, owners of those papers and Sky Television among many, many other things, to get his hands on the market now served by non-commercial broadcasting. Murdoch, born Australian but who, for business reasons, became a US citizen, is a fierce opponent of the European Union, in particular British membership of the single currency. The power of his media organisation means he has access to, and influence on, the most senior politicians in the country on that issue and many others. When John Major unexpectedly won the general election in 1992, the *Sun* carried the headline: "It's the *Sun* Wot Won It". While the truth of that claim was difficult to establish, no one thought it was absurdly far-fetched, something apparently underlined by Tony Blair's landslide victory in 1997 shortly after the *Sun* had urged its readers to vote Labour.

Murdoch's views of life are to a large extent rooted in his business interests: "Rupert follows the money," one senior Labour figure told me, a philosophy that's at least fairly easy to understand. It's rather more straightforward than many of the delusions and obsessions of many newspaper proprietors over the years, often outsiders of piratical character. Given the influence many of them wielded it's not reassuring to realise that mental stability didn't always appear to be their distinguishing characteristic. Lord Beaverbrook, for example, a Canadian who sat in Churchill's War Cabinet, told a Royal Commission on the press that he ran the *Daily Express* "purely for propaganda and with no other purpose". One problem was that his pursuit of propaganda often involved conducting vendettas against people to whom he'd taken a dislike, most notably, perhaps, Lord Mountbatten. In his book on the press, Roy Greenslade writes that "one observer claimed that the [*Daily Express*] had six reporters following Aneurin Bevan wherever he went.... The *Express* was not alone. When Bevan was dying in hospital in 1960 reporters from the *Daily Mail* and the *Daily Telegraph* were found in a neighbouring ward."

Cecil Harmsworth King, chairman of a great publishing empire which included the *Daily Mirror,* was in 1968 ejected from his job by fellow board members after attempting to organise a coup to overthrow the then Prime Minister, Harold Wilson. King's chosen instrument, coincidentally, was Lord Mountbatten. One of King's newspaper-owning uncles, Lord Northcliffe, known as the Napoleon of Fleet Street, became convinced at the end of his life that he was being poisoned by Belgian ice cream. He died in a Paris hotel shortly after being discovered pointing his pistol at a dressing gown hanging on his bedroom door, under the impression it was a German assassin. Another Canadian, Conrad Black – Lord Black of Crossharbour – one time proprietor of the *Daily Telegraph* and *The Spectator,* remains, at the time of writing, in prison in the United States. Rupert Murdoch dyes his own hair.

On the whole, then, this has not obviously been a class of men to whom you would turn for advice on, for example, critical matters of economics or diplomacy, or to whom you would lightly entrust the care of a small dog. Over the years this has been a club which has had more than its fair share of crooks and fools. Yet they and their successors continue to be perfectly happy in their self-appointed role as moral guardians of the nation. Anyone who thinks that adultery, for example, is in general a private matter of concern only to the parties involved is denounced as lacking proper, traditional values. Paul Dacre, Editor-in-Chief of the *Daily Mail,* explained in a speech in November 2008: "Since time immemorial public shaming has been vital in defending the parameters of what are considered acceptable standards of social behaviour, helping ensure that citizens – rich and poor – adhere to them for the good of the greater community."

It's vigilante justice but that's what newspapers do and there's no point in complaining about it. It's not even that someone should prevent them doing it. It's just that they shouldn't try to persuade themselves and the rest of us that they carrying out some kind of sacred duty that will protect society from terminal decay. The truth is that behind all the self-generated romance to which journalists and their employers are particularly addicted, they are commercial enterprises that daily give the lie to George Orwell's view that the most hateful of all names to the British people is that of nosey parker. Nor is this state of affairs really a problem, even if it is something that has increasingly come to affect the character of all newspapers. It is no longer a surprise, for example, to find in the *Sunday Telegraph* speculation about the state of some celebrity's marriage. But as long as there are plenty of sources of information, including newspapers, then contending arguments, even contending gossip, will be heard and work their way into public debate. The real difficulty lies elsewhere: the menacing shadow that hangs over the idea of an informed democracy isn't quality but quantity.

That is evident when you look at the structure of British journalism in the context of the emerging new political order. Its metropolitan character has intensified, not just in newspapers but in broadcasting too. In the 1950s ITV was established with a specifically regional character. Granada Television and the idea of the North West as Granadaland was the most striking example of the way in which the varied nature of the United Kingdom was reflected in national television: *Coronation Street* is an obvious and continuing example of how it was done. At the same time those companies told their own regions – some more than others admittedly – about the nature of their communities. Most of the original fifteen companies have now been absorbed into the single company, ITV, with only Scottish Television and Ulster TV surviving independently. Their obligations to broadcast local programmes have been sharply reduced to reflect their parlous financial state. Regional commercial television is clinging on by its fingernails but is only delaying the moment when it finally loses its grip and falls on to the rocks below.

The London-based press is also under pressure. By no means every title is expected to survive recession. In general it operates almost entirely from London; the reporters that once were based in cities and territories around the country have all but disappeared. In fact the majority of national newspaper journalists aren't simply confined to London but to the screens and telephones in their offices. The rest of the world reaches them through electronic filters.

Worse still is the condition of local papers, in particular the kind of regional dailies that once illuminated the political world – national and local – to their readers. They have been fundamentally altered by large groups in pursuit of an electrifyingly high level of profit. In 2006, for example, Trinity Mirror, which owns 186 titles around Britain, made a profit of 42 per cent on turnover; other regional newspaper groups weren't all that far behind. These kind of figures have been achieved by a traditional method: ruthless cost cutting, in particular a drastic reduction in the number of staff. Fewer people have to produce more copy, much more copy, as the papers try to turn themselves into what are called multi-media platforms, with journalists expected to turn out video reports as well as the traditional written stories. And they do so at very low levels of pay – starting salaries for new entrants to the trade range from £11,000 to £13,000 a year. That compares with the average starting salary for a graduate in the UK of just over £20,000. Once upon a time novels about journalism were called things like *Street of Adventure*. Bright lad wanted, the job advertisements used to say. Any bright lad today would find something better to do.

Professor Bob Franklin of the Cardiff School of Journalism has written extensively on the condition of the non-London press and has identified in particular what he calls McJournalism, a form of newspaper publishing in which reporters are given rigid templates for the effort they are allowed to devote to any story. They do not have the time or resources to research their own work but are expected to use agency copy, the internet and press releases as their main sources. Now that the massive profits have stopped rolling in, a trend intensified by recession, the big newspaper chains are under increasing pressure. Franklin thinks this means that most of the regional dailies will disappear within five years. He thinks the weekly press has better prospects, but what sort of newspapers will it produce? He's less optimistic about that. "They're very different. Every aspect of design and the way they're written is changing. Their contents are shifting. They are too much of an economic organisation and their profitability has been won at the cost of their editorial integrity."

What that means is that their editorial agenda is now almost exclusively concentrated on lifestyle and what's known as human interest. Matters considered boring by editorial directors – local authorities and the courts, for example – are too expensive and complicated to cover compared with the ready-made stories coming in as handouts or written centrally in the company machine. What is now rapidly disappearing is the constituency of journalism which once meant that there was a dispassionate account available of huge swathes of life throughout the United Kingdom. When I worked for the *Luton News* in the 1960s, for example, no court of any kind sat without a reporter being present. No matter how dull the proceedings, every case was written up and published in the paper. Full council meetings were covered by five of us working in relays. At a general election I was attached for the duration of the campaign to the Communist candidate – embedded, you might say – attending and reporting on his public meetings night after night.

Much of the material thus acquired wasn't very interesting although a surprising amount was recycled for the national press. The point is it provided a form of public scrutiny that underpinned the democratic process. Such sources of information have largely disappeared now. The greed of proprietors is one reason, but another, as Bob Franklin says, is that the world we once reported has also changed beyond recognition. "We've destroyed a lot of the fabric of everyday life into which a newspaper was interwoven. People don't work in the way they used to. Buying a newspaper was always a habit related to employment. You bought it on the way to work, you read it in your breaks at work. We've split up cities, we've put people in suburbs. Changes in everyday life account for a lot of this change in newspapers."

There are commentators who think that a form of rescue will come from the internet. Online editions of newspapers are becoming increasingly popular, but what goes online needs the support of what is being written for the traditional, printed newspaper. Most independent blogs fade away after the first flush of the author's enthusiasm and those that remain are essentially a form of running commentary on life rather than a serious attempt to gather fresh information and analyse it. Most of the best of them come from the people who are already writing for the newspapers or working for the BBC, not as a substitute for basic reporting but as an extension of it. The phenomenon known as 'citizen journalism' – pictures taken on mobile phones, accounts of events, opinions on this and that, all emailed to newspapers is not journalism at all, but a haphazard form of evidence-gathering. Bob Franklin argues: "My particular view is that what I call the digital optimists have no cause for such optimism."

No doubt during the fifteenth century, in monasteries all over Britain, monks fretted away over their illuminated manuscripts when that Mr. Caxton started messing about with moveable type. Industries change and develop and disappear. But it's particularly ominous in what's sometimes known as the 'information age', at a time when Britain is becoming more politically diverse, people have fewer reliable sources of information available to them.

It's already possible to see from the example of Wales the seriousness of the problem that arises when power is exercised in what is fast approaching an information vacuum. The *Western Mail*, which has long styled itself the national newspaper of Wales in fact circulates almost entirely in the south of the country. It sells around 37,000 copies a day to a population of three million. The *Daily Post*, the morning paper that covers north Wales sells around 40,000. Both these papers belong to Trinity Mirror, as does *Wales on Sunday*, the *South Wales Echo* and a number of important weeklies. They have all been subjected to the squeeze I've discussed above. Numbers of staff have declined steeply. The group has reinvented itself as *Media Wales* and most editorial staff work across the group's titles. Most people in Wales who read newspapers – more than eighty per cent of them – read papers published in England, although they'll rarely find anything about Wales in them. Thirty years ago all those papers had correspondents based in Wales: the priorities of the post-Fleet Street world mean that now there are none.

In 2008 ITV announced that 429 people out of just over 1,000 working in its regional news operations were being made redundant. ITV Wales, part of the group, planned to cut its news output by a fifth to four hours a week, and its non-news programmes from four hours a week to one and a half hours. It's unlikely that much of that will survive the disappearance of the old licensing system when television moves completely to digital transmission, a change that is already under way. More than that, the publication of ITV's grim results in March 2009 suggested that even this modest output might be in further difficulty.

It's a nasty paradox. A new political system that desperately needs to be reported thoroughly has been greeted with the hacking down of most of the organisations that ought to be doing the reporting. There aren't many of them in Wales and they've never been awash with money, but now there are hardly any that can seriously tackle the job. This lack of pluralism looks like the most serious threat of all to the proper development of an uncertain new democratic system where demands for more power have become commonplace in a largely perfunctory public argument. At the heart of the new dispensation, the national assembly's building in Cardiff Bay, the Senedd, you won't find many reporters. The Press Association has one there, as do the *Western Mail* and ITV. Others drop in from time to time in search of a story or a few quotes but of an afternoon it's quite possible to find yourself alone in the press gallery, often an entirely appropriate reflection of the quality of debate on offer.

There is one exception. BBC Wales does have substantial resources, although it's under pressure too, and a big political team that serves a large number of outlets in two languages. But it can't be healthy for the BBC almost alone to carry the burden of keeping three million people intelligently informed about the way in which they are governed. It threatens to become a kind of monopoly by default. It seems to me that's a dangerous state of affairs. Without pluralism, without competition, journalism inevitably lacks its proper vigour and a necessary sense of adventure.

It's difficult to see how this central problem of the new devolved system can be resolved. Conscientious and thoughtful people conduct investigations into possible solutions but invariably come up with something that involves spending public money. That's what everybody in this game is after. A Welsh media commission, for example, has asked for £50 million to fund an additional English language channel. What, *more* public money for, Welsh broadcasting, people might ask. This is a country which has lavished money on S4C, the Welsh language television service that gets £100 million a year, something like £200 per head for everyone who speaks Welsh. That money doesn't just come from Wales, but from every taxpayer in the United Kingdom. Channel Four also wants public money; so, too, does Scottish Television which has asked for 'a small public subsidy', to keep news and current affairs running 'effectively'. The BBC, nervously hearing the knives being sharpened on the whetstone, campaigns against 'top-slicing'; the government, over its head in financing the banks, isn't, in any foreseeable future, going to fork out cash for what will inevitably be portrayed as frivolous purposes. And even if it did, what would

Rupert Murdoch and the BBC's other influential competitors have to say?

But can the BBC and the government afford not to act? In Scotland, a country much, much better served by newspapers than Wales, the SNP government won't have forgotten the affair of the Scottish *Six*. People who know Alex Salmond say the reason he doesn't like the BBC is simply because it is British. He believes that whatever the corporation has done in Scotland in the last ten years has been dragged from it rather than been given willingly. The futuristic new BBC building at Pacific Quay in Glasgow, a physical statement of investment in Scotland, can be portrayed as evidence of guilt for past neglect. One of the first acts of the SNP administration when it took office was to set up a broadcasting commission. Its main conclusion was that a separate Scottish digital channel should be established. The cost? Say, £70 million or so. Where should the money come from? Public funds. Whose public funds? That's not our concern. The BBC's? Maybe. How much did you say you were giving to Welsh language television?

It's an astute proposition. It's expensive without seeming to be unimaginably so. It may be a test of how seriously metropolitan England and its institutions take Scotland. In particular those institutions will have to calculate the possible political consequences for the whole of the United Kingdom of failing to react appropriately. If it happens it's another triumph for the SNP. If it doesn't happen it's another example of a London failure to do anything much for Scotland without being forced to do to do so at the ballot box. John Birt, the man who, in alliance with Tony Blair, saved *British* broadcasting in 1999 by heading off the Scottish *Six* has spent a lot of his subsequent career working as an adviser to the government. Perhaps they ought to ask him what to do next.

The Right Prescription

SOMETIMES IT'S THE very small things that make you realise how much the world has altered while you weren't paying attention. You see a movie from the 1960s and practically everyone is smoking all the time, offering bulky cigarette cases, flicking metal lighters. Unthinkable now. When did you last even see a cigarette case? Some television news footage from the seventies is included in a documentary and you laugh at the formality of the reporter's suit and the luxuriance of his sideburns. What did he think he looked like? Not only that, but there in the background is a miners' picket line. What's a picket line, for goodness' sake? What's a *miner*?

Some aspects of life, though, remain resolutely unaltered. Politics, for example, despite the fact that people have regularly announced that things will never be the same again. They said it in 1945 and again in 1959; in 1983 and in 2001, only for the wheel to come round once more and restore a sense of natural rhythm. Nowhere was this clearer perhaps than in the House of Commons in the middle of 2007 where the Conservatives were once more smoothly led by an Old Etonian. Opposite him was the new Labour Prime Minister, a studiously unpolished figure with an unmistakably regional accent. Not much of a revolution there, then, despite the coarse interruption of a series of grammar school types as Tory prime ministers and leaders, and the stupendous achievements of a public schoolboy in taking Labour to an unprecedented period in power. It was easy to think that British public life had, after an unsettling interval, resumed a familiar shape in which class still played a key role.

As the Brown-Cameron passengers buckled up their seat belts for the flight to the next election it took on even more clearly the traditional character of British political dispute. When economic crisis struck the government more or less nationalised some of the banks – admittedly out of necessity rather than conviction. It spent previously unthinkable sums of public money in an effort to shore up the system. It began to look very much like Old Labour behind a new shop front. The Conservatives also resumed their familiar place as opponents of public spending and of the tax increases that would inevitably follow as a result. Quite what should be done instead was not so clear, the Conservatives being rather more decided about what the government should not have done in the past. That, though, is the proper privilege of opposition.

However, there was something else in this cosily familiar configuration of British politics. There was a new element. The political structure of Britain had been rebuilt and new arguments had emerged. If the confrontation of gentlemen against players, toffs versus proles, had lost much of its passion, even if superficially still in evidence, it began to look as though the United Kingdom might now be divided less by matters of class and more by arguments about place. If the Etonians had made a spectacular comeback, what about the significance of all those Scots – four of them in the Cabinet, including the Prime Minister, all representing constituencies in which the UK Parliament had only limited authority? In the changing rooms of Westminster and all around Britain the teams were learning the rules of a new game: England v the Rest (of the United Kingdom).

It was a coincidence that the argument should be so neatly embodied in the two men who faced each other across the chamber of the House of Commons. It was made for the cartoonists. David Cameron, the grandson of one baronet and son-in-law of another, posh enough but not ridiculously so; someone to whom status and privilege clearly didn't come as a surprise; and, as a man who had worked in public relations, someone modern enough to fit snugly into twenty-first-century politics, a trade in which image had become rather more important than principle. On the other side Gordon Brown was about as Scottish a politician as you could imagine without tumbling over the edge into grotesque parody; a son of the manse, the traditions of which he proudly carried with him; a Stakhanovite intellectual; a forbidding presence of old-fashioned Nonconformist rectitude; one of only two Prime Ministers, and the first for a century, who had been to a university – Edinburgh – other than Oxford or Cambridge. Too Scottish for his own good, you might be tempted to think. Yet far more than

David Cameron he was the one who worried away persistently at the idea of Britishness, what it was and how it might be saved.

Paradoxically, that insistence might have made him seem even more of an alien figure. Real British people, critics muttered, are at ease with their nationality; they simply don't harp on about being British any more than most of them would dress up and go morris dancing on a spring afternoon. Naturally sceptical, they began to wonder why someone would go on like this. What was the subtext, the hidden agenda? If a man of undiluted Scottishness was banging the British drum in this unnatural manner perhaps it was because the national identity of which he spoke with such enthusiasm was already leaking away.

When Michael Foot was in charge of the Labour government's devolution plans in the seventies he argued that, far from threatening the solidarity of the United Kingdom, they were in fact a method of strengthening the Union. What was wrong, he asked, with a measure of home rule, a proposition ridiculed by his friend Neil Kinnock as being the same as talking about a measure of pregnancy or a measure of measles. Nevertheless it was a seductive idea in the political circumstances of the time. Set up some kind of parliament in Edinburgh and the Scottish nationalist threat would evaporate in the warmth of the new democratic institution. In the case of Wales a rather less powerful parliament of some kind and ditto the rather less powerful nationalist threat. Michael Foot, a notably honest man, might have believed this line, but did anyone else?

It wasn't put to the test at that stage, one good reason, perhaps, why Tony Blair pulled out the same argument twenty years later when he said that Scottish devolution would be "the salvation of the United Kingdom". But so far and no further isn't a strategy with a particularly good track record. For example, it suited people to insist that British sovereignty would not be impaired by Britain's joining the Common Market in 1973 even though it could not conceivably have been true. Every international treaty involves someone yielding some sovereignty in some way. To contradict the obvious in this manner is to undermine your arguments on everything else. How could the European Union function, never mind develop, if member governments could continue behaving exactly as they pleased? The fact is that over these years sponsors of constitutional change have preferred to deny what is self-evidently true and to ignore inconvenient consequences because they have lacked sufficient confidence in their own arguments.

This is not to say that Britain shouldn't have joined the European Union or have embarked on a programme of devolution. In fact these two matters are intimately connected, but governments have preferred to treat them as separate constitutional rearrangements, each of which can be kept safely in its own box. The convention is that voters should be asked to pronounce only on the simplest of questions and not be troubled by intricate patterns of change or the philosophy that lies behind them. But those voters have become aware that power is on a flight from Westminster and they might as well grab some of it for themselves as it rushes by.

The great challenges of the twenty-first century are international terrorism, globalisation and climate change. In the early years of the century it's dawned on even the least alert citizen that, far from being able to solve them, the power a British government has in relation to these matters is limited, sometimes to the point of virtual invisibility. At the same time the nature of political argument has changed almost beyond recognition. Left and right have become meaningless distinctions, party loyalties largely pointless. In the new administrations of the United Kingdom unfamiliar systems have obliged people to establish a new form of political dialogue. In government in Scotland, Wales and Northern Ireland, nationalism has come to assume an unprecedented authority.

Elsewhere in the world old identities are changing or reasserting themselves in a way that sometimes reaches everyday lives. Croatia keeps England out of the European Championship and old rivals celebrate. But it was only the other day that Croatia re-established its separate existence, never mind an international football team. And the man in the Millennium Stadium understands only too well that, thanks to the number of nations emerging from the wreckage of the Soviet Union, the prospects of *his* team qualifying for the World Cup finals for the first time in more than half a century is even dimmer than it's generally been during that period. Or again, sitting in the audience for the BBC Cardiff Singer of the World in 2007 you suddenly realised that when that competition began, less than a quarter of a century previously, many of the performers taking part would not have been there representing independent countries. Ukraine, for example, Uzbekistan or Estonia or Lithuania. And even if the same individuals had been present there'd have been plenty of minders around to make sure they didn't defect. The world is nothing like it was even in the immediate past. There is more than an echo of this process in the changing nature of Britain and the unfamiliar way in which people think of their place in it.

People who take a particular interest in such matters understand these things and their relationship to each other perfectly well. How the poor old voter finds out and what he or she makes of it is all too often, as I say, through the small things. Like car parking.

In March 2008 the Welsh Assembly Government announced that all car parking charges at Welsh hospitals were to be abolished. Even by the modest standards of the ministers of Cardiff Bay this was not a momentous event. There was a bit of an argument about it, but there aren't many things you can do in Wales without having some kind of row, and in the normal course of events it would have been forgotten quickly enough. But then something unexpected happened. A government minister called Ben Bradshaw, a man with responsibility for health matters in England, went on the radio and explained what a terrible idea it was. He felt strongly about this, he said, because his view was that the health service in Wales wasn't performing very well, unlike that in England which everyone knew, and I paraphrase, was running with all the unobtrusive efficiency of an expensive Swiss watch.

The most interesting thing about this intervention, perhaps the only interesting thing about it, was that hospital car parks in Wales were none of Bradshaw's business. More than that, they were *specifically* none of his business. What was going on? What did he think he was doing, this Labour minister in England, rubbishing a decision by a Labour minister in Wales? Was this what newspapers like to call a gaffe? Or even a split? Had he simply stumbled into this breach of protocol because he hadn't yet grasped, nine years after the event, even the broad outline of the nature of devolution within the UK? Not a bit of it. Ben Bradshaw wasn't speaking to Welsh voters who, poor dabs, would have to look after their own interests. No, his message was to the people of England who were starting to take a closer interest than they had previously (closer than none at all, that is) in what was happening in those exotic nations of Scotland, Wales and Northern Ireland. In particular he was addressing a growing sense of unease that, in some devious way, those places were getting away with something. Worse, getting away with it at the expense of the English taxpayer.

How was it, this taxpayer might have asked, that the Welsh could have free car parking in their hospitals while he couldn't? The burden of Bradshaw's answer was that this state of affairs arose from the fact that the people who ran such things in Wales had no proper sense of priorities. The more money a government spent on car parking, obviously, the less it had to spend on clinical procedures. No wonder then, that when it came to something like waiting lists, the Welsh lagged a long way behind the more fortunate English. You could almost hear his sigh of disbelief at the folly of his Celtic colleagues as he emptied a bucket of irony on to the whole affair. "If that's what Scotland and Wales want to do," he said, "that's one of the joys of devolution." Exactly. It's their money and they can spend it as they choose. Except for one thing. Perhaps it's not *their* money after all.

One of the decisions taken by the Welsh Assembly Government that took office in 2003 was to introduce a policy that would eventually lead to the abolition of all prescription charges. In a British context this was a change that passed largely without comment, as indeed did practically anything happening in Wales that wasn't Dylan Thomas, Charlotte Church, rugby, multiple murder or some aspect of sexual misbehaviour by a public figure. However, when at the end of 2007 Scotland announced that it was to do the same thing the response was very different. In England it was the cue for an outbreak of a new consciousness by a public prodded out of its indifference by a bunch of politicians and journalists carrying sharp sticks. It's not their own money the Scots are spending on this lavish extension of the welfare state, the message was, it's your money. And the reason for this was down to something called the Barnett Formula. Fortunately, the details of the Barnett Formula needn't detain us here. It is a method (meant to be temporary when it was devised in the 1970s) of fixing the levels of some public spending in the component parts of the United Kingdom outside England. That is the very, very short version of the matter. But when the argument broke out all you really needed to know to be able to join in was that its provisions gave Scotland £1,500 more per head of population than England. For Wales the figure was an extra £1,000 per head. This was by no means the whole story but it was good enough for the English electorate or, more specifically, its representatives in Parliament and its guardians in some parts of the media.

Until this point English voters had been largely in the dark about this state of affairs, not least because over the previous decade they would have found little or nothing on the subject in their traditional sources of information, network television and radio and the national newspapers. Occasionally one or other of the big name commentators would turn out a sentence or two saying that devolution was destroying Britain, but rarely pausing long enough to explain why. In the *Daily Telegraph* in February 2008, for example, Simon Heffer devoted an emotional paragraph to the wonders of the long defunct half-crown. You could almost hear the sound of sobbing as he considered the planned disappearance of the figure of Britannia from the coinage. It showed, he pronounced, how devolution policies had effectively buried Britain.

Now, suddenly, a light bulb of comprehension flickered on above the heads of the English electorate. What these simple figures meant was that free prescriptions in Scotland were in effect to be subsidised by the taxpayers of England. And to a somewhat lesser extent the Welsh were getting away with the same trick. Even worse than that, those in England who might have liked a similar prescriptions regime themselves came to realise that one reason they couldn't have it was that they were spending so much money on Scotland, Wales and Northern Ireland. Of course this is a simplistic argument, but simplistic arguments are often the things that make the wheels go round in politics. The consequence was that, in the eyes of the *Daily Telegraph* at least, this state of affairs lost much of its snooze content and suddenly became the 'controversial' Barnett Formula, to be promoted briskly up the league table of Things That Are Wrong With Britain.

"There is growing resentment among English MPs and voters," the *Telegraph* observed, "over perks handed to Scots but denied to them. These include the scrapping of tuition fees for all Scottish students at Scottish universities, free personal care for the elderly, free eye and dental checks and the abolition of prescription charges for the chronically ill."

You might think it's a funny world in which free prescriptions for the chronically ill can be described as a 'perk', and a demand for an even spread of misery throughout the United Kingdom isn't much of a slogan. But it was, as is traditional in these affairs, a way of missing the point. Or, rather, two points. The essential problem wasn't that Scotland and Wales had too much money but that they didn't have enough. And what they had didn't come from the right place. They got proportionately more than the English under the terms of the clapped-out Barnett Formula, and the budgets of the two countries amounted to billions of pounds. In theory they could spend those billions as they pleased, but the reality was that they had only the minimum room for manoeuvre. The big things, like health and education, took the big money. A government looking to make a splash had to spend small sums in an eye-catching way.

Which explains the particular attraction of doing something about prescription charges. It was no coincidence that this idea first emerged in Wales. It was a specific nod in the direction of Aneurin Bevan, the founder of the National Health Service, and in particular to the socialist principles that New Labour had made so unfashionable. And, since eighty per cent of the population already qualified for free prescriptions, it was also affordable. Scotland was to come to that policy rather later, at an estimated cost of £70 million pounds a year. Northern Ireland was to join in by reducing charges from January 2009 with the aim of abolishing them altogether. But both Scotland and Wales also found money to reduce the level of fees paid by university students, another policy rooted in an old Labour principle, in this case the aim of liberating poor people through free education. The message was clear, if limited in application: the harsh, market-driven policies of the UK regime could be mitigated by the principled egalitarianism of politicians who were more in tune with what their people wanted and deserved. Vote for us and turn the clock back.

That's not to say there weren't other ways of analysing the merits of these measures. Providing free prescriptions for all, critics argued, was simply a way of giving some more money to people who already had plenty. Introducing lower university fees could be presented as a benefit for young people from affluent as well as from poor families. And in Scotland a system of free personal care for the elderly, which was not only expensive but perhaps unaffordable in the long run, was also a method simply of preserving an inheritance – the houses parents wouldn't have to sell to pay for care – for middle-class children. You could certainly argue that there was as much sentiment as there was practical benefit in these policies. In particular they contained the message that here were administrations that really cared about the sick, the young and the elderly, unlike, the implication was, those cold-eyed guys in

Whitehall. It's difficult to think of how anything more irritating for English taxpayers could be contrived than the idea that they were paying for a bunch of second division politicians in Scotland and Wales to indulge in smug displays of moral superiority. No wonder they began to talk about getting their money back.

The trouble was that, once this argument had arisen, it was hard to see what anyone could do about it without creating a different and even more serious problem for the main UK political parties – the pro-Union parties as they came to be called in the Scottish context. The difficulty was this: devolution had created new identities and new rivalries within the British Isles. The distinction between England, Scotland, Wales and Northern Ireland was clearer than it had ever been, not least because it could be expressed in cash terms. And, when people began to look at the system, they began to realise that it was ridiculous to suggest that twenty-first century Scotland was poorer than, for example, the north east or the north west of England, regions excluded from the bounty of Lord Barnett's patent public spending device. There was an obvious answer, particularly in the case of Scotland: cut the subsidy, give them less money.

But how could the Conservatives, a party totally steeped in unionism, embrace enthusiastically a policy which, however equitable, would further undermine Scotland's place within the United Kingdom? In 2007 they had only a single Westminster seat in a country in which a nationalist government was setting the tone. Half a century previously they'd had thirty-six seats; even as recently as 1983 they'd held twenty-one. To argue that the Treasury should hack away at Scottish revenues would be suicidal, among other things a gift to the separatist ambitions of Alec Salmond and the SNP. But not to do so was to risk inflaming the resentment of many English voters whose weight would be decisive at the next general election. At the end of 2007 David Cameron was aware he was walking a tightrope.

"I don't care whether pandering to English nationalism is a vote winner," he told the *Daily Telegraph*. "The very fact that in my two years as leader I haven't ripped open the Barnett Formula and waved a banner shows you that I am a very convinced Unionist and I'm not going to play those games."

His answer, or non-answer, to the problem was a 're-examination' of the formula but, more significantly, an insistence that it didn't really matter very much anyway.

"Increasingly it looks unfair and increasingly people are questioning it. But I always say to English audiences of course the time will come when we have to look at it, but do not believe there's some pot of gold here. It's not those perfidious Scots taking all our money.... Don't treat it as a big grievance. It's not the biggest thing since the Wars of the Roses. Get it in perspective."

Cameron's reference to the Wars of the Roses, which had nothing to do with Scotland, was perhaps an indication of how confused people can get over the issue. But he wasn't alone. The government were also at a loss and, like Cameron, sought shelter under the much-prized umbrella of 'perspective'. Early in 2008 the Chancellor, Alistair Darling, agreed that the government would publish an account of the way in which the Barnett Formula had worked over the previous thirty years. Later he made it clear that this was by no means a *review* of the formula but something that would *inform debate*, one of those semantic distinctions behind which politicians like to lurk. What it meant was that the government intended to do something and nothing at one and the same time. Meanwhile in Scotland itself those pro-Union parties decided to set up a 'commission', a word carefully chosen, in an era of language inflation, to show how seriously they were taking the whole affair. So Labour faced a dilemma. Take money away from the Scots and both fuel talk of independence and face a further kicking at subsequent elections. Do nothing and confront the accusation in England that the government were sucking up to Scotland because (i) the Prime Minister was Scottish and (ii) they were afraid of the nationalists and were bribing the Scottish electorate to stay in the UK. The lesson obviously was the less you voted Labour the better they treated you.

There are people in the world who think the answer to this question lies in staging a form of poverty contest. They point out that the present mechanism is based on population and argue that it should be replaced by a needs-based system. The detail of such a scheme has yet to be worked out. Presumably researchers would put together a socio-economic analysis based on, among other things, the Gross Domestic Product of a country or region, unemployment, housing, health and crime statistics and many other things. The result would be a form of United Kingdom deprivation league table with, for example, a base of 100 in which the Home Counties might would come out at, say, 150, and Wales perhaps at something like 75. Central government money would be distributed (or presumably withheld) according to relative poverty or affluence.

This idea is particularly popular in Wales where many politicians maintain that such a system would inevitably yield more money than Barnett. There's good reason for their optimism because the Gross Domestic Product figures show Wales at not much over three quarters of the United Kingdom average. Not only that, but in these terms relative poverty has increased since the establishment of the national assembly. Even so, whether Wales would get any more, never mind lots more, is problematical because any new arrangements would now include the regions of England. Scotland might well get less but, even according to David Cameron, not a lot less. It is, perhaps, a way of moving the problem around rather than solving it. A more fundamental solution will eventually be necessary, even if it's not yet hammering on the door. When it comes it could alter the whole nature of government in the United Kingdom. It's not often discussed at present, but it looms ominously over one of the core principles pursued by traditionalist politicians.

One central political question isn't put to the people of Scotland, Wales and Northern Ireland when they go to the polls to elect their devolved administrations. It's this: what is the connection between how you vote and the taxes you pay? The answer is: none. But if there is no relationship between these two things then what are described as governments in Edinburgh, Cardiff and Belfast aren't actually governments at all. They are not accountable to their voters for the raising of revenue, one of the most important aspects of what real governments do. In this regard they are little more than pensioners drawing their allowances at the Westminster post office. They have to allocate a large part of their income to the fundamentals of everyday life – food, power, accommodation – and with what's left over they can choose between cat food or a couple of pints of beer.

The truth is that no government can be worth the name if it has no control over raising revenue as well as spending it. The Barnett Formula is an anachronism not simply because it comes from another political era, and not because it might be unfair to England, but because its continuation represents a failure to address a central issue of devolution. This is a matter that strikes terror into the hearts of British governments of any colour. Since 1979 in particular, the fiscal imperative has been to keep a tight, centralised grip on public expenditure. This is why, for example, local government, subject to a stringent capping regime, has ceased in any real sense to be either local or government.

In the same way the various new administrations of the United Kingdom can fiddle around with, say, free prescriptions or free car parking; or they can make changes that effectively cost nothing, like ending assessment tests for schoolchildren, as they have done in Wales; or they can move money from one place to another, as Scotland has in introducing free personal care for the elderly. What they can't do is demonstrate any connection between those modest measures and the figures in the income tax column of a worker's payslip. And if they could? Well, in Wales and Scotland in particular the administrations tend to be of a leftish character, much inspired by the social benefits of the public sector and somewhat in thrall to the more sentimental aspects of old-style socialism. A decision in May 2008 to restore free NHS care to failed asylum seekers in Wales fits that template exactly. The message is: we are good people. In Wales politicians are inclined to believe that the voters would be glad to cough up a bit more in the interests of progressive policies. Perhaps they are right, but their freedom to put that idea to the test would make something of a hole in the principle of any Westminster government's ability to impose a UK-wide economic policy. And that, governments from Thatcher to Major to Blair to Brown have insisted, is the road to ruin. If you don't keep your hands firmly round the throat of public spending, even when you're increasing it, the entire strategy risks collapse.

Some political analysts think the importance of such a change shouldn't be exaggerated. They point out that Scotland, Wales and Northern Ireland represent less than a fifth of the UK population and that some changes in fiscal arrangements needn't wreck the system. But once it starts, you have to ask, where would it end?

The acute sensitivity to this issue was revealed with great clarity in the devolution settlement applied in Scotland after the referendum of 1997. Yes, a Scottish government would be allowed to vary levels of income tax. But Labour, which dominated the first two Scottish administrations, swore that its ministers would cut off their hands rather than do any such thing. It was a power of taxation modelled on the lines of a nuclear weapon, threatening in theory but something no one dared use. Not even the SNP, indeed, when they took power in 2007. In part that was due to the very limited authority granted by this aspect of the Scotland Act. Income tax could be raised (or lowered) by up to three pence in the pound. One problem was that if it were increased by, for example, 1p, the cost of collecting the revenue would eat substantially into its value. So there would be limited advantage in what was hardly likely to be a popular move in the first place.

At the same time, though, it wasn't an entirely useless virility symbol and when the SNP formed a government it devised a plan to use it as the basis of a local income tax that would replace the unpopular council tax. Not an increase, but one form of payment being substituted for another. Once again, however, nothing was as simple as it seemed. A local income tax would, by definition, bring relief to poorer people who would no longer have to pay council tax. In the UK Treasury eyes lit up, as if they'd had been given an opening by a careless opponent in a game of chess. If you do that, the argument shot back, then Scotland wouldn't be needing the £400 million a year provided for council tax benefit. After all, you could hardly say that people would need assistance to pay a tax that had been abolished. Now it was time for Scotland to say, "Hey, that's *our* money". But then, if you were of a separatist cast of mind it was also, in the long run, a useful argument to have. There they go down in Whitehall, as usual seizing every available opportunity to make us poorer.*

It was another illustration of the instability of the original devolution arrangements. UK Government ministers liked to call it the devolution 'settlement' when it was clearly anything but settled. It looked increasingly as if eventually a new financial system would have to be devised under which Scotland, Wales and Northern Ireland raised a substantial part of their revenue from some form of local taxation – a sales tax, perhaps, or, more likely, something based on the income tax system. Whatever it was, it would have to be a way in which organisations that called themselves governments could take substantial responsibility for their financial affairs and from time to time, submit those decisions to the judgement of the people who elected them.

In the process there would have to be an arrangement to establish some kind of financial balance between the different parts of the United Kingdom, something on which the SNP had a specific

---

* Early in 2009 the SNP had to drop this idea because it couldn't get suport from other parties in the Scottish Parliament.

idea. England could have the Barnett money back, an independent Scotland would take the oil. The world economic crisis in 2008 and the fall in the price of oil made the calculations rather less convincing, but it nevertheless gave some economic credibility to the argument for an independent Scotland, in particular if that argument was supposed to be chiefly about prosperity.

In all this there was an even greater problem to be resolved: England. The matter of how much money the devolved administrations should get from the central UK government was clearly something that couldn't be ignored indefinitely. Taking the heat out of it would demand careful political judgement, but it hardly amounted in itself to some kind of constitutional crisis. What it did, nevertheless, was underline the inescapable fact that such a crisis did in fact exist. The problem was this: Scotland and Wales were clearly entitled to spend their own resources as they chose, however much the system that delivered those resources might be in need of reform. But it was a very different matter for those countries then to interfere in English financial questions. Free prescriptions were one thing. Scottish and Welsh politicians voting at Westminster to impose university top-up fees in England – fees their own constituents wouldn't have to pay – was quite another. As with the Barnett Formula we were on a return journey to the Seventies and to something that had haunted devolution ever since it had moved seriously onto the political agenda at that time.

It emerged first as the West Lothian Question, named after the then constituency of Tam Dalyell, the Labour MP who deployed it so effectively as he and many of his colleagues subverted and demolished their own government's desperate efforts to hand over some power to Edinburgh and Cardiff. The actual question was simple enough: could it be right for Scottish and Welsh Members of Parliament to vote at Westminster on questions that related to England only, while English MPs had no authority in the same areas of government in Scotland and Wales?

No coherent answer was forthcoming either at that time or in the referendum debates of 1997. The result was that the Conservative Party, perhaps without too much real enthusiasm, at least at first, began to argue that Parliament would have to devise a special system for dealing with legislation that affected England only. The particular appeal of this idea might have had something to do with the fact that Scotland and Wales had in recent years sent only tiny numbers of Conservatives to Westminster; sometimes none at all. So the creation of a specifically English political constituency had something to recommend it. The fact was that, entirely predictably, devolution created an English question to which there were no coherent answers.

For some time the government seemed to think it could simply be ignored because so many of the crucial issues of modern life – economic policy, defence and so on – were decided at Westminster that the West Lothian matter could be relegated to the status of just another minor anomaly in the famously rackety British constitution. It wasn't even a new problem. Since 1921 Northern Ireland had been devolved, un-devolved and devolved all over again. Westminster representation was adjusted accordingly, but no-one suggested that the existence of the United Kingdom was under threat because special arrangements were made for one part of it.

It's also the case that very few people exercise significant political power in Britain for more than a short time, and when it comes to particular responsibilities hardly anyone presides over a ministry for more than a year or two before being moved on or out. The result is that a problem deferred, even comparatively briefly, is a problem handed on to the next guy. One day someone will have to come up with an answer, an English parliament, perhaps. Labour and Conservative politicians might not want it, but at the same time they might not be able to think of a way of not having it. Some senior figures in the Labour Party think the solution might lie in regional government for England. The only problem is that the English have shown no interest of any kind in such an arrangement. But if exactly what should be done remains uncertain, the need to do something is an increasingly pressing question.

That state of affairs was illustrated in a leading article published, symbolically, for St. George's Day in 2008, in which *The Spectator* reported on the way in which the once arcane theology of devolution had moved into mainstream political argument.

"Issues which were once debating points for constitutional theorists – the West Lothian Question and the Barnett Formula – are now live-political issues. In the 1970s, Tam Dalyell asked the highly technical question: why should a Scottish MP be able to vote on matters relating to England when an English MP cannot vote on matters solely relating to Scotland? In 2008, the English ask, more generally, why the Scots and Welsh have their own assemblies, but not the English; why the government can spend £1,500 less per head per annum on public services south of the border; why, in short, the English voters who made the New Labour electoral coalition possible in the first place in 1997 have been given such a raw deal?"

None of this was particularly new but now, suddenly, people were becoming aware of the electrifying consequences that might lie just around the corner, something of enormous political significance. As that *Spectator* article was appearing, the government's fortunes were in steep decline. Week after week the Conservatives surged ahead in the opinion polls. A general election had to be held within the following two years. A dramatic Tory revival was taking place. Boundary changes and regional differentials made precise predictions uncertain but, particularly in the midst of world economic gloom, with Britain teetering on the brink of the recession into which it was later to plunge, a meaningful Labour revival seemed unlikely. But then the unlikely happened in the most dramatic manner. Instead of consigning the Government to certain oblivion, the worst economic crisis in living memory revived its fortunes. One week Gordon Brown was hopelessly inept, the next he was a world statesman. Suddenly his whole career seemed to have been an ideal preparation for disaster. The handsome Conservative majority that had seemed to be almost in the bag for 2010 was being washed away by the tide of imminent financial ruin. Maybe Labour wouldn't recover enough to win but one prospect seemed increasingly likely to follow the next general election: a hung parliament.

Then, within a matter of months, it began to look once more as though Labour would be in for a shattering defeat at the next election, but these violent swings of public opinion only reinforced the uncertainties of political soothsaying. It meant that Brown would have to hang on until the last possible moment, the late spring of 2010. Suppose the recession wasn't as prolonged as had been forecast? Perhaps a more cheerful public would take a more charitable view. And then, John Major had stuck it out to the end of his term in 1992 and pulled off an unexpected victory. In 1964, Alec Douglas-Home, leading an exhausted and unpopular government, and with the country apparently desperate for change, had persisted to the very end and lost by only a handful of seats.

What could happen as a result is that a Conservative Party with a substantial majority in England could be denied office by Labour MPs returned from Scotland and Wales. It seems impossible to overstate the resentment and frustration that would follow if such a result put Labour back in power. There would inevitably be questions about the legitimacy of such a government in a post-devolution Britain. Labour, the Conservatives would be bound to argue, had no mandate to govern England. They might even enjoy a wry smile when they reminded the electorate of how often that slogan was used in Scotland and Wales to justify attempts to deny the authority of Mrs. Thatcher's governments. *The Spectator* forecast might still hold good: "Gordon Brown's astonishing political freefall means that – even if Labour recovers partially before the general election – he might find on the morning after polling day that he was notionally Prime Minister of a country in which the Conservatives had a majority of seats in England. At that point, to put it mildly, the chemical compound of the United Kingdom would become distinctly unstable."

It might not happen, but it wouldn't be very sensible to use the holiday money to bet against it. In 1974, for example, the Conservatives won 268 seats in England against 237 for Labour. But the UK result had Labour on 301, the Conservatives on 297 and the Liberals on 14. After Ted Heath had failed to do a deal with the Liberals that would have kept him in office, Labour formed a government. The difference was made in Scotland and Wales where Labour outnumbered the Conservatives by 64 to 29. It's difficult to believe, a generation on, that such an outcome would be patiently waved through by the Tories as simply another British electoral anomaly.

That's one consequence of the changing nature of the United Kingdom – hypothetical maybe, but by no means ridiculous. But there's another, less explosive, that might be just as important in determining the shape of future British governments: whether, indeed, there will continue to be British governments at all. It arises from a combination of social upheaval, a dislocation of political ideology, parliamentary arithmetic and a change in electoral mechanisms.

When in the nineties arrangements of various kinds were being devised for the new devolved institutions, it was clear that if the whole business were not to be a complete farce it was crucial to include some form of proportional representation. In Northern

136   << A Useful Fiction

Ireland it couldn't be otherwise because power-sharing had to be a prerequisite of any deal between republicans and unionists. No other system was acceptable. At the same time it was obvious in Scotland and Wales that without PR the whole business would have been a travesty. In the 1997 general election in Scotland Labour won 56 of the 72 seats; in Wales 34 out of 40. If results of that kind had been translated into the new bodies it seemed likely that they would swiftly have descended into some of the worst excesses that had long disfigured local government where in the past huge majorities had maintained authoritarian, and frequently dishonest, one party rule. Far from the democratic process being extended, it would have been strangled.

There were plenty of people in the Labour Party who couldn't really see the problem. They grumbled, they protested, but in the end they bought it, however grudgingly, and in an unprecedented display of open-mindedness and inclusiveness a government volun- tarily gave away power. Specifically it meant that a single party had no prospect of winning a majority of seats in Scotland and was unlikely to do so in Wales (fifty per cent was the best Labour managed there). The result was that Wales and Scotland began to develop a more distinctive political character because of the inevitability of compromise built in to the new electoral system. It took a while, but soon enough it began to erode some of the voting traditions that had been established over generations.

In Scotland in 2007 the SNP won 47 seats – just over a third of the Scottish Parliament but, crucially, one more seat than Labour. The consequence was that the SNP formed a government despite being heavily outnumbered. In Wales Labour's vote fell and the party won only 26 out of the assembly's 60 seats. For a while it looked as though the three other parties would form what came to be called a 'rainbow alliance', led by Plaid Cymru, the common ground of which would be that they disliked and distrusted Labour even more than they disliked and distrusted each other. That it didn't happen was due in part to the traditional flakiness of the Liberal Democrats, who agreed and disagreed with the scheme more or less on alternate days, but also to the undiminished potency of the Thatcher legacy.

There has been nothing more useful to the old lefties in Wales, a group that includes practically everyone in Plaid Cymru, than the idea that a malevolent Margaret Thatcher, with the assistance of a few stooges, had unleashed on the country a typhoon of destruction which had wrecked whole industries and their associated communities almost overnight. That is how the story was often told, untroubled by history or nuance. It was in any case part of a narrative in which the Tories, in particular landlords, coal owners and ironmasters, had down the centuries become wealthy as a consequence of wrecking the lives of hundreds of thousands of decent men and women. Now that the government was in many cases the owner – of the coal and steel industries, for example – Mrs. Thatcher could plausibly be portrayed as one of their number.

In those circumstances it was simply too much for some members of Plaid Cymru to contemplate any kind of formal association with her Welsh successors. To share power with the Conservatives would have brought an unbearable sense of shame upon them. They stopped singing Somewhere Over the Rainbow, pulled back the duvet, and got into bed with the Labour Party instead. And how snug they were. When it came to matters of government, even in a good light it was hard to discern where one party ended and the other began. In Wales politics had traditionally been raucously partisan, particularly in recent years in the rivalry between Labour and Plaid Cymru. Now we could see why. It wasn't because of the differences between the two parties but because they were actually two factions trying to push one another from the same piece of left (but not very left) of centre common ground. The differences between them, it emerged, were essentially narrow issues of belief, the gap between High and Low Church, perhaps, rather than being matters of much practical consequence; the question of Welsh independence, for example, being about as significant as the fierce dispute between the Big-endians and Little-endians of Lilliput over how to break open a boiled egg. At the same time, though, it was becoming clear that the Thatcher legacy wouldn't last for ever. In the 2007 elections to the Welsh Assembly, the Conservatives got exactly the same proportion of the vote as did Plaid Cymru. In Wales the argument was now beginning to devolve to the one reasonably clear distinction you can make – between the moderate right, the Tories, and the moderate left, the rest. Although superficially it looked like four party politics what was emerging was a new version of old-fashioned two-party politics in which traditional party identities were being redefined.

But neither the Welsh deal nor a nationalist government sitting

in Edinburgh was the most startling public demonstration of the
revolution that was taking place in what you might call the non-
English sector of British public life. In Belfast, Ian Paisley and
Martin McGuinness walked into government together, not as a way
of continuing by other means forty years of bitter and bloody hostility, but laughing. They even became known popularly (if that's the
right word) as the Chuckle Brothers. That was a piece of black irony
perhaps, and Northern Ireland might have remained as implacably
sectarian as it had always been, but this was an event and an atmosphere so extraordinary that it was possible to believe that almost
anything might happen in politics, anywhere.

What it revealed above all was that what was once unthinkable
can swiftly become matter-of-fact. In the same way the assumption
of power by the SNP in Scotland and the deal between Plaid
Cymru and Labour in Wales has suddenly normalised the place of
the nationalist dimension in those two countries. One of the most
revealing aspects of these events was that there was no sense of
revolution in the air. The lights were still on, the buses were
running, government hadn't collapsed, life for the man and woman
in the street went on almost entirely unchanged and daylight gave a
new perspective to the much-advertised terrors of nationalism.

It might well be that this kind of change owes far less to shifts
of political opinion brought about by argument or experience than
it does to the erosion of traditional party allegiances. People don't
vote the same way in elections for the devolved assemblies as they
do when it comes to Westminster. It's also the case that they vote
less than they used to, presumably because they understand the
outcome of an election in a post-political British world of liberal-ish
consensus won't change their lives very much anyway. For example,
if by some miscalculation a Labour government inadvertently
raised income tax, recent history shows the public can be certain
that ministers would rush through measures to bring it down again.
The pursuit of genuinely distinctive ideas by the major political
parties is no longer an identifiable characteristic of British life.

Similar reasons may account for the fact that the electorate also
votes in even smaller numbers for the devolved authorities than it
does when it comes to choosing a UK government. And rather than
being converted by any powerful arguments providing a sense of
clear choice, maybe they're happy to take a lucky dip approach to the
ballot box in a world in which, thanks to proportional representation,

the usual outcome of an election is almost inevitably going to be compromise. The SNP might be governing in Scotland, for example, but it can do only what the other parties will allow it to do.

Even that, though, is enough to prompt fresh ideas about the nature of Britain and what it might now become. In an article in the *Guardian* shortly before the London mayoral election of 2008, Ian Jack explored the implications of a victory for the Conservative candidate, Boris Johnson. Jack, a Scot living in England, once editor of the *Independent on Sunday* and later editor of the literary magazine *Granta*, was particularly exercised by the idea that victory for Johnson would put another Old Etonian in a position of great power, alongside the Tory leader, David Cameron and the shadow Chancellor, George Osborne. Not only that, but those three men had also been members of the Bullingdon Club, an Oxford University dining club particularly noted for extravagance (its blue tailcoats cost £1,200 each), ostentatious condescension and drunken bad behaviour on the part of its members.

"You must wonder," Jack reflected, "why the leadership of the likely next British government has been drawn from such a narrow and privileged seam of English society." He went on: "If this is what England is, if this is what England wants, do I want to belong to it?"

He suggested that Scotland might be to the United Kingdom what Canada had in difficult times been to North America, a place of refuge from an unsympathetic regime. "Scotland is becoming to England what Canada has long been to the US, at the very least since Vietnam draft-dodgers crossed the border."

Jack went on to list the radical social reforms adopted in Scotland by successive administrations, in particular, but not exclusively, under the SNP, reforms the UK government felt unable to offer to the people of England: free personal care for the elderly; the eventual abolition of prescription charges; the abolition of university tuition fees; opposition to nuclear power and the new generation of Trident submarines and an ambitious programme of building council houses. He might have echoed the American journalist Lincoln Steffens on the Soviet Union in 1919 by writing: I have seen the future and it works. Or is it the past they're reconstructing in Scotland?

All this wasn't quite compelling enough to persuade Ian Jack to pack up and go home. But: "I think that if Cameron wins he will be the last prime minister of Great Britain. If he goes two terms he will become the first prime minister of England. Our United semi-states will be no more. Then there really will be a new Canada in the north."

H'm, as R.S. Thomas once said. You've got to leap an awful lot of crags to get from here to there, but the very fact that such an argument can be seriously advanced reveals the extent of the change that has already occurred in the constituent parts of the United Kingdom and the uncertainty over the future direction it might take. Not long ago Jack's thesis would have been dismissed as a humorous fantasy. Now it's at least a realistic possibility. And the idea at the heart of that essay, the description of the better life that's available just up the road, might emerge as the most seductive element in the whole business of constitutional reconstruction.

Throughout the United Kingdom, it's now well understood, politics has become a matter much more of style than of substance. There are good reasons for that state of affairs. In particular many of the most important factors that decide the nature of daily lives in Britain are beyond the control of Downing Street and Whitehall. Oil prices reach record levels, the cost of food soars and all they can do is shrug their shoulders. It's not us, they say, but people like the Chinese and their expanding economy. At the same time, of course, we want the Chinese economy to expand because it means we can sell them stuff. Then oil and food prices fall rapidly and another economic disaster descends on the British. This time it's the fault of the Americans and their wretched sub-prime mortgages, something hardly anyone without a grasp of the technical complexities of the financial world can really understand. Those who are supposed to be in charge look on, scratching their heads like Stan Laurel. They take action but no one in the entire world really knows if it will work. It becomes clear that to a greater extent than ever our destinies are in the hands of other people entirely.

Why should anyone be surprised? After all, it was more than thirty years previously that, by joining the Common Market, Britain abandoned the concept of the unchallenged authority of a sovereign parliament sitting at Westminster. Some people believe that position can be restored by leaving the European Union, but in the meantime laws made in Britain must conform to the stipulations of EU law. The origins of devolution might have been in a fairly disreputable effort in the nineteen seventies to halt the advance of nationalism rather than devising a route to better government, but

by the nineties it could be embraced instead as a natural development of the way in which power was being redistributed more
generally. If you argued within the EU about the principle of
subsidiarity, that's to say making decisions at the lowest appropriate
level, it was difficult to be entirely convincing when taking the
opposite view about running affairs in Scotland or Wales.

The consequent temptation might be, therefore, to turn your
back on the intractable problems of a wider world and get on with
cultivating your own garden. You can distance yourself from those
aspects of UK government policy to which you object – nuclear
power stations, for example, polyclinics, city academies and so on –
introduce a few, inexpensive, liberal policies, particularly in a
feelgood way in the health service, denounce any aspects of foreign
policy you don't care for and blame any failures on the neo-
Stalinists up at Westminster whose addiction to Big Government
and the central state means they refuse to give you the appropriate
resources and powers to carry out your enlightened programme.
This is clearly the route to eventual independence that Scottish
nationalists have begun seeking, grievance politics on a massive
scale. They were able to start the process in 2007 because any
London government was alien to the SNP. When we get to the
stage, which probably won't be all that long delayed, when there's a
Conservative regime running things in London and an anti-Tory
administration of some kind in Cardiff, Wales will also seek, probably not independence, but at least greater and greater autonomy.

One further factor will add to these pressures. There's growing
evidence that in places like Wales old political habits are slipping
away. It's been a gradual process but an inevitable one. The disappearance of the great industries (the last deep mine in Wales closed
in 2008) and the fragmentation of the communities they supported,
as well as the consequent decline in influence of the trade unions
mean that Labour's grip on both practical authority and mass sentiment has been permanently loosened. The exact repercussions are
not yet clear. The Welsh local government elections of 2008 seemed
to reflect an unaccustomed lack of certainty in the minds of many
of the voters. Labour ended up controlling only two councils –
unnervingly for them, the same number as the Conservatives – and
lost control in places where the party was practically invented –
Merthyr, for example, once the seat of Keir Hardie, and Blaenau
Gwent, where (when the constituency was called Ebbw Vale)

Aneurin Bevan had been succeeded by Michael Foot. Independents of various descriptions took control of one council in three, the Liberal Democrats once more led the local authorities in Cardiff and in Wales's second city, Swansea. Odd characters re-emerged. Ron 'Moment of Madness' Davies, driven from a Labour Cabinet by his adventures on Clapham Common and later from the assembly by the publication of some outdoor photographs in the *Sun*, was restored to his local council, now as an independent. His wife joined him, but as a representative of Plaid Cymru. Everyone, except Labour, claimed victory. It was difficult to discern any particular trend – except an anti-Labour one. In Scotland too, in 2007 and then in by-elections, the political mood was at least as much against Labour as it was in favour of the SNP. Maybe, you thought, the nature of politics was at the beginning of radical change, something given momentum by the establishment of devolved institutions and further accelerated by a disaffection from the old politics. In the UK general election of 2001 there was a disturbing fall in turnout to less than sixty per cent. It didn't recover much in 2005. People didn't bother to vote. Now, perhaps, they were beginning to vote differently.

Not enough evidence exists yet to say any such thing with confidence but it's clear that plenty of people are willing to make a break with the old allegiances of place and class. It's possible that some of them are being capricious in the face of the sheer impotence that characterises the relationship between the ordinary citizen and the nature of his everyday life as decided by government. If this is true, you're bound to ask, how long will it be before it leaves the boundaries of the non-English nations of the UK and is reflected in the people sent to Westminster from those places? The nature and style of politics in the United Kingdom are changing rapidly and the eventual consequences are unguessable. If you take a few bricks out of a wall you still have a wall. The question is how many you have to remove before you are left with a pile of rubble and you have to start rebuilding another, rather different, structure.

Tiger Tiger

ON SUNDAY, OCTOBER 12, 2008, I went to Glasgow to look for myself at the events and ideas that, I was assured by some shrewd observers, could well lead sooner rather than later to the establishment of an independent Scotland. When I got up the next morning it was to discover that particular ship was now floating upside down in the Clyde. Two of the country's most important financial institutions were on the verge of collapse, saved from complete disaster only by the intervention of the government in London. Overnight the fragility of the dream of a prosperous Scotland breaking free of the United Kingdom had been ruthlessly exposed by an international financial crisis on a scale that hadn't been seen for at least sixty years. As Bill Jamieson put it on the front page of *The Scotsman*: "From proud banking icons to two humiliated, nationalised rumps: Scotland's two largest banks are being pulled from the brink of an economy-destroying collapse – but at the price of proud, centuries-old independence."

The news was that the Royal Bank of Scotland was being saved by the injection of £20 billion by the government, a move that would effectively put the bank under British state control. (There was even more of that sort of thing to come in the succeeding months.) Only a few weeks previously intervention by Gordon Brown, which involved tearing up competition regulations, had opened up the route by which HBOS (Halifax Bank of Scotland), Britain's biggest lender and another of Scotland's great financial institutions, could be rescued from extinction. Also falling as steeply as the stocks of these organisations was the share price of Scottish independence, harshly exposed by the market as being offered for sale on the basis of a false prospectus.

A headline in *The Times* a couple of days later put a widely accepted view with undiluted clarity: "Crunch has put paid to

Scottish independence." Underneath, the columnist Magnus Linklater, a former editor of *The Scotsman*, was scornful of the view of Scotland's First Minister, Alex Salmond, that he intended to press on with his plan for a referendum on independence in 2010. "Self-delusion is, of course, an occupational hazard for those who prefer dream over substance, but this time it sounds as if the leader of the Scottish National Party has lost touch with reality.

"Around him, and his party's flagship policy, lies the wreckage of Scotland's independent banking sector, the very symbol of his future hopes for a robust economy. Worse, the two main Scottish banks have been saved from collapse by a Westminster government drawing on the resources of the United Kingdom's taxpayers. They are now British, not Scottish, banks and their future strategy will be determined from the City of London and not Edinburgh."

Plenty of other people argued in much the same way, adding to the case against the SNP's ambitions the collapse, a few days earlier, of Iceland's banking system, something that effectively meant the entire country was bankrupt. The critics reached eagerly for one particular item in the SNP's literature. "Off our east coast lies Norway, the second most prosperous country in the world. Off our west coast lies Ireland, the fourth most prosperous country in the world. Off our north coast lies Iceland, the sixth most prosperous country in the world."

This was what Alex Salmond liked to refer to as the "arc of prosperity". On that October day the Secretary of State for Scotland, Jim Murphy, jeered that it was more like an arc of insolvency. In the Scottish papers, apologists for the nationalist position wrote letters saying, in effect: when we said Iceland what we actually meant was Norway which, as everyone knows, is doing particularly well because, like Scotland, it has oil. Even the writers themselves seemed unconvinced by this argument. It looked very much as if the independence game was up, at least for the foreseeable future. But that, I think, would be to jump too fast to the wrong conclusion.

Nationalist politicians in Scotland and Wales have always liked to point to the Scandinavian countries as models of what small nations can achieve, but perhaps there was always more wishful thinking than hard-headed policy in this admiration, no serious belief that their social and political systems could be copied whole-sale. What unexpectedly turned their heads was the example of Ireland, transformed from economic dead cat to Celtic Tiger in not much more than a twinkling of those smiling Irish eyes of song and legend. Across the water, politicians – and not just nationalist politicians – have looked on in amazement and envy. What's the trick? they ask. Can we do it? And, for some people the most telling aspect of all: see what not being British can do for you.

There have been some who have been totally dazzled. When he launched his economic policy in 2001, the Welsh First Minister, Rhodri Morgan, was questioned about his ambition over the following ten years to raise Welsh Gross Domestic Product from eighty per cent of that in England to ninety per cent. Was this really achievable, he was asked. Surely, he said, surely it wasn't asking too much to achieve forty per cent of what Ireland had done in a similar period.

You sometimes wonder whether politicians say such things because they believe them to be true or because they think other people will believe them to be true. If there were a Nobel Prize for missing the point they'd have been on the phone from Stockholm almost before he'd finished the sentence. There were any number of self-evident reasons why Wales could not be Ireland. As it was the relative decline in the Welsh GDP continued, as normal, rapidly downhill.

The Irish story was all the more extraordinary because it was so unexpected. After all, it wasn't all that long since the windows of lodging houses in parts of London displayed exclusion notices: 'No blacks, no Irish, no dogs'. Perhaps this attitude arose in part from the fear aroused in the poor by people who were even poorer. Labourers and servants, large numbers of women and girls as well as men, crossed from Ireland to find work. Much of the money they made was sent home to support families who had even less. Nor were they invariably treated sympathetically, even by their own people. Between the wars, my father's cousin Luke, from the village of Gurteen in Co. Sligo, wrote for help to a man called Sir Patrick Hannon, another Sligo man, who had become a prominent British industrialist and Conservative MP and who, family legend had it, was related to us in some unspecified way.

"What Sir Patrick did," Luke told me long afterwards, "was to send me the address of the biggest labour exchange in London." So he became one of the countless numbers of Irishmen who dug the tunnels for one of the London tube lines.* Something like sixty

---

* Luke later followed another way of life that was part of the Irish tradition. For many years he served in senior ranks in various British colonial police forces

years later, though, one of *his* cousins, only one generation on, was recruiting labourers from Wales to work on building projects in Dublin. What took place in Ireland in the late twentieth century was, by any standards, quite breathtaking. In his book, *Luck and the Irish*, Roy Foster summarises in a single sentence the astonishing measures of growth. "Output in the decade from 1995 increased by 350 per cent, outpacing the per capita averages in the UK and the USA, personal disposable income doubled, exports increased fivefold, trade surpluses accumulated into billions, employment boomed, immigrants poured into the country."

To the susceptible such statistics are a form of political seduction and it was clearly tempting to believe that the very fact of its independence must have been crucial in Ireland's economic leap forward in the last years of the twentieth century. Clearly there was a great deal in that argument, in particular Ireland's freedom to set its own economic policies, unlike Scotland and Wales which, even post-devolution, have scarcely any room for manoeuvre in that area. Small can help too. One of the reasons given for Ireland's success is what's been described as its open, accessible, responsive government. In Ireland, just as has become the case in Scotland and Wales, politicians are everyday figures, referred to in familiar terms. On the journey in from Dublin airport, for example, taxi drivers would invariably point out Bertie Ahern's constituency office and the bar across the road where the *Taoiseach* would drink pints of Bass. But you would also be told by someone else, in the way of small communities, that he didn't really like beer at all but pretended to do so in order to cultivate a man of the people image. In Britain, in a similar way, when he was Prime Minister Harold Wilson had made a great public display of his halves of bitter and his pipe whereas in private he preferred brandy and cigars. It was just that the British system was too big for the ordinary voter to get to know such things. However, it's also the case that the electrifying political scandals, mainly over money, that have emerged in Irish politics in recent years should make people recognise that, despite Ernst Schumacher, when it comes to government small is by no means invariably beautiful.

---

before, equipped with a British government pension and an MBE, he retired to Dublin where died in the night that followed his ninetieth birthday party. His career was another small illustration of the fluidity of relatonships within these islands.

One of Ireland's most substantial advantages, which was all the more striking in a country where history is a kind of industry, was that it had no industrial history to speak of. It could reinvent itself in the late twentieth century without being waylaid by an economic past that nagged from beyond the grave. In the United Kingdom, in contrast, there was always a sense that the old certainties of work and community could somehow be maintained. Inventive government and sheer determination could mean that wholesale change could be avoided, the unpleasant realities of the modern world by-passed. In Scotland and Wales and the great industrial areas of England, trade unionists and politicians manned the barricades year after year in a sustained effort to keep things as much as possible as they'd always been. Mighty industries like coal, steel and shipbuilding, dead on their feet in many instances, were treated as much as instruments of social policy as they were as commercial enterprises. And not just by Labour governments. In the early seventies Ted Heath broke his own resolutions by intervening to save Upper Clyde Shipbuilders. In the early sixties another Conservative Prime Minister, Harold Macmillan, had taken a hand in the affairs of the part of the steel industry that had remained nationalised. A scheme to build a big new steelworks in South Wales was turned into a plan to divide the investment and build two new works – one in Llanwern, near Newport, and a second at Ravenscraig, in Motherwell. The calamitous consequences of this bright idea became legendary throughout the industry.

There were other interventions. The way it worked is summarised by Andrew Marr in his history of modern Britain. He writes of a Conservative Secretary of State for Scotland in the sixties... "doling out industrial plants such as the Ravenscraig steelworks and obliging the British Motor Corporation to build cars in Bathgate and the Hillman Imp to be constructed at Linwood." This regime was followed by that of a Labour Scottish Secretary, Willie Ross... "whose gifts included a nuclear reactor at Dounreay, the Invergordon aluminium smelter and rescuing a Clyde shipyard. He set up the Highlands and Islands Development Board and the Scottish Development Agency. If planning could make a country rich, Scotland would be paradise."

Over the years Wales also got, among other things, an aluminium smelter, two nuclear power stations, the Royal Mint (thanks to the then Chancellor, Jim Callaghan, representing a Welsh constituency) various motor factories, a development agency, a rural development agency and, as I've said, half a publicly-owned steelworks. Rather cruelly, poor old Northern Ireland had to put up with the DeLorean car company, a device through which its owner, John DeLorean, helped himself to millions of pounds of government money. The question of Scottish and Welsh devolution had hardly been raised at this time but here was the answer to it, a UK government distributing industrial development to the hard-up regions of Britain, like a duchess visiting the poor. Down the years various regulations – industrial development certificates, for example, regional development grants, selective employment tax and other measures – reinforced the system. The message from Conservatives and Labour alike was a simple one: you might be hard up now but without the intervention of a centralised government you'd be even worse off.

Essentially, though, these interventions didn't really add up to what might be called a strategy. A familiar world was being dismantled and many people inevitably felt that they would be abandoned with it. And who can blame hundreds of thousands of workers and their representatives for exerting every last fragment of their influence to save their economic and community lives? Looking at what they were being offered instead, bits of the decaying British motor industry and the rest of it, you can see they were right to be suspicious. What else could they do but defend the status quo as best they could when government had no coherent vision of a new economic structure for the country, certainly not one that involved investing in the future rather than shoring up the past? It was better to stick with the familiar since there didn't seem to be much else on offer. Not least because in the years from 1959 to 1979 there were two Conservative governments and two Labour governments plus two more bits of Labour governments, almost all of which, from 1964, were in more or less a permanent state of crisis. The chief consequence was strategic inertia. Those smelters and factories being sent off to the north and the west were the instruments of finger-in-the-dyke economics. That state of affairs was reinforced by the fact that some of the great employers, like steel and coal, were publicly owned industries. Others were nationalised in desperation: for example what became British Leyland, an important component of the proverbially incompetent and loss-making motor industry. These were employers subject to the slightest political breeze. As a result such ideas as they had about how to modernise the UK economy tended to shrivel up under the continuing pressure of everyday events.

There might, too, have been one largely unspoken aspect of this state of affairs. Radical industrial change, if it came, would mean snapping the thread that connected contemporary Britain with the Industrial Revolution, with the structures that had given much of the country its particular character and its reputation around the world for two hundred years. However much that image had diminished in the last part of the twentieth century, its end would perhaps have represented a kind of defeat. It's a feeling that seems to persist in the personalising of that change, specifically the demonization of Margaret Thatcher and, for example, the persistent idea in places like South Wales that, if it hadn't been for her, the pits would still be open. The fact remains, though, that the comparative success of the UK in the ten years of the Blair government, economic growth, high employment, had a great deal to do with the enforced break with the past engineered and enforced by the Thatcher government.

Ireland had no such problem. It had no industrial past to shake off. Instead there was a long history of rural poverty scarred in particular by the potato famine of the eighteen forties which led to the death of a million people and forced another million to emigrate. In 1844, more than eight million people lived in Ireland. A century and a half later the population of the whole island of Ireland is fewer than six million. In the nineteen-eighties it was ready to leap the centuries straight from the agricultural to the post-industrial without a foot touching the ground. It was every bit as much of a miracle as one of those moving statues.

If you look at why it happened you can see at once why it's unlikely ever to happen again, in Ireland or anywhere else. One of the country's great assets was its comparative lack of economic development. In the nineteen eighties it also had a specific advantage over practically every other country in Western Europe: a large, low-wage labour pool. But it was also a well-educated labour pool, thanks to a push in the 1960s to improve and modernise the education system. The school leaving age was raised, new colleges and universities were established. Between 1961 and 1971 university attendances doubled while those at technical colleges increased fourfold.

Famously, of course, Ireland embraced membership of the European Community with fervent enthusiasm. It was hardly surprising, since the Common Agricultural Policy, a boon to small, hard-up farmers, might have been designed with the country in mind. Within a short time the symbol of rural Ireland changed from banks of freshly-cut turf to the smartly-painted, modern, EC-financed bungalow standing in a large plot of land. But that was only one tangible benefit of membership. Access to the European market was one of the factors that persuaded expanding industry from abroad to locate in Ireland, an advantage reinforced for Americans in particular by it being an English-speaking country in the right time zone. It was a combination that unrolled the red carpet for the great growth enterprises of the late twentieth century, in particular electronics, software and pharmaceuticals. The United States was crucial in this development. By 1993, a quarter of the entire manufacturing workforce in Ireland was employed by American companies. In the nineteen nineties the Irish growth rate outperformed all other member countries of the European Union.

It's evident from all this that the particular circumstances of Ireland at a particular time were at the heart of the economic revolution that swept over the country. It all looks rather different now, not least because footloose industrialists from booming countries have disappeared. Other countries, in eastern Europe in particular, now have the edge in crucial resources, notably lower wages, so that jobs move away from the richer countries that once attracted them.

It's easy enough to see why no other small country could hope to be Ireland, or to do what Ireland did in those astonishing years that brought such an explosion of economic growth. It's also clear enough that Ireland hasn't found some magic formula that insulates it from the chill economic winds blowing round the rest of the world. Recession arrived there in 2008 just as it did everywhere else in Europe. There's just as much gloom in Dublin as there is in London. More, perhaps, because of the contrast with those stupendous years of growth and prosperity. Even so, it remains as an important symbol of one thing above all: it is possible for a small country to seize an opportunity and transform itself utterly. The details don't matter, only that it can be done. It's one reason why the arrival of a severe economic recession shouldn't be assumed to mean that Scottish independence overnight became unthinkable. And there is one special circumstance in Scotland that's taken to suggest it could enjoy a kind of prosperity not available to most other countries. That factor is oil. Or, as they sometimes call it in the heightened language of sensual political arousal, "Scotland's black, black oil".

How much is it worth to Scotland? No one really knows, because, until it reaches the point of serious negotiation, it's impossible to say what proportion of North Sea oil would come under the control of a Scottish government. One piece of research, quoted by the SNP, says that if Scotland got 82.5 per cent of the revenue it would have a budget surplus of £4.4 billion. At 95 per cent that figure would be £6.2 billion. But if less, of course, less. How much is left in the North Sea? Maybe as much as already been extracted. But maybe not. Perhaps what remains is not all that accessible. A low oil price, which helps other sectors of the economy, reduces the economic practicality of exploiting the more difficult reserves. And, like coal, from the day it begins to come ashore it is a diminishing asset. One day, in thirty years perhaps or even sooner, it will all be gone. Sixty years ago, it's worth remembering, there were still almost 100,000 miners employed in South Wales alone. Nevertheless, in the intervening period, it's argued, it would be possible to lay the foundations of a stable and wealthy nation by implementing policies designed to encourage investment, to develop other forms of energy and, among other things, to create a form of giant national piggy bank on the model of the multimillion dollar oil fund established in Norway. Perhaps it really could be Ireland all over again, with oil instead of people the natural resource to sustain an economic boom. It's just possible, but the economic milk curdles quickly enough.

Because of this emphasis on oil it's easy enough to characterise Scottish nationalism as being essentially a programme of economic opportunism. Not least because there's more than a little truth in the idea. At the same time it's no more self-serving a philosophy than the response the discovery of oil prompted from the UK government once it had reached out over the border and started to exert a significant influence on UK political life. As often happens in politics, the arguments weren't really about what they were supposed to be about. Although governments have traditionally wrapped up the question of devolution in the language of history, democracy and cultural identity, it has essentially been about money and power and continues to be so.

The first gas from the North Sea came ashore in the nineteen sixties; the first oil was discovered at the end of that decade. Soon it was clear that there really was wealth beyond the dreams of even the Scottish avarice of legend, something put into words by the SNP's slogan: 'It's Scotland's Oil'. Now, the party claimed, people had the choice of being rich Scots or poor British, an idea that persisted unchanged into the next century. Suddenly it was possible to argue that there was a practical dimension to a campaign for self-government, something underlined by the particular circumstances of the time. In the autumn of 1973, as a consequence of the Yom Kippur War, the price of oil was increased almost threefold. That was the vital element that gave the miners their decisive lever in the dispute that led to the defeat of the Heath government in the following year. In first election of 1974, seven Scottish Nationalist MPs were elected, as well as two from Plaid Cymru. In the second election three Plaid Cymru members were elected. The SNP won eleven of the seventy-one Scottish seats but, even more significantly, came second in forty-two others.

The parliamentary arithmetic and the increased economic importance of Scotland demanded drastic action or, at least, some kind of diversion. Harold Wilson, running a minority administration, found it in the debris of an old policy devised the last time a Labour government had been scared by the nationalists. In the nineteen sixties he'd set up a Royal Commission on the Constitution to examine questions of devolution to Scotland and Wales. The Kilbrandon Commission, as it came to be called, didn't report until the end of 1973 when its eight hundred complex pages, including a memorandum of dissent, seemed to be some kind of survival from another era; only suitable, perhaps, for keeping the boilers going during the three-day working week introduced as a response to the dispute then under way between the government and the miners.

A matter of months later, though, and devolution became the answer to the most pressing problem facing Wilson who was, unexpectedly, Prime Minister once more: survival. Kilbrandon was at least a fig leaf, its very existence suggesting that the government wasn't suddenly grasping at constitutional change in a desperate attempt to keep the Scots and Welsh in order and itself in office. There you are, the implication was, look at how consistent we are in our support for devolution. We've been working on it for years. No one was fooled, though. It was a political fix and its sheer insincerity has perhaps coloured the devolution arguments ever since. It gave rise to the entirely unsatisfactory nature of the separate schemes dreamt up for the two countries – not enough for supporters, too much for opponents – that tormented the tottering administrations led by Wilson and then by Jim Callaghan right down to their last days in 1979.

The Kilbrandon Commission understood well enough what this was really all about and put its collective finger on the sense of economic grievance that existed in Scotland.

"New political initiatives, including the adoption of strong regional policies, have been taken, but have not succeeded in raising the prosperity of Scotland and Wales to the level of that of the Midlands and the South East of England. In these circumstances political nationalism has grown and put down stronger roots. As economic prosperity can never be absolutely assured, the possibility of a nationalist revival in times of economic adversity will thus always be present."

That was how it looked at the time, but Kilbrandon understandably missed the twist that North Sea oil was about to bring to this argument. In nationalist eyes it was to reverse completely the nature of the relationship between Scotland and the rest of the United Kingdom. Where once Secretaries of State had waltzed through the country distributing charity in the form of dud motor companies, toxic power stations and incomplete steelworks, now the English middle classes lived comfortable lives on the proceeds of an oil industry that by rights belonged to Scotland. In the twenty-first century the 'economic adversity' of Kilbrandon's analysis was no longer needed to inflame political resentment.

A more homely, if less obviously practical, version of a similar policy exists in Wales, although Kilbrandon was among those who observed that there was a less materialist aspect to Welsh demands for self-government. The commission reported: "In Wales the general sympathy for nationalist ideas seems to be more widespread, even among leading figures in Welsh public life. This sympathy seems to be vested, however, in a desire not so much for independence or home rule as for a recognition of the need to foster Welsh economic and cultural interests and for a greater say in the way in which Wales is governed."

The emphasis of cultural matters in the character of Welsh

nationalism, in particular the Welsh language, gave it a moral strength but a political weakness. The vast majority of the population believed they would inevitably be disadvantaged by any kind of home rule regime in which a further premium was put on the ability to speak Welsh. But that didn't mean then, and still doesn't mean, that Wales ignored the economic aspects of self-determination. It's just that they took a rather different form, in particular the idea that the Welsh language could be numbered only as one item in a long list of things of which England had robbed Wales.

In those more innocent days when Kilbrandon roamed the streets of Britain, Plaid Cymru sometimes persuaded itself that, if you did the sums right, Wales would actually turn out to be better off separated from the United Kingdom. In the first place it wouldn't have to pay for all those English extravagances: armies, nuclear weapons and so on, things a civilised society would be better off without. Then there were Welsh natural resources: the country was 'energy-rich' it was sometimes asserted, despite the fact that the coal industry was in steep decline and some of that energy-richness, two nuclear power stations, would not have been there at all if Wales hadn't been part of the United Kingdom. In those days, though, it was virtually impossible to say where anything that might be called the Welsh economy began and ended, so such arguments were difficult either to substantiate or refute.

There was another aspect to this argument. That was the sense that Wales was somehow owed something by England; that the industrial history of Wales was essentially one of exploitation, where Welsh labour and Welsh natural resources had been used for the benefit of capitalists who took the proceeds away from the country. They are denounced from political platforms to this day, most notably the Scottish Bute family who built Cardiff. Others, great ironmasters like the Crawshays from Yorkshire, or the Guests from Shropshire, arrived in Wales and stayed; and there were the home grown coal owners, like the Lords Rhondda and Merthyr, but the theory was probably sound enough. Whatever the ultimate destination of the wealth they generated, it wasn't ordinary Welsh people who benefited from it.

In a sense this lost treasure is a vanished and intangible Welsh equivalent of Scotland's present-day oil. At the heart of it is this argument: Wales is poor and socially deprived at least in part because of the conduct of previous generations. Therefore a British government has a duty to make reparations through a rather more generous financial arrangement than currently exists. It would not be some kind of charity but a recognition of what is properly due.

This is sentiment rather than any kind of coherent political strategy, and it's not put strictly in those terms by most nationalist politicians. But when they are talking about a Westminster government meeting the needs of Wales, they are also talking about that history. And it is a way of portraying Wales, not as some kind of pensioner dependent on the generosity of a London administration, but as a form of historical creditor, simply seeking what is due to it. It has many obvious shortcomings and it's not as immediately appealing as the SNP's robust claim to something that really exists, something that is even more compelling when, as in 2008, economic adversity makes a spectacular comeback. Oil is readily understood and promises large quantities of jam, not tomorrow, but now.

But it leaves one central question unanswered. It's this: would Scottish independence still be worth having if there were no oil at all? Or if the oil were going to run out next month or next year? What might the voters think if, instead of living in the third richest nation in the European Union, as the hypothetical figures have it, they were going to be citizens of the tenth richest nation, or the twentieth? The crucial point is that there is absolutely no reason why, even without oil, Scotland shouldn't become a self-governing country if that's what its people want. The same goes for Wales. The question is, though, what is independence *for*? What is the principle that drives those who seek it? Is it simply a way of getting a bit richer? If it's worth having, is it worth being poorer to achieve it?

What people said in Ireland in 1921 was, in effect, that, yes, independence was worth that sacrifice, although it's impossible to assess to what extent and with what enthusiasm that idea was endorsed by the average citizen rather than by their political leaders. It was clearly a view held by Eamon de Valera, one of the most important of those leaders, a man who was to be the country's prime minister three times between 1932 and 1959, later serving as president until he was ninety years old.

In his history of Ireland between 1912 and 1985, J.J. Lee writes that de Valera "had compared Ireland before independence to a 'servant in a big mansion'. If the servant wanted his freedom he must 'give up the luxuries of a certain kind which are available to him by being in that mansion.... If he goes into the cottage he has to make up his mind to put up with the frugal fare of that cottage'."

But, as Lee points out, what are presented as the necessary sacrifices of one generation are less compelling for its successors. Thirty years on that was clearly the case.

"The injunction may have been good enough for the sometime servants. It was no longer good enough for their children. 'The luxuries of a certain kind' for which those children yearned in 1957 included the 'luxury' of a family of their own, the 'luxury' of a job where they need not constantly touch the forelock, the 'luxury' of decent medical treatment. Some even dared contemplate the obscene 'luxury' of the opportunity, denied them in the morality of the cottage, of providing decent education for their own children. An affluent society might be a squalid society. It did not have to be. That was a matter of choice. A frugal society had little choice."

It was to be a further thirty years before much of that frugality was chased away by the Celtic Tiger and now it's impossible to imagine any western politician embracing the austere views put forward by de Valera. Not in Scotland or Wales where devolution has become an argument about how to become richer, but only in part. The idea is that everyone in Scotland, and maybe even in Wales, can, as in Ireland, at least aspire to live in the big house. At the same time, though, it would be a mistake to think that the SNP's case for independence rests on something as simplistic as economic advantage. Inevitably it's an important element of the argument but only one aspect of it. John Curtice who is Professor of Politics at Strathclyde University is one of the UK's leading experts on opinion polling. He says that the second crucial part of the case lies in the question of Scottish identity.

"SNP leaders say it is because we are a nation and like all nations we should have the right to be an independent state and, by the way, guys, we used to be one anyway. It's straight assertion of the nation state. You want to be able to reflect your distinct separate national identity."

To a very large extent, Curtice says, that identity is a powerful force in Scotland, an emotional if not political distance from the British state. "Britishness is a secondary identity for most people in Scotland. There are lots of people who will acknowledge both, but if you force them to choose they are more likely to prioritise their Scottishness over their Britishness. And in a sense if you actually force people to choose, about eighty per cent of the people in

Scotland say they are Scottish and about twenty per cent say they are British. In that sense Britishness is already dead in Scotland."

Alan Taylor is associate editor of the *Sunday Herald* and editor of the *Scottish Review of Books*. He's a former Labour supporter who's moved towards the nationalist position, a shift that's been endorsed for him by the arrival in government of the SNP. As you might expect from a writer and literary critic, his emphasis on the potential future of Scotland is essentially a cultural one. He's angry about Scottish writers who don't think Scotland is worth writing about. He is dismissive of the reputations of best-selling Scottish novelists like J.K. Rowling and Ian Rankin. He's small and red-headed and combative. He explodes with contempt at the low level of expectation encouraged by politicians.

"Too many people in the country follow the politicians' lead which is the man with the *Daily Record* in one hand and a pie supper in the other. What ever happened to enlightened, sophisticated, intelligent Scotland? Where did it go? I've no idea. It just evaporated.

"The kind of country I would like it to be is a sophisticated, intelligent, well-behaved, civic-minded, independent-thinking, enterprising, inventive place. They're all the qualities that we think Scots have but I'm dubious that they use them at the moment. We need to state what are our values and find a way to return to them through education from the way people are brought up, through the way society's run and ordered."

It's an elevated view of an independent Scotland. But what would the man with the *Daily Record* and the pie supper make of it? I asked him: "What does a guy who goes to see Glasgow Rangers say to that?

"I don't give a toss what he thinks."

"He's got a vote, just like you."

"Alas he does. He's got to earn that vote. He's got to carry it through in his own daily life. I would like them to think about what they're doing in their daily life instead of hitting people over the head with bottles or stabbing people or shouting sectarian chants or gumming the streets up with their dead chewing gum."

Other Scottish journalists take a rather cooler view of the current state of play. Mark Douglas-Home, a former editor of the *Herald*, says that, yes, he sees the argument about Scotland as a nation, the 'blood' argument, but says: "It's a very appealing argument but it needs to go hand in hand with the economic argument and the nationalists know that and they've been using the economic argument recently much more than they have the emotional blood argument. You need both with nationalism but the economic argument is fundamental to making people take the risk. People can be nationalist in their hearts and want independence but when they look at their jobs and their security and investment for schools and hospitals then there's a common sense side to it. The nationalists have been arguing that the common sense argument has been on their side. You can argue that when times are good, but when times are bad you need to belong to a bigger economy."

And that, he thinks, marks a decisive shift in the mood in Scotland. "I thought that we were on the verge of independence but this banking crisis has changed that. There's a big problem for the nationalists. It doesn't mean that people are going to feel more British but they may think, well, the sensible route at the moment is to stay under the British umbrella. I don't think that means that people feel more British but they may regard Britain as just a wise choice when times are hard. They may feel as passionately Scottish as they did before but that may not translate into votes for the nationalists."

John Curtice, the man who knows the figures better than anyone, also seems inclined to agree that in the end the persuasion must be economic. "It has to be because at the end of the day if you are a realist within the nationalist camp you know you've got about a third of the population on your side. You've got to work out how you get another third to a half. You also know that basically speaking it remains the case that people are not convinced that Scotland would be better off as a separate economic entity. That is the debate you have to win."

At least in the short term, Curtice thinks, the SNP might be content to settle for some expansion of the powers of the Scottish Parliament. The planned referendum on independence might never happen and instead the parliament would have wider authority, particularly over fiscal matters. "It's the possibility that the Scottish Parliament will get some kind of assignment of fiscal revenues, perhaps getting greater control over setting tax rates. That's the big game, the real game in town. If the SNP by 2011 have got in office in Westminster a UK government that's committed to doing that they will say, 'God, didn't we do well'."

That prospect seemed to recede in December 2008 in the interim report of the commission set up by the non-nationalist parties to look into the further development of devolution in Scotland. The chairman, Sir Kenneth Calman, a former chief medical officer for Scotland and later for England, released an interim finding which was doubtful about the idea of devolving full fiscal autonomy to Scotland. That doesn't rule out some, even quite a lot of extra fiscal power eventually being handed over to the Scottish Parliament, but by 2011, the date of the next Scottish elections, the political map might have been much more drastically redrawn. Before that date there'll be a UK general election which, according to Mark Douglas-Home, could change everything.

"If Cameron wins that election and he wins it in England and he has virtually no seats in Scotland then he will have the Scottish election coming after that and you will have the situation in which the nationalists can say: 'We're being ruled by a Conservative government with English seats. Why should Scotland stand for that? This is your moment to express your outrage that the British constitution can throw up this anomaly and vote us in with a huge majority'."

The prospect of events unfolding like that is increased by the weakness of the other political parties in Scotland. It would be wrong to say the Conservatives have been obliterated, but with hardly any representation at Westminster (they won only one Scottish seat in the 2005 general election) and only 17 of the 129 seats at Holyrood, their influence is tiny and reduced even further by the fact that they are not seen as a Scottish Party. The Liberal Democrats, who formed a coalition with Labour in the first two parliaments, refused to work with the SNP and so undermined their own influence and profile. What are the Lib Dems up to, people ask. A party devoted to the idea of coalition working in an electoral system that inevitably delivers coalition then turning its back on coalition is, to say the least, inconsistent. Meanwhile Labour, it's generally agreed, is in serious trouble. The party has had five leaders in the first ten years of the parliament's existence and a constant complaint about it is the ambiguity of its Scottish character.

Mark Douglas-Home points out: "Labour's got a structural problem that effectively means that the Labour leader in Holyrood has to defer to London all the time and is seen to be doing that. When Jack McConnell was first minister he wouldn't criticise

Labour if it wasn't a devolved matter. He wouldn't express an opinion. Now that we've had Alex Salmond with an independence of mind and spirit saying, look, London, you're getting this wrong, you're messing this up, I think it's very hard for us to go back to having a Labour leader who isn't able to do the same thing."

The tensions in this relationship were starkly exposed in May 2008 when Wendy Alexander, then the Scottish Labour leader, challenged Alex Salmond to hold an immediate referendum on independence. In Westminster Gordon Brown distanced himself from her to the extent that he claimed that she had never called for the referendum, even though she had done so in the clearest possible terms.

John Curtice's analysis shows that Labour's difficulties in England and in Wales have been substantially to the advantage of the Conservatives, but in Scotland it's been different. "In Scotland it is quite clearly to the benefit of the SNP. The Conservative Party are going nowhere in Scotland. We've had recent polls that put the SNP ahead of Labour in Westminster voting intentions – which is unprecedented."

The political shifts of even a few months in the second half of 2008 illustrate just how difficult it is to predict the political state of Scotland in the years 2010-2011 and thereafter. It's by no means impossible that in Scotland the way the cards fall could renew the momentum of the independence movement. There will be fewer arguments about the collapse of the Scottish banks and more about the idea that as an independent country in the European Union it would have done no worse, and perhaps better, than as a part of the United Kingdom.

Even if that argument carries weight, however, there is a whole series of complex and time-consuming obstacles in any route to independence. If a Scottish referendum voted in favour, expert opinion insists that it would be only the beginning of the process. It would be just the starting gun for negotiations with the United Kingdom Government. If terms of independence were agreed then it's likely that there would have to be a second referendum to determine whether they were acceptable to the people of Scotland.

As for membership of the European Union: an examination by the Constitution Unit at University College, London, of the whole question of Scottish independence concludes that Scotland would have to reapply for membership. It would not necessarily succeed.

There are other views particularly, as you might expect, in Scotland itself.

At present the idea of Scottish independence is a proposal of broad principle. Even if a majority of the Scottish people come to support it there would be complicated political and diplomatic riddles to be untangled. When the details began to emerge, as they would have to, it's impossible to say then how voters would respond, whether, for example, they might come to have second thoughts or, conversely, they might be swept along on an exhilarating tide of change. Amid the uncertainties one thing is clear enough. It could happen. And the inescapable conclusion is that what happens in Scotland will have a profound influence on the future of the United Kingdom and the whole idea of Britain and Britishness.

Crossing the Border

AS WELL AS PROVIDING an enticing if misleading example of the benefits of being a small, independent nation on the western edge of Europe, in recent years Ireland has also, almost unnoticed, been instrumental in subverting the traditional ideas of nationality within that territory once known as the British Isles. It's nothing short of astonishing that, despite a bloody civil war being fought for more than thirty years over the Britishness or otherwise of a section of UK territory, attitudes on mainland Britain towards the Irish Republic have remained for the most part amicable and even, in recent times, envious. It's difficult to think, for instance, that many people outside Ireland either knew or cared that for sixty years the constitution of the Irish Republic maintained that country's claim to sovereignty over the whole island. Yet it was at the core of what the fighting was all about: republicans believing in the legitimacy of this claim, unionists resisting it with all the means they could deploy, each side murdering large numbers in the process, many of the victims, as always, being innocent bystanders. Two sovereign governments stood on opposite sides of this argument but, apart from those directly involved, the general population of the UK seemed perfectly capable of separating the act of terrorism from the nationality of the terrorist.

One reason might have been that, despite the reservations British people might have about the Catholic citizens of the Irish Republic, many nevertheless seem more sympathetic to them than to the chilly Protestants of the North. Yes, the Southern Irish were traditionally characterised as rambunctious, priest-ridden, feckless and prolific, but somehow even those were more attractive qualities than the grim rigidities of the implacably sober unionists, the stony-faced, bowler-hatted Orangemen who sometimes looked like another intergalactic enemy invented for Doctor Who.

Peripheral matters have sometimes illustrated this. One of the most popular and accomplished people in broadcasting is Terry Wogan. To many people his style, soft-spoken, funny, inclusive, ironic, his status as a secular saint and honorary knight represents the best of what it is to be British, even though, of course, he is not British. In previous years it was Eamonn Andrews who performed a similar role as British broadcasting's reassuring Irishman. Like a lot of their countrymen, whose legendary charm and fluency are by no means a tourist board invention, they seem to pay a compliment to the English language by the care with which they use it. In that regard it's no coincidence that across the centuries Irish people have been some of the greatest and most inventive writers of the English language: essayists, poets, playwrights and novelists from Swift to Wilde, Joyce, Beckett, Heaney and many, many more.

In broadcasting, far from southern Irish accents serving as some kind of reminder of ancient hostilities, it's frequently argued that such a way of speaking smoothes out some of the trickier aspects of class that continue to haunt life in England in particular. As George Bernard Shaw, an Irishman, wrote in *Pygmalion*: "It is impossible for an Englishman to open his mouth without making some other Englishman hate or despise him." It's also the case, I think, that even at the height of the Troubles if you heard an Irish accent when travelling on the tube, you wouldn't wonder nervously what the man was carrying in his bag.

In contrast, when a very accomplished and accessible Northern Ireland broadcaster, Gerry Anderson, was given a high-profile afternoon programme, *Anderson Country*, on Radio 4 in 1994, it provoked an unprecedented number of complaints. Was it just because of his accent? Almost certainly not, but it didn't help, as David Hendy records in his book *Life on Air*, a history of Radio 4.

"Some correspondents made it clear that it was Anderson's accent that grated. They were at least being consistent in their prejudice since Northern Irish accents had always attracted partic-ular opprobrium from a section of the Radio Four audience. The more general charge, however, was banality."

This is no more than anecdotal evidence but the people who run broadcasting naturally reflect the prejudices of the people to whom they broadcast. They try not to be enslaved by them, but it's inevitable that audiences are resistant to what they suspect is supposed to be good for them, or what advances some inclusive agenda in which they're not particularly interested. If they get bored they find something else to do or something else to listen to. It's a fact of life that has meant that, for all the headlines over so many decades, to many people Northern Ireland has remained a kind of foreign country. And that's despite the fact that, for many of its inhabitants, it seeks to be one of the most British places in the entire world.

When governments try to emphasise the virtues of Britishness and urge greater displays of patriotism, perhaps they don't like to think too long about that part of the country in which a majority of the population want to be British above all else, where national identity is a kind of uniform rather than an old coat carelessly thrown over the shoulders. To be British with such a passion is, in a sense, very non-British. Which is one reason perhaps why the Protestants of Northern Ireland aren't invariably seen as the embodiment of patriotism but more often as an incomprehensible and alien race.

"To the rest of Britain the Protestants of Northern Ireland are the yokel country cousins who happen to bear your name." This is the view of one southern Irish broadcaster who spent many years working in the North. "You mentioned them as little as possible, you visited them as little as possible. Every year, perhaps, you sent them a distant Christmas card. Britain was increasingly embarrassed by the version of Britishness adopted in Northern Ireland – in particular its rigidity. A culture based on the revealed word in scripture finds politics very difficult. In particular it makes it difficult to make deals."

That commentary might be dismissed as the kind of partisan view you inevitably get on the divided island of Ireland. But from the beginning of partition the exasperation often spread through the British political establishment. In a speech in the House of Commons in 1922, for example, Winston Churchill reflected on the intractable sectarian divide, something that was unchanged even by the momentous events of the First World War.

"The whole map of Europe has been violently altered. The modes of thought of men, the whole outlook on affairs, the grouping of parties, all have encountered violent and tremendous change in the deluge of the world, but as the deluge subsides and the waters fall short we see the dreary steeples of Fermanagh and Tyrone emerging once again. The integrity of their quarrel is one of the few institutions that have been unaltered in the cataclysm which has swept the world. That says a lot for the persistency with which Irishmen on the one side or the other are able to pursue their controversies."

The Labour Prime Minister Harold Wilson was to adopt a similar attitude half a century later, although he put it in rather less elevated language. He used the most wounding terms to denounce the Ulster council workers' strike of 1974 which wrecked the power-sharing agreement painfully put together at Sunningdale the previous year.

These were people, Wilson said, who "viciously defy Westminster, purporting to act as though they were an elected government, people who spend their lives sponging on Westminster and British democracy and then systematically assault democratic methods. Who do these people think they are?"

Government files made public in 2006 revealed that, thirty years earlier, Wilson had been so fed up that he had drawn up a plan to cut Northern Ireland loose from the rest of the United Kingdom, making it an independent dominion subject to the Queen, but outside the Commonwealth. It was a scheme that would probably have meant a terrible civil war. Did Wilson mean it, or was he trying to scare other people, in particular the Irish government? Then again, he was within a couple of months of leaving office: was he already at the beginning of a serious mental decline, starting to lose touch with reality, as was evident later? In the end the idea came to nothing, but its very existence revealed the lack of sympathy with the fundamentalist intractability of the Unionists.

The sponging remark in particular was bitterly resented, but there was to be an echo of it almost thirty years later from Peter Hain when he was Northern Ireland Secretary. In a speech in September 2005 he talked a great deal about money, pointing out that public spending in Northern Ireland was almost a third higher than the average for the United Kingdom. He threatened to introduce water rates and pointed out that people there contributed to local services at well under half the rate of Wales and Scotland. The message was clear enough. Failure to reach a deal on power-sharing, he implied was, would be very expensive.

"Hain behaved like an eighteenth-century governor," I was told. "He set about pissing people off. Did he do it on purpose? Was he winding them up?" Perhaps he was. Buried away in all the rhetoric of political fundamentalism, there is in Northern Ireland a keen appreciation of financial advantage. The Northern Ireland Executive got back to work and the water rates were not imposed.

Elsewhere in the UK it was difficult to detect much criticism of the need to fix things in this manner. Perhaps, indeed, no one noticed. In any case it seemed the price of comparative peace in Northern Ireland was worth paying. Which is no doubt why, when English newspapers and politicians complain about the public spending advantages enjoyed by Scotland and Wales, they say nothing about the condition of Northern Ireland, which does better out of the Barnett Formula than anywhere else.

What generally passes people by, however, is the way in which the peace process in Northern Ireland has changed the structure of the United Kingdom. In its turn that is also a consequence, at least in part, of the altered condition of the Irish Republic, a further key element in a changed constitutional world. The economic revolution that swept through that country in a matter of a few years also revealed important aspects of the nature of the United Kingdom and, for that matter, the nature of Britishness. Ireland has lost part of its distinctiveness, a shift that has become an important factor in obscuring the outlines of nationality in all in the countries of these islands.

What has happened in Ireland is that to a great extent economic success has made it more like everywhere else, most remarkably in the matter of religion. When I went to Dublin in the nineteen fifties, even as a Catholic child I was startled by the ostentatious observances all around. On a journey through the city, for example, every time the bus passed a church most of the people on board would cross themselves. Years later, grownups who didn't believe would at least keep up the pretence, leaving the house on a Sunday morning for a Mass-sized interval in the pub so that a devout mother (who'd been to church early) wouldn't suspect their godlessness. A disgruntled Protestant son-in-law, with no religious imperative to go out, would have to stay with her, thirsty. By 2008, a cousin was leaving detailed instructions about his funeral and the fastidiously non-religious character it should have. One of his daughters put a copy of the *Irish Times* into the coffin, something perhaps for the short journey across Dublin to the crematorium, the existence of which was itself an innovation of revolutionary religious modernity in the city. As the coffin lid was lifted into place there was a brief sense of shock. Despite what had clearly been specified, the undertakers had put a crucifix on it. "Ah well," the deceased man's sister said, "it was probably more expensive without."

It isn't prosperity that has brought about this kind of change, although it's accelerated it. Before the Celtic Tiger ever stirred there was the women's movement in the Republic and its spectacular campaigns. The most famous of them was the Contraceptive Train, organised by the Irish Women's Liberation Movement. In 1971, forty-seven women went to Belfast where they bought condoms. On their return to Dublin they challenged customs officers to arrest them for the illegal importation of contraceptives, in Ireland then a crime for which they could be sent to prison. The customs men let them pass. Seven years later some of the restrictions on contraception were lifted but it wasn't until 1993 that it became freely available.

If the most Catholic state in Europe was eventually forced to give way on that central aspect of faith it was the Church itself that took an axe to its own authority. It did so by its response to the exposure of the widespread sexual abuse of children by priests. As in other countries, like the United States, the Church didn't publicly condemn and punish the men concerned, but tried to pretend it hadn't happened. Among the offenders was Father Brendan Smyth who eventually died in prison, having been convicted in both Northern Ireland and the Republic. He was a rapist of children who had continued his activities for thirty years, despite the fact that they were known to his religious superiors. Others who were less obviously vicious still destroyed lives. Father Michael Cleary, priest and TV personality (favourite joke: "You can kiss a nun but you mustn't get into the habit") was famous throughout Ireland, not least as the warm-up man for the Pope's visit in 1979. But he also lived in a sexual relationship with his housekeeper. A television documentary broadcast long after his death illustrated vividly the wreckage of her life and that of their son.

The Catholic Church's terror of exposure, its apparent indifference to suffering and its isolation from the demands of truth, justice and humanity, repelled huge numbers of ordinary people who, in the modern world, were in any case no longer in awe of the institution and the black-suited thought police of the priesthood. In less than a generation the call of the religious life rapidly began to die out. In 2007 in Ireland 160 priests died but only nine men were

ordained. In the same year only two nuns took vows. The erosion of
the Church's place in society was already in train, but without the
sexual scandals, some observers believe, its relegation would have
taken at least another generation.

It was through such dramatic changes that, as Roy Foster puts
it in his book, *Luck and the Irish*, the Catholics became Protestants.
In simple terms, they weren't going to be pushed around any more.
Attendance at Mass plunged. As in the UK, many Irish couples
stopped getting married, even when they had children.

Foster writes: "Traditional Protestant attitudes to Catholics as
brainwashed pawns of a totalitarian religious system could not
survive the spectacular demonstration of individual conscience and
judgement by Irish reformers of one kind and another since the
1960s."

To say that that in Ireland the Catholics have become
Protestants is clearly not to suggest that the Irish have in some way
also become British. It's obvious that *not* being British remains a
crucial part of the definition of being Irish. But it is also a country
whose history was for centuries inextricably and unwillingly
entwined with that of Britain. The result is that its social and
economic revolution, taking place over a few decades, has in at least
one important way altered the character of the United Kingdom.

The change in Ireland was intimately bound up with the arrival
of tangible prosperity, something that in its turn affected traditional
political attitudes. The ending of partition was one of those aspirations that politicians came to understand could never be achieved,
in particular because there was no way in which a Dublin government could exercise authority over a million Protestants in the
North. A booming economy made even the theoretical objective
much less desirable. Who would actually want to take on the North,
described by Foster as "an ailing, unprofitable and expensive
backwater." And if the South wouldn't touch the North with a
bargepole then the IRA was left with no ultimate objective. In a
transformed world, north and south, the pressures of the past
subsided in the face of the realities of the present.

The former *Taoiseach*, Garret Fitzgerald, thought that a
younger British politician like Tony Blair, born in 1953, was greatly
helped by being free of the burden of the traditional antagonisms
between Britain and Ireland. Older people still probed away at
ancient resentments like the refusal of neutral Ireland to let Britain

use the country's ports during World War II. Every so often a newspaper would remind its readers that President de Valera had sent condolences to Germany on the death of Adolph Hitler. The new generation of politicians like Blair, although he once talked about "the hand of history", had moved on. You can say the same, too, about Bertie Ahern, born 1951, the *Taoiseach* who was Blair's key partner in the peace deal.

The vigour with which the 1997 Labour government immediately set about a programme of constitutional change looks even more astonishing in retrospect than it did at the time. Blair was eventually undone by his foreign adventures but on the domestic front he greatly altered the familiar world in which most of us had lived until then. Fewer than six months after Labour took office the people of Wales and Scotland had voted to establish devolved administrations. Not much more than another six months after that, the Good Friday Agreement was signed. And, while most of us might not have seen it at the time, these two great changes were closely connected. More than that, they were also linked to events in Europe, the fall of the Berlin Wall, the break-up of the Soviet Union and in particular the growth of the EU. Borders ceased to matter in the same way.

When the devolved governments began work in Scotland and Wales at the end of the1990s, one of the first responses of the Irish government was to establish consulates in Edinburgh and Cardiff. Not some small passport office above a shop, but a genuine international presence staffed by real diplomats of energy and enterprise. The message was this: despite getting on for a thousand years of conflict, in the modern world matters of national status were becoming significantly less important.

In these circumstances the idea was that while Scotland and Wales might not be sovereign countries as such they nevertheless had some vague equivalence of status with Ireland. And there was a lot more of this kind of thing. Among the new institutions created under the Good Friday Agreement was the North-South Ministerial Council in which British ministers now sit alongside those from the Irish Republic to deal with matters of cross-border co-operation. David Marquand, the historian and former Labour MP who later became a senior official of the European Commission, writes in his book on Britain since 1918: "The implications were startling. Hard-edged, monolithic British notions of sovereignty – both national and parliamentary – had given way to soft, porous ones. The sovereign British state had given the sovereign Irish state a role in the governance of part of the United Kingdom."

More than that, the British government had in effect abandoned its sovereignty over the people of Northern Ireland. If at some future date the people of the North voted in a referendum to leave the United Kingdom and instead become part of the Irish Republic, that was a choice entirely for them, something with which no British government would interfere. As the Good Friday Agreement says: "The participants... recognise that it is for the people of the island of Ireland alone, by agreement between the two parts respectively and without external impediment, to exercise their right to self-determination on the basis of consent, freely and concurrently given, North and South, to bring about a united Ireland, if that is their wish, accepting that this right must be achieved and exercised with and subject to the agreement and consent of a majority of the people of Northern Ireland."

This long, single sentence is a constitutional revolution designed for a specific purpose. But the issue of the sovereignty of the Westminster parliament has been altered not simply in the case of Northern Ireland. In theory, as Anthony King points out, Westminster could choose to make laws for Scotland on any matter it chose. It could abolish the devolved administrations in Scotland and Wales. The crucial words are *in theory*. Any attempt to move in that direction without the clear consent of the people of Scotland and Wales would provoke huge protests. As King writes: "If London's writ were to run north of the border or on the far banks of the Severn, it would almost certainly have to be carried by English policemen with the backing of English troops."

It is one of those powers that Parliament cannot exercise and so the nature of the countries we live in is changed without anyone noticing very much. Power, actual or imagined, no longer resides at one address. It also lives in Brussels, for instance, and, whatever their views of the European Union, British politicians have had to engage in its operation. Many of the anti-marketeers of previous generations soon enough came to recognise two things: the importance of the European institutions in the lives of British people and the opportunities they offered for exercising influence outside the British governmental system. Who in the Seventies would have predicted, for instance, that Neil Kinnock would one day become vice-president of the European Commission and his wife Glenys a long-serving member of the European Parliament.

The importance of Europe in everyday life might even have shaped the attitudes of Ian Paisley, a man with an inexhaustible appetite for getting elected to any institution in which he could wield influence and state his case. As well as being an MP he was a member of any number of versions of the Northern Ireland assembly and, for twenty-five years, also sat in the European Parliament. Paul Murphy, a former Secretary of State for Northern Ireland, believes the European experience was a crucial influence on all the politicians involved in the peace process.

"I think that the common membership of Europe has blurred those distinctions of Irishness and Britishness. Ireland sees itself as a European country. In the North too, where the three MEPs work together as one. During the two years I was Europe Minister, the fact was that they were members of the same club, the two prime ministers kept meeting, ministers kept meeting. Europe I think was key in blurring those borders. Not just the physical border but the border of Britishness and Irishness."

Other cross-border institutions created as a result of the Good Friday Agreement have also begun to erase old distinctions. For example, the establishment under the Good Friday Agreement of the British-Irish Council. Among those who sit on it are representatives of the British and Irish governments, the devolved institutions in Scotland, Wales and Northern Ireland. Also in the system are representatives from the Isle of Man, Jersey and Guernsey whose place in the intricate machinery of the British Isles led Anthony King to write: "The Channel Islands and the Isle of Man enjoyed home rule, but no one paid much attention to them."

The influence of the British-Irish Council seems to be about as great as the excitement it generates in the countries it represents. It would be surprising, indeed, if the vast majority of people outside the political loop had ever heard of it. It discusses what are described as matters of mutual concern, which seems to be very much anything it feels like, including, in September 2008, the global economic climate. What impact it can have on any of these matters is not strictly relevant. What is important is the fact that Alex Salmond and Rhodri Morgan and Peter Robinson can sit down on terms of equality with people like the Irish leader Brian Cowen, and before him Bertie Ahern (Ireland takes the affair seriously enough for the *Taoiseach* to make a point of being there), and a senior figure from the British government including, in 2007, the Prime Minister, Gordon Brown. It's not the United Nations, but it's a start, a way of saying that the differences between these countries are less rigid than you might think. Salmond and Morgan and Robinson represent what have come to be called governments and that's significant in itself. Despite the differences in their titles, the First Minister of Northern Ireland and the Deputy First Minister – Peter Robinson and Martin McGuinness – in fact enjoy equal rank within the system. And when they go abroad, to Dublin for example, they are accorded the status of heads of government.

It's also the case that in Northern Ireland, in a break with every convention and regulation of the past, nationality has become a matter of choice. People born there can decide if they want to be British, or Irish or, if they like, both and, if they want to, carry the passports of both countries. This is such a remarkable development that the rest of the world has sometimes struggled to keep up. When, for example, footballers born in Northern Ireland exercised their choice of citizenship and opted to play instead for the Republic, FIFA, the international football authority, refused to allow it. It took the intervention of the Irish government to persuade them that the world really had changed that much.

While the political structures have been rebuilt, though, the question remains of whether Northern Ireland itself has changed. The historian and *Irish News* columnist Brian Feeney thinks it has done so in one particularly important way. "People on both sides now realise it is a place apart," he says. He believes that while Unionists no longer feel they live under the threat of being integrated with the South, nevertheless some aspects of the divisions between the communities are as powerful as ever. In working-class areas even now new walls are being built to divide Catholics and Protestants. Teenagers stone each other, indulging in what the police describe as 'recreational violence'.

Many of the civil rights issues that were intimately bound up with the Troubles – among them discrimination over jobs and the allocation of housing – have been resolved, but many cultural and political ravines remain to be bridged in some way. For example, Sinn Fein wants to end academic selection at eleven, the Democratic Unionist Party wants to keep it. Smaller issues are just as passionately disputed. A plan to build a sports stadium on the

site of the old Maze Prison has become controversial because Sinn
Fein has proposed that it should include a museum of the conflict.
The Unionists say that would simply glorify the IRA. There's
probably nothing they can't argue over but at the same time the two
sides have to come to agreements, otherwise nothing can be done.
Each of them holds a veto over the other. Both Peter Robinson and
Gerry Adams say government is going to be a battle a day. In a
sense it's the old fight continued by different means.

Some of the disputes have occasionally seemed to threaten the
very existence of the devolved government, a situation that Brian
Feeney thinks makes the politicians draw back. "They have done
deals. It's in both their interests to do deals. They don't want people
thinking they can't run the place."

How much things have changed but at the same time have not
changed in Northern Ireland was illustrated in the extraordinary
sight in March 2009, unthinkable only a few years ago, of Peter
Robinson and Martin McGuinness standing alongside the Chief
Constable of Northern Ireland, Sir Hugh Orde, to condemn the
murder of a policeman. But the show of unity by the politicians also
emphasised the fragility of the structure that has been devised to
end sectarian killing. The policeman was shot by members of a
dissident republican group. Two days previously two soldiers died
in an attack on the Massereene Barracks in Antrim, victims of
another, separate, republican organisation. McGuinness, once a
leading IRA man, now spoke on behalf of the rule of law.

"These people are traitors to the island of Ireland, they have
betrayed the political desires, hopes and aspirations of all the people
who live on this island," he said. And demonstrating just how much
attitudes had altered, he urged people with information about the
killings to come forward to the police, words that would once have
choked any member of Sinn Fein.

The soldiers who died were the first to be killed by terrorists in
Northern Ireland for twelve years. Paul Stephen Carroll, the policeman who was shot, was the first member of the Police Service of
Northern Ireland to be killed since it had replaced the Royal Ulster
Constabulary eight years previously. The central question raised by
these events was whether it remained a place where, as many
believed, periods of comparative peace would continue to alternate
with episodes of violence. Would it prove to be the case, as Conor
Cruise O'Brien had once suggested, that Northern Ireland's

violence abated cyclically as its leaders approached old age? Martin McGuiness was born in 1950, the Sinn Fein president, Gerry Adams, in 1948. Would a new generation of violent republicans, who portrayed these men as having sold out, wreck the peace process and bring mayhem back on to the streets? The killings of the two soldiers drew attention to sensitivities and resentments that haven't disappeared, notably the fact that republicans still regard the British army as an alien force in Northern Ireland and resent its presence. This is tormented territory and predictions are futile. I asked an Irishman who is normally overflowing with opinions and explanations informed by experience and history. What is the future of Northern Ireland?

"I absolutely don't know," he said.

In the aftermath of those killings there was a great deal of optimism that this was just a spasm engineered by organisations that had few members and little support in the wider community. Had the whole long process of war and peace finally revealed that traditional habits of thinking about borders, nationalities and the limits of self-determination were coming to an end? If that turns out to be the case in Northern Ireland it's a lesson that is unlikely to be wasted in Scotland and Wales. And perhaps in England too.

The Whale in the Bathtub

The English, the English, the English are best,
I wouldn't give twopence for all of the rest.
– Michael Flanders, 'A Song of Patriotic Prejudice'

When, by a single vote in the summer of 2008, the SNP emerged as the largest single party in the Scottish Parliament and proceeded to form an administration in Edinburgh, a sense of horror swept through the highest levels of government in London. One observer says: "The mood of panic amongst Labour ministers was quite extraordinary. You would have thought the barbarians were at the gates."

What those ministers were thinking, we have to assume, is that they had brought this particular roof down on their own heads. A Scottish parliament was meant to put the nationalists in their place, reinforce the traditional authority of Labour and, in the process, make majorities in Westminster that much more secure. When you imagine them running round the place with their heads in their hands wailing: "What have we done? What have we done?" you realise how naïve intelligent and experienced politicians can be.

If they'd had any sense, they might have begun thinking, they'd have left that devolution stuff alone. Yes, it could be presented as a high-minded extension of democracy within the United Kingdom, a mechanism that would respond to the national aspirations within it without wrecking the whole enterprise. In May 2007 it looked as though they'd got that badly wrong. Wales and Scotland were key areas in Labour's hold on British power. Now the SNP was forming an administration in Scotland and, a few weeks later in Wales Plaid Cymru were to become part of a coalition government. In both places they were leaking support at an alarming rate.

Of course Labour didn't really have much option but to pursue a policy of devolution for Scotland. There was a clear demand for it and it had long been promised as an integral element of the party's programme. It had also been embraced with enthusiasm by Tony Blair's predecessor, John Smith, so there was a strong emotional content in carrying out what people liked to describe as Smith's legacy. It's just that they don't seem to have been quite smart enough to understand how it might all turn out. But then, they were not alone in that.

If there's a theoretical case for Labour being at least wary of devolution, there's an opposite argument that suggests that the Conservatives, instead of opposing it so vehemently, might sensibly have embraced it with enthusiasm. Why didn't Margaret Thatcher and then John Major decide it would be very much in the interests of the Conservative Party to abandon the unsympathetic territories of Scotland and Wales? That question is raised by the historian David Cannadine in his book *Making History Now and Then* in which he asks why the two prime ministers insisted on a constitutional arrangement for the United Kingdom from which they did not benefit in electoral terms "...when it would have been more sensibly self-interested for them to advocate the complete devolution of Wales and Scotland by making them independent nations, thereby leaving a no less independent England in which they would have a much greater prospect of enjoying a permanent, inbuilt majority."

The simple answer is that British political parties, Conservative or Labour, don't in reality have choices of that kind. Actively participating in the break up of Britain, however it was wrapped up for public consumption, would have been unthinkable for the Conservative and *Unionist* Party, even if the union to which the title specifically referred was that with Ireland, something that had been dissolved decades previously. But the Conservative Party is wedded to the idea of continuity even when it is contradicted by the actual events of history. It was for such reasons, perhaps, that in 1997 John Major warned that devolution would mean the end of a thousand years of British history. Didn't it sound a little familiar, an echo of Churchill, in 1940: "If the British Empire and its Commonwealth last for a thousand years, men will say, 'This was their finest hour'." Calling on a thousand years of this or that is a handy rhetorical device, but in Major's case he was talking nonsense since there had not been anything like a thousand years of what might be described as British history. He was talking about *English* history but, like a lot of people, he didn't get the distinction, or maybe didn't think it worth making.

For her part, Mrs. Thatcher was so insensitive to the deep differences between the various countries of the United Kingdom that in the case of Scotland she carelessly managed to add to that country's ample stock of anti-Conservative resentment. In his memoir *Cold Cream*, Ferdinand Mount, who was head of her policy unit, writes of her determination to reform local government finance. Replacing it, he says, it became a crusade. "Her obsession was with the widows living on reduced incomes in large houses who could not afford to pay the rates at their new exorbitant levels."

Mrs. Thatcher's answer was the poll tax, a scheme that her ministers recognised would inevitably be a disaster and which was to play a crucial part in her eventual downfall. But by this stage of her leadership, Mount records, ministers and MPs had been reduced to "such a spineless condition" there was scarcely any serious opposition. Did anyone dare suggest to her that, even if the poll tax were to emerge in the end as a brilliant stroke, it still might not be a very good idea to use Scotland as a test bed for it? If they did she didn't listen.

David Cannadine points out that historians recognised the changes that were taking place in the United Kingdom long before Conservative politicians in particular had grasped them. Once upon a time British history had been contained in series after series of mighty volumes that announced themselves as histories of *England*. Now a different school was adopting a different perspective in writing about Britain.

"The exact relation between the rise of the new British history, and the simultaneous advent of the new British politics, is not yet clear, but it cannot have been just coincidence that they happened at the same time: for while English history was being reformulated as British history during the 1970s and 1980s, English politics was simultaneously becoming preoccupied with the British question."

One reason might have been that the focus of much writing about history was changing as a much greater emphasis began to be put on the lives of ordinary people, a counterweight to accounts of the dominance of court and parliament in London. Politicians had a lot of catching up to do, as became increasingly clear to the Conservatives after the end of the Thatcher/Major years. In

Scotland and Wales people had stopped voting for them. They didn't win a single seat in either country in the 1997 general election and there was good reason to believe that, in Scotland in particular, they might never make any serious recovery. Labour was the chief beneficiary although that wasn't to last. Excluded from those important territories more radical thinkers among the Tories might at least have examined fresh ideas about how they might respond to the fragmentation of British politics. They might have considered, for example, that in that 1997 election, while they were a long way behind Labour, ninety of the Labour seats that gave Tony Blair his massive majority were in Scotland and Wales. Nor was there any compensation to be found in Northern Ireland. Until 1972, the Ulster Unionists, who dominated politics in the province for so many years, took the Tory Whip in the House of Commons. Some years later David Cameron might not have entirely appreciated just how long ago those days were, how much the province had changed. In 2008 he set off to woo the Ulster Unionists once more, but by that time they had been reduced to a single member at Westminster, crushed under the wheels of the Paisleyite DUP. In all these circumstances surely the bold move would have been to cut the Celtic fringe adrift and plan to rule England, perhaps indefinitely.

Although it's not invariably a good idea to rely on historians as guides to the future, this is an area in which they have been in advance of conventional political thinking. In particular because the study of history takes a considerably longer view of the world than does politics – rather longer than the next election. And some historians, knowing that what looks like the settled story of the UK has been in place for only a relatively short time, take a strikingly robust attitude towards the idea that change within Britain is a continuing process.

In her book *Britons*, for example, Linda Colley writes about the creation of Britishness brought about by the Act of Union with Scotland in 1707, which gave rise to a "widespread though never uncontested or exclusive belief that the unity which Britain constituted, as one eighteenth-century Scot put it, an umbrella, a shelter under which various groupings and identities could plausibly and advantageously congregate. Great Britain became a workmanlike nation of sorts, albeit one that encompassed other, smaller, nations."

The consequence was, she writes, "It worked and prospered because for a long while it was able to convince many (never remotely all) within its boundaries that it offered ways for them to get ahead, whether in terms of commercial opportunity, or enhanced religious security and constitutional freedoms, or greater domestic stability and safety from invasion or access to improved job opportunities at home or abroad, or less tangible forms of betterment."

Many of those things, you might now say, are the benefits, the usefulness of the British umbrella, that are being questioned three hundred years later, in particular by the SNP. And so: "If Great Britain fissures in the future into autonomous Welsh, Scottish and English nations – and it may – this will be in part because its different peoples have decided that they can get ahead better without it."

Elsewhere, even before the new devolved administrations had opened their shops for business, another leading historian, Norman Davies, wrote enthusiastically in his book *The Isles* about the possible consequences.

"The resurgence of pride and consciousness among the 'popular nations' of the Isles causes me no unease. Patriotism is a healthy quality and patriotism is one of the things that has been seeping away from the state-backed 'British Nation'. England is a great country with enormous resources of fine people, high culture, economic wealth, and worldwide support. It would probably do better on its own than at the head of unwilling satellites."

Well, you don't read that very often. Home rule for England. Its sheer novelty makes it seem implausible, in particular because it shatters the idea of England and Britain being interchangeable terms. Many English politicians don't seem to have understood that change. Apart from arguments about levels of public subsidy and the emergence from time to time of debates about English votes for English laws, they seem to treat devolution as a phenomenon that leaves their own parish untouched and unaffected. The truth is, though, that since the last days of the twentieth century, England as an identifiable, separate country has to some extent had to be invented. By the BBC, for example, which has its own unique constitutional place in the scheme of things. "Schools in England…" newsreaders now say, "The health service in England…" instead of referring just to schools and the health service and assuming that meant everyone in Britain even when it didn't. It draws attention on a daily basis to the rebuilding work that's taking place behind the scaffolding and tarpaulins of Britishness.

In the same way you can discern the disappearance of a specifically British point of view when it comes to some central issues of
politics. The European Union, for instance, once reviled by many
nationalists as a power bloc that would further endanger their
identity and national interests, is instead now portrayed as exactly
the opposite, an organisation in which the small British nations
could stand, out of the shadow of England, on equal terms with
other independent nations. In a sense it might be another, larger,
umbrella. In Wales, too, the EU is also seen as a very handy source
of large sums of money, Wales being so comparatively poor that it's
qualified year after year for help in catching up with everyone else,
which it never does. These are places in which the fortress nation
stuff is dismissed as imperialist claptrap, and not just by members
of the SNP and Plaid Cymru.

In Scotland it is at the centre of the nationalist project.
'Scotland in Europe' is the SNP's key slogan. John Curtice of
Strathclyde University thinks that far from being abashed at the
blows apparently rained on the cause of independence by the 2008
recession, the SNP Leader, Alex Salmond, who wants Scotland to
be part of the single currency, would turn the argument on its head
and say: "You know what? You're quite right. It's no good being a
small country in a big world and the United Kingdom is too small.
What we need is an independent Scotland which is at the top table
of international negotiations as a member of the Euro."

From this point of view hostility to the European Union, the
constant efforts to portray it as an organisation whose first thought
is to act against British interests, takes on a particularly English
character. The idea seems to persist in some sections of the
Conservative Party in particular that membership of the EU is a
temporary (if long-running) aberration that can in due course be
corrected or even abandoned. It is the anti-foreigner rhetoric of the
Sun and the *Daily Mail* rather than any kind of coherent political
philosophy. This is a country in which you rub your eyes with
amazement when, on Radio 4, you hear a caller complain about the
Euro, not on economic grounds, but because the aesthetic quality
of its currency is so poor – 'like monopoly money'. And immediately afterwards you can hear a mainstream right-wing
commentator agreeing, and regretting the passing of pounds,
shillings and pence, a system as remote to most listeners as the days
of the farthing and the groat.

The character of some of the debate over Europe has been nailed by David Marquand, who resigned as a Labour MP in 1977 to work as chief adviser to Roy Jenkins when he became president of the European Commission. In 2008 Marquand wrote about the civil war in the Conservative Party over the ratification of the Maastricht Treaty in 1993, a key event in the internal conflicts that were to wreck the party at the 1997 election.

"For much of the time the issues at stake seemed technical and rather tedious, but at bottom the quarrel was over the explosive questions of identity and nationhood. However, the identity in question was essentially, even uniquely, English. Ostensibly the irreconcilables fought to save the British State and Britain's identity from a continental embrace, but when they spoke of Britain they meant England. Their rhetoric had little resonance in Scotland or Wales and no real counterpart in most of continental Europe."

Fifteen years later it's even easier to see how a particular set of attitudes towards Europe doesn't necessarily serve the needs and ambitions of the non-English countries of the United Kingdom. The nationalist parties of Wales and Scotland see the EU as an alternative source of power to Westminster, a club they might aspire to join at some stage. On the other hand British nationalism clings to the central idea of the undiluted sovereignty of Westminster, even though it has long since fled the city and the country.

Contemporaneously, though, other powers have been moving towards the English centre as the traditional structure of government in England has been substantially reduced in influence and authority. England is a much more centralised state than it was in 1979, but the English voters, unlike those in Scotland, Wales and Northern Ireland, have nowhere to look except Westminster when it comes to locating many of the levers of power that increasingly operate much of the machinery of their lives.

The emasculation of local government was an inevitable consequence of the political, philosophical and economic attitudes adopted by Mrs. Thatcher. She might have wanted a smaller state but she was also determined that what happened in that state should be much more closely regulated by her government. The poll tax belonged in that plan. As described by Anthony King in his book on the British constitution you can see why.

"In 1979 when the Thatcher Government came to power the local government army mustered more than three million men and women, well over ten per cent of the entire British workforce. Moreover, it probably *is* fair to say that the local authorities' bias tended to be in the direction of benign and often unthinking collectivism. Some sort of clash between the Thatcherite philosophy of free-market capitalism and the more paternalistic philosophy that pervaded local government was inevitable."

The result of that clash was a big reduction in the autonomy of local government. Most important of all was the financial squeeze that means that local government now raises only about twenty per cent of its own revenue and is subject to constraints on how it can be spent. King writes: "Local government was effectively imprisoned and cast in irons. To this day, despite changes of government, it has not begun to escape."

These changes have diminished very substantially the political character of local councils, although the difference can't always be seen with the naked eye. King states: "The onlooker is left with the impression that two worlds exist: the shadow world of local politics – a noisy and colourful world of election, parties, candidates and councillors – and the real, corporeal world of extremely complex arrangements that are either under central government's control or under no one's control. Local government has gone along with local identities."

This amounts to an English problem that is largely unacknowledged in England: the erosion of representative democracy. The lives of more than fifty million people are largely controlled, in terms of policy if not administration, by a centralised government in London. It isn't solely devolution and the new tensions created by the existence of other governments in Scotland, Wales and Northern Ireland that is the source of the English question. It is also the lack of connection between the details of people's daily lives and the system that decides what those lives are like. The arrival of devolution has sharpened the point of this question because it's possible to look at the new structure of the UK and to get cross about the way in which, it's often argued, it puts the English at a disadvantage.

The changes in the governance of the United Kingdom have been introduced on a pragmatic basis designed to answer one of the most persistent questions of politics: what's the least we can get away with? The result has been different arrangements for different countries: quite a lot of devolution for Scotland, rather less for

Northern Ireland and less still for Wales. And for England? Well, nothing. When referendums were under way and then the system began to operate, no one seemed to think there was much of a problem. Later, when Wales was getting a little more power, I asked a cabinet minister about it. What about poor old England, then? He was brisk. He didn't want to see the "balkanisation of Britain".

A couple of years later he'd changed his mind. Then he told me: "In my view the English question can only be addressed properly by English regional government and English regional identity. The future of England constitutionally and politically as part of the UK will either be a progressive future or it could become a little England anti-European, anti the rest of the world, racist at the edge and sometime in the middle kind of agenda. Therefore I think what we do about this is really, really important. It's the unfinished business of devolution. The unfinished business of devolution is actually England."

If that's true, and it looks as though it is, how do you resolve the problem? The central difficulty was put very clearly by Anthony King in his 2008 report on the BBC's news and current affairs coverage of the United Kingdom: "England... resembles a huge whale in a small bathtub."

The solution identified by the cabinet minister was to introduce regional government into England. One of the UK's greatest experts on this subject agrees. Professor Robert Hazell is head of the Constitution Unit at University College, London.

"It could help to give England a louder voice within the Union; and it would help to decentralise the government of England. But it could achieve the first aim, of giving England a louder voice, only if there were elected assemblies with strong powers and functions – the stronger the better. The stronger the powers the louder would be England's voice within the Union, because those powers would be a closer match for the devolved assemblies in Scotland, Wales and Northern Ireland. And the stronger the powers the greater would be the decentralisation of England."

This raises an even knottier problem. There's good reason to think that the people of England are indifferent to the idea of regional government and quite probably actively opposed to it. You can't be absolutely certain because there's not all that much evidence about what the English actually think. A single referendum, in 2004 in the North East, was held on a proposal for a

regional assembly in England. It got a decent turnout by the
standards of these things – 48 per cent – but a big majority against
– 78 per cent of those voting. It was a conclusive enough for that to
be the end of that little exercise in temperature-taking.

Even so, supporters of English regional government say that
perfunctory experiment doesn't really tell us very much about the
state of public opinion. Despite the fact that it had been included in
Labour's 2001 manifesto, it was a little orphan policy left on John
Prescott's doorstep, shunned by his Cabinet colleagues. A properly
thought out programme might do rather better, especially one
wholeheartedly supported by ministers.

That might not be quite as far-fetched as it seems. Devolution
is not only different in different parts of the United Kingdom but it
has a number of separate histories. In Northern Ireland, after a long
and tortured period of violence and intransigence it amounted to
the restoration of a system that had first been established in the
1920s. Devolution in the sense of a part of the United Kingdom
having a separate Prime Minister and government had thus been an
established fact of public life for more than eighty years. In
Scotland, already attuned to the idea, at least some of the momentum came from the sense of having been unjustly denied a
parliament in 1979. In Wales, sections of the political class, by no
means all of them nationalist, looked at Scotland galloping away
and desperately tried to catch up. The fact that in 1997 Scotland
voted for a parliament a week ahead of a yes vote in the referendum
in Wales was no coincidence. If the two countries had voted on the
same day it's very likely Wales would have said no.

Some kind of change seems certain to happen in England. For
example, David Cameron is keen to increase the number of elected
mayors although that's something that would clearly be relevant only
to towns and cities above a certain size. Then it's quite possible there
could be a new arrangement at Westminster that would allow English
issues to be dealt with separately by English MPs. It's not straightforward because it's not easy to decide what pieces of legislation
affect England exclusively and have no bearing on the government
of the other countries of the UK. Even more important is the fact
that it would change the whole nature of the UK parliament.

What becomes increasingly clear among these diverse
arguments is that altering some aspects of the structure of government has inevitably created instability and uncertainty in other

parts of the system. Shouldn't this have been anticipated when it all got under way in the 1990s? That it wasn't shows the extent to which constitutional change was a leap in the dark.

Further problems that jostle in the crowd of anomalies and uncertainties on which the British system is built begin to suggest that other parts of the structure might in any case be in urgent need of repair. It emerged at the beginning of 2009, for example, that new devices for turning position into cash were apparently available in the House of Lords. The allegation was that some Labour peers were taking money in return for trying to amend legislation as it went through the House. Maybe they were and maybe they weren't but, remarkably enough, even if they had been there wasn't much anyone could do about it. Although they have a special place in the legislative process, peers who break the rules can't be suspended and can't be sacked.

There was uproar, as there usually is, and the traditional calls for reform and promises of change. Old wounds were reopened. Jeffrey Archer, Lord Archer of Weston-Super-Mare, was perfectly entitled to attend the Lords and draw his allowances, despite having spent time in prison for perjury. Conrad Black, Lord Black of Crossharbour, the former proprietor of the *Daily Telegraph* could rejoin the legislative system eventually, once he'd been released from his American jail. Michael Watson, Lord Watson of Invergowrie, who had been both an MP and an MSP, had become a particularly assiduous attender in the upper house as soon as he'd completed his prison sentence for arson.

Some people began to think that the sheer absurdity of all this, the lack of dignity, the lack of probity it revealed at the very centre of the British constitution, would really, this time, persuade someone in authority to do something about it. But what would that something be? The question exposes the inertia at the heart of the system. A fully-elected second chamber, perhaps; or a partly-elected chamber with a number of distinguished, nominated members; or a wholly nominated affair, a solution which, it will surprise no one at all, is the answer favoured by most of the members of the present House of Lords. If history is anything to go by nothing much will happen because doing something makes people's heads ache.

Experience shows that if any serious change is to take place then it'll have to done fast, without too much time for debate. That's what happened with the partial reform that got rid of most hereditary peers. It's also what the government did with the devolution referenda of 1997 where people were rushed to the ballot box on the principle, details filled in later. And, since the referendum has become firmly established as part of the British constitutional landscape, perhaps a way forward would be to hold one on the future of the House of Lords, a democratic judgement on an undemocratic institution.

It's possible, however, that this question and many others about the way in which we are governed could be swept up in a more dramatic change than any we have seen so far. All three major political parties at Westminster are officially committed to introducing a UK bill of rights which could be an important first step towards a written constitution for the United Kingdom. Gordon Brown called the idea "a new chapter in the British story of liberty", but once again stirring words may turn out to conceal something less admirable. A bill of rights might bring some clarity to the nature of the relationship between citizens and the state. The first move could even be to make the people citizens, a word that implies equality, rather than subjects as they are at present, buried under an anachronistic sense of hierarchy under the Crown. The basic idea would be to give everyone a broad range of social and economic rights, including health care, housing, education and an adequate standard of living. In the summer of 2008 a cross-party parliamentary committee backed the idea and urged the government to get on with it. Since it has so much support perhaps there's a real prospect of something actually being done, even if it would fly in the face of history and the lessons of experience.

It's not very British, perhaps, an architect designed construction amid the ramshackle collection of outbuildings and extensions within which such change has traditionally been accommodated. Nor is it quite what it seems. Tucked away beneath an apparent consensus on the principle there are some rather less liberal forces at work. David Cameron in particular, is keen to make alterations to the Human Rights Act, the measure that incorporated the European Convention on Human Rights into British law, sometimes revealingly referred to by ministers as 'the criminals' charter'. Jack Straw, the Justice Secretary, calls for 'rebalancing', a word menacing in its apparently neutral implication of fairness. Any changes along those lines would be problematical since, as long as the UK is a member of the European Union it will remain bound by the terms of the human rights convention.

In any case, when in March 2009 Straw produced an outline of what such a bill might contain it looked more like a modest statement of aspirations rather than a programme for action. There were to be no new rights enforceable through the courts. An emphasis on responsibilities seemed simply to be a way of urging the people of the United Kingdom to be better, more community-minded people. For example, they would be reminded of their duty to vote but would not be put under any legal obligation to do so.

It seemed to lack ambition, another illustration of the fact that the debate over a British bill of rights tends to get subverted by the persistent political imperative of make populist gestures and put a sticking plaster on an immediate problem rather than considering what kind of country we would like to live in and how we might create it. If it's impossible to reform or even regulate something as manifestly ridiculous as the House of Lords, the prospect of achieving something as serious and principled as a bill of rights backed by law seems unattainable.

Nevertheless the need to consider such questions is perhaps more urgent than ever. Under Tony Blair there was more significant reconstruction of relationships between the countries of the United Kingdom than there had been for centuries. Taken with the fundamental change involved in membership of the European Union it's no exaggeration to describe the last thirty years of the twentieth century as having brought about a constitutional revolution in the United Kingdom. It was the biggest upheaval since the acts of the late seventeenth and early eighteenth centuries, including the union with Scotland, that were to establish the essential character of the country for the following three centuries.

Blair's intervention in this way didn't really settle anything definitively – except, possibly, in Ireland – but rather created a series of new problems that have yet to be resolved. Perhaps you've got to live within the new system, in Scotland or Wales, to appreciate the extent of what's happened. A serious measure of national self-determination within these countries has ceased to be the weekend hobby of political treasure hunters but an established fact of everyday life. The voters there have discovered they need no longer look to Westminster for answers to many of their everyday problems. The power is now held much nearer home. They may not even like it very much, but they can't avoid the reality of it. The nature of the United Kingdom, and with it the idea of Britishness, has been irrevocably altered.

Nor has the journey come to an end. Before the autumn of 2008, plenty of rational and well-informed people, both in Scotland and outside it, believed that country would become independent in the foreseeable future. That project took a battering from the economic hurricane but it would be foolish to insist that it could now never happen. Those old enough to remember the time when Labour came to power in 1964 will have lost track of the number of economic crises they've lived through since then and which were all more or less forgotten until the next one turned up. In any case, what happens in Scotland might depend as much as anything on what happens in England, in particular the character of a government returned by English votes. Permanent political warfare between the SNP in Edinburgh and a Conservative administration in Westminster could have a decisive effect on the state of Scottish public opinion.

What happens in Scotland will in its turn colour political attitudes in Wales, even if it seems unlikely that the country will ever become an independent state. It's not simply that the economic realities are firmly against it, but also that it's impossible to detect any substantial public appetite for such an outcome. Nevertheless, in due course government in Wales seems certain to take on greater powers, including the capacity to legislate in devolved areas, very much on the Scottish model established in 1999. That change can be triggered by a referendum already provided for in the system and in the end, even if at a later date than its more enthusiastic supporters would wish, it will probably prove irresistible. Particularly, once again, if there is a Conservative government in London.

The dangers of predicting the path of constitutional progress are demonstrated all too clearly by the example of Northern Ireland. The intransigence of both sides, their inability to shake off the grip of history, for a long time suggested that there might be no end to the bombing and the shooting. But the world changed, in particular the Republic of Ireland changed, even Ian Paisley changed, and agreement, however fragile, was reached between antagonists who had previously seemed entirely irreconcilable. For the time being at least the war has become chiefly one of words, exchanged in a parliament in which the two sides have been put into a constitutional yoke, neither able to achieve anything without the agreement of the other

The recent experience of these three devolved countries suggests it would be foolish and presumptuous to attempt to forecast the future pattern of events, particularly in Northern Ireland where history and experience aren't all that reassuring on question of whether violence might again overwhelm politics. In any case the British population might not yet have entirely come to terms with the fact that so many decisions about the United Kingdom aren't actually United Kingdom decisions at all. They are taken in Brussels or through the global machinery of diplomacy and negotiation. To judge from what has happened so far it seems at least likely that the constituent parts of Britain will be increasingly inclined to seek to take responsibility for those elements of life over which it is possible to exert direct control. They can create their own countries in a form with which they are more at ease, in which political decisions are not always necessarily more congenial, but more easily understood, less remote and more readily influenced. It's a process that's inevitably being driven by the political classes; the next stage is to see how quickly the voters catch up and join in.

The first ten years of the devolved administrations persuaded quite a lot of people to modify their attitudes towards the principles involved. Some of them are active politicians, like many of the Conservatives in Wales, who briskly grasped the futility of pretending that devolution hadn't happened or that it could somehow be put back in its box. More unexpected was the conversion of Leo Abse, a brilliant parliamentarian and one of the great social reformers of the last decades of the twentieth century. From the backbenches of the House of Commons, he conducted a dazzling one man assault on what he saw as prejudice and intolerance. Through a combination of force of personality, technical and legal skill and tireless persistence, he was instrumental in changing many of the laws he believed contributed to the unhappiness of large numbers of people. Divorce, adoption and family planning were among them. I have never known anyone with quite such unshakeable certainty about his own causes and his own opinions. He was perhaps the last man you would expect to change his mind about anything.

During the devolution debates of the 1970s he was one of the most formidable opponents of the government's plans. He used his expert knowledge of parliamentary procedure and his arresting powers as a debater to ambush the scheme wherever he could. He was a fierce opponent of nationalists and their fellow travellers, and a shrewd judge of the argument that would reverberate among the people in the street. His image of any number of politicians climbing aboard a devolution gravy train was unquestionably influential in a country like Wales where local government corruption had long been a national sport.

Almost thirty years after those debates I went to see him at his home in Chiswick. He was a few months away from the end of his life, but he was astonishingly vigorous for a man of ninety. In an interview that lasted many hours the fact that he was now completely deaf in no way interfered with his compelling account of his life. Nor had he lost his capacity to spring a surprise. Devolution, he told me, hadn't turned out to be quite as bad as he thought it might.

Since it was Leo, though, this change of heart wasn't as straightforward as you might have imagined. It wasn't so much that he'd been converted to the cause of devolution but that it served in a small way as a useful antidote to New Labour, a creation he felt had wrecked the party he had served for so long. He was particularly caustic about Tony Blair. "The first time I met that boy," he said, "I rumbled him." And so we got to the practical point. In those circumstances, he explained, a Welsh assembly could act as a check "against the delusions of metropolitan London".

That Leo Abse of all people should have come to that conclusion revealed the extent of the change that had swept over Britain in a matter of only a decade or so. Other people are also revising their views of devolution in the light of the present British experience. Politicians in particular have to adapt to the environment in which they find themselves, rather than worry about how they got there in the first place. New frameworks have been created in Scotland, Wales and Northern Ireland and they're not going to be dismantled. In these circumstances England, or the regions of England, may join in. What is clear is that Britishness, being British, is something that in only a dozen years or so been radically reconstructed. It isn't going to stop there. The builders are still at work.

Was Enoch Right?

IT'S HARDLY SURPRISING that when he was looking for sources to use in his exploration of Britishness Gordon Brown was urged to turn to George Orwell. Orwell exemplified many of the qualities Brown believed characterised the British people, in particular in his passion for liberty and tolerance and, in the words of his biographer Bernard Crick, the duty of speaking out boldly. Crick describes the themes that ran through Orwell's work; among them his enthusiasm for plain language, plain speaking, the good in the past, decency, fraternity, individuality, liberty, egalitarianism.

There was also patriotism of a clear-sighted kind. Crick writes: "He was almost alone among Left-wing intellectuals in stressing the naturalness and positive virtues of loving, not exclusively, but none the less intensely and unashamedly, one's native land." Orwell was, Crick says, a revolutionary patriot, a man who when he died was described as "the wintry conscience of a generation". Above all there was his refusal to be silenced, most famously as a tireless and incisive critic of totalitarianism, something that made him plenty of enemies among other left wing intellectuals. He himself wrote: "If liberty means anything at all it means the right to tell people things they do not want to hear."

For such reasons Orwell, long after his death in 1949, remains a hero and an example to many people in the modern Labour party. They admire what he said and his courage in saying it. He can now safely be held to represent the best of what it is to be British. But many of those virtues described by Bernard Crick, patriotism, a refusal to be silenced, for example, can be called into service of other causes which give a very different picture of Britishness. Orwell is one outstanding political symbol of his country, but to other people, so is another controversial figure whose passionate arguments still reverberate through Britain long after his death: Enoch Powell.

Powell began a debate about nationality and identity that still isn't over. A speech he made more than forty years ago remains a matter of fierce dispute. He was a Cabinet Minister for only fifteen months, but generations after he last held office he is vividly remembered when most of his political contemporaries have long entered oblivion. Even ten years after his death it was possible for a member of the Conservative Party to get the sack as a parliamentary candidate because he used the inflammatory phrase: "Enoch was right". Powell himself never had any doubt about that. He was a man whose extraordinary certainty and firmness of purpose could leave you breathless.

One winter Saturday afternoon, for example, I heard him speak to a group of elderly Conservative farmers and their wives, taking as his subject the money supply and even less accessible aspects of economic policy. It didn't apparently occur to him to make any concessions to his listeners' idea of what might make an interesting day out. The best known Midlands accent in Britain just flowed on, gripped by a passion no one else in the room could share, defying anyone to look away or drop off, even for a moment. A man who can believe like that, it was easy to think, must know something concealed from the rest of us. Someone so indifferent both to public opinion and the conventional demands of his own party carried a moral authority denied to practically everyone else in the political trade. With his staring eyes, his authoritarian Brigadier's moustache and his clipped, intense manner of speaking, in the years of his greatest fame he was to many people a kind of comic book madman. To others he was a visionary, a man whose brilliance of intellect allowed him to understand and describe the world with almost supernatural clarity. Whether he really was right or not was, as always, another matter.

At the core of Powell's self-belief was what David Marquand describes as his faith in the "unshakeable sovereignty of England", a thread of Englishness carried from medieval times. It was summed up in a few phrases in a speech he made in the summer of 1969: "We have an identity of our own, as we have a territory of our own... the instinct to preserve that identity, as to defend that territory, is one of the strongest influences planted in mankind."

There was an unshakeable passion about his devotion to the story of England. When I heard him speak about Europe at a Conservative conference in the seventies, he seemed to be physically seized by emotion. As another observer pointed out, you might not remember what he said but you couldn't easily forget the way he said it. In fact his concern wasn't exclusively about England although he seemed very English. Powell was proud of his Welsh ancestry, but Wales was also subject to the institution which to him embodied nationhood, the sovereign parliament at Westminster. We were all in it together.

In these circumstances it was almost inevitable that the matter of Europe led to his final break with the Conservative Party after a turbulent period during which his relationship with his leader, Ted Heath, resembled a crumbling marriage. The split became irrevocable when he intervened in the first general election of 1974 with a stroke of theatrical brilliance. He declined to fight his Wolverhampton seat that time and instead effectively urged people to vote Labour. That way we might get a referendum on Britain's membership of the Common Market, he said. Well, enough people did vote Labour and we did have a referendum and nothing changed because by that stage most of the population didn't see the world in the way he did. But it was one of the great themes of Powell's life: he did what he thought was his duty, whatever the personal cost.

On Europe his view was at least in the political mainstream even if he didn't reflect majority opinion as revealed by the referendum. Later, in another centrally British cause, he was to be substantially more idiosyncratic, even if not totally isolated. In the second election of 1974 he returned to parliament, but this time as the Ulster Unionist member for Down South. It had some logic to it. Powell and his new colleagues could at least agree on the central importance of Britishness and the need to maintain its traditional character. However, he managed to out-British even most of the unionists with his answer to the problem of Northern Ireland: an end to devolution and complete integration within the United Kingdom. This, he said, was the way to stop the IRA. It's difficult to think of anything more inflammatory in the circumstances and it perhaps illustrated how accurate his old colleague Iain Macleod had been when he said: "Poor Enoch! Driven mad by the remorselessness of his own logic."

Today Powell isn't remembered for his stand on the European issue, something that cost him a place anywhere near the official centre of British politics. Nor would many people be able to recall his big idea for Northern Ireland which, however rational he might have considered it to be, was viewed by most of the rest of the world as little short of demented. What both issues underline, though, are his obsessive zeal for the particular character of Britishness and his unshakeable conviction that there was an obligation on a politician to speak out about what he believed to be true. When inconvenient, difficult, matters arose and people thought silence might be the best course of action, he replied: "I simply do not have the right to shrug my shoulders and think about something else." That was the principle he laid out in the most famous speech he ever made, one of the most sensational public pronouncements of post-war British politics.

On April 20, 1968, at the Midland Hotel, Birmingham, Powell made the speech that was to wreck his ambitions as a Tory politician, but which at the same time made him immensely famous, someone who remained at the centre of a furious controversy even after he died thirty years later, at the age of 85. His subject was immigration and his message was that some areas of Britain, like the Midlands, were undergoing "the total transformation to which there is no parallel in a thousand years of British history". The inevitable result, he argued, would be social conflict and, ultimately, violence. The remedy, urgently needed, was twofold: stopping, or virtually stopping, further immigration and promoting what he called re-emigration, something otherwise known as voluntary repatriation.

He'd spoken in these terms previously, but there were two particular aspects of this speech that captured public attention and made it the focus of argument down to the present day. More than forty years later it can be seen as a case against what has become the fashionable cause of multiculturalism. Powell said that there were simply too many immigrants in the country to allow them to integrate with the rest of British society. Their numbers and physical concentration, he said, meant the pressures towards integration which normally bear upon any small minority did not operate.

"Now we are seeing the growth of positive forces acting against integration, of vested interests in the preservation and sharpening of racial and religious differences, with a view to the exercise of actual domination, first over fellow-immigrants and then over the rest of the population."

Which brought him to one of the most remarkable oratorical moments of the twentieth century, remarkable because it was as far from a rabble-rousing peroration as you can imagine. Its force came from the sense of measured seriousness it carried, along with the reminder of the weight of intellect carried by Powell the great classicist. "As I look ahead," he told his audience, "I am filled with foreboding. Like the Roman, I seem to see 'the River Tiber foaming with much blood'."

It was a particularly chilling warning because it rose above the everyday language of a world in which even the rudiments of a classical education were giving way to more utilitarian studies. By that time not many young people would have had the vaguest idea of who Powell's Roman, the poet Virgil, was. His cultural alienation from most of his audience, his refusal to talk down to them, his self-appointed role as a seer, gave his words particular force. The next day Edward Heath sacked him from the shadow cabinet but in the weeks that followed he received thousands of letters agreeing with him. London dockers and porters from the Smithfield meat market marched on the House of Commons in support.

After that speech an unquenchable argument arose: was Enoch a racist? He denied being so, insisting that he talked about immigration and never about race. That was a rather other-worldly view to take. Powell the thinker divorced himself from Powell the politician. Immigration and race were inextricably linked in the minds of his audience around the country who would not make the linguistic distinctions he employed. As a shrewd and tireless operator in the media world he must have known that people infinitely less subtle than him would use his words to prosecute a cause he publicly disavowed.

There was another aspect of the speech that shocked the country. That was Powell's use of a letter about the plight of an elderly woman living in his own Wolverhampton constituency. In eight years, his correspondent said, every other house in the street in which the woman lived had been bought by immigrants. Her life had been wrecked by noise and harassment.

"She is becoming afraid to go out. Windows are broken. She finds excreta pushed through her letter-box. When she goes to the shops, she is followed by children, charming, wide-grinning piccaninnies. They cannot speak English but one word they know. 'Racialist', they chant."

Many people found something odd about this letter. The language had an unexpected element to it – the word piccaninnies seemed rather jarring in an old-fashioned way; the idea that small children who spoke no other English would shout out a word as formal as 'racialist'. Analysis of this kind, and the way in which the letter fitted so perfectly into Powell's argument, led to suggestions that it was a piece of fiction. Perhaps, one theory was, he had been the victim of a hoax. Powell himself refused to give the identity of the woman because to do so, he said, would be a breach of the important bond of confidence between an MP and his constituents. In his essay in the *Dictionary of National Biography*, Simon Heffer records that, although Powell was meticulous about documents, no trace of the letter was found in his papers after his death, something that raised further doubts.

It wasn't until much later that an investigation by BBC journalists came up with evidence that suggested very strongly that Powell's widow was indeed genuine. Mrs. Drucilla Cotterill was the only white resident in Brighton Place, Wolverhampton, and people interviewed by the *Document* programme on Radio 4 confirmed much of what had been contained in the letter, including incidents in which excrement had been pushed through her letter-box. Powell's much advertised scrupulous honesty was posthumously vindicated. Even so, there are other reasons for saying that Powell wasn't invariably as straightforward in all matters as his reputation and his own defence of it would suggest.

The intellectual Enoch had a great talent for languages. He became a professor of Greek at the age of 25 and later learnt a considerable number of others, including Russian, as well as some during his service in India. According to Simon Heffer he had also studied medieval Welsh, an accomplishment which was about as much use in twentieth-century Wales as Chaucerian English would have been in contemporary Southwark. Even so it had its place in serving his eagerness to put his case in any medium that would have him. A general belief grew up in Wales that he could actually speak modern Welsh and, as a result, during the nineteen-seventies he was occasionally invited to appear on *Heddiw*, the daily Welsh language current affairs programme run by BBC Wales.

The system ran like this. The interviewer would write down the questions he wanted to put and they would be sent off to Powell. Powell would write out his answers in English and send them back. A third party would translate the answers into Welsh and they would be put on to autocue. Powell would sit in the studio and answer the interviewer by reading the answers from the screen attached to the camera in front of him.

He gave a credible if not entirely convincing performance. He used words that were recognisably Welsh but which could not really be described as coming from a Welsh speaker. It was a bit like Ted Heath speaking French. I know because I once sat next to Powell in the studio as he delivered his lines with his familiar intense confidence. Who would dare tell him he was wrong, anyway? Thus was established another tiny addition to the legend of his big brain. You know, awed bystanders would say, Enoch can even speak Welsh.

It was something you often find in politics. It wasn't a lie but it wasn't exactly the truth either. It added, as if it were needed, just a bit more to the messianic character of Powell's public persona. His relentless drive, his utter certainty sat uneasily among the doubts and compromises that keep the political wheels turning. His use of any opportunity, however obscure, to pursue his argument seemed unbalanced. It was not, frankly, very British.

At the same time, however controversial his views, Powell could certainly claim a better grasp of principle than Labour and Conservative governments of his time. Indeed, the Labour government that was in power in 1968 had some reason to be grateful for what became known as the 'Rivers of Blood' speech because it diluted criticism of its own efforts to keep particular immigrants out of Britain. In that year the Kenyan government began making changes that threatened the status of 200,000 Asians in the country. But those people were the holders of British passports and so, if they were driven out of Kenya, they had the right to settle in the UK instead. This state of affairs unnerved the British government and James Callaghan, the Foreign Secretary, introduced a Commonwealth Immigrants Bill abolishing the freedom of entry of those passport holders. It was met with severe disapproval in some sections of the Labour Party and among some traditionalist Conservatives who were shocked at this cynical breach of the promises implied by the possession of a British passport. Two weeks later, though, Powell made his Birmingham speech. His views, portrayed as extreme, somehow made the government's intervention seem less offensive.

Four years later, in 1972, another problem arose in East Africa. Idi Amin began expelling the Asian population, including 27,000 British passport holders, from Uganda. The UK government, led by Ted Heath, was obliged to allow them into the country, but not before making strenuous efforts to keep them out. Heath even contemplated the idea that emergency legislation might have to be introduced to deprive them of their British nationality. Then the government toyed with a scheme that would have sent the refugees to a remote island territory where they could wait until being allowed gradually into Britain under some kind of voucher system. Only the Falklands expressed any interest and the plan was abandoned.

As usual, Powell was clear about the proper way to proceed. The government was under no legal obligation to let the Uganda Asians in, he said, and should not do so. He was ingenious in the way in which he obtained the most prominent platform from which to oppose his own party on the matter. A motion opposing the entry of the refugees was put down for debate at the Conservative conference in October. It came from a constituency association – Hackney and Shoreditch – and in the normal course of events some obscure office holder from the constituency would have gone to the rostrum to propose it. Suddenly it was revealed that the Hackney and Shoreditch association had an honorary president. His name was Enoch Powell and he'd be opening the debate.

In those days the Conservative Party conference made plenty of room for the convivial side of politics and the afternoon session didn't begin until half past two. On the day of the Uganda debate, however, lunches were curtailed and the Winter Gardens in Blackpool was packed long before the debate was due to begin. In decades of attending political conferences I never knew such feverish anticipation over a single speech. In the end even Powell couldn't live up to the expectation, not least because he made his audience intensely aware of the ambiguities that tormented them. A majority of them might have agreed with him on the principle of immigration, but at the same time many of them would not have wanted to have been publicly identified with such an uncompromising position. They admired Powell but owed loyalty to the party and its leader, a course they did not invariably follow over sensitive matters. In those circumstances the leadership won the vote, but at the same time Powell could not be said to have lost the internal argument. He had an unerring instinct for the traditional accommodations of politics, the finessing of opinions, the small dishonesties employed in search of one deal or another, and he wrecked his career by refusing to have anything to do with them. Who could feel anything but uncomfortable in presence of such rectitude? And who could fail to identify his great weakness: the moral superiority he clearly felt as a consequence?

Today many of the arguments he put forward in Birmingham in 1968 are out of date. Immigration remains an issue, although a much more diverse one than he described. Who would have imagined, in 1968, that Poles and Romanians would be considered a threat to British identity and prosperity, thanks to Powell's other menacing shadow, the European Union? Voluntary repatriation, probably always a chimera, has become a meaningless idea as succeeding generations have become British-born. That among them are numbered some home-grown groups of Islamic fundamentalists may be disturbing because of the extent of the havoc they can inflict. But then, the country has over the years contained plenty of seriously anti-British elements, from Communist spies to Irish terrorists. The tribal wars of the white people of Northern Ireland have been much more lethal than the difficulties caused by immigration from the Commonwealth. Racial discrimination persists from the golf clubs that continue to find methods of excluding Jewish members to a constitutional bar on Catholics that remains in force.

The phenomenon of alienation within Britain is nothing new. It perhaps applies in particular to the poor of all races. There has been violence in some cities. There are problems of integration. What the solutions might be is not clear. Politicians talk a lot about multiculturalism although it's sometimes difficult to pin down what they mean. Are they suggesting a society with mutual respect for any number of independent cultures and traditions, or one with an agreement on the umbrella of secular society with a common structure of law and language within which everyone can shape their own lives? Both, perhaps.

It would be absurd to pretend that there are no serious racial issues in Britain today even if they are whipped up by some newspapers and the British National Party. They follow Enoch Powell in their grim forecasts of national oblivion and say that, even if the details of the problems change, his analysis still stands. One day he'll be proved right. National identity, the very existence of the nation, will be swept away, just as he forecast.

Yet to be British as Enoch Powell was British was almost a psychiatric condition, a delusion about the state of a world in which outcomes aren't invariably, or even usually, determined by logic. He never wavered. His apocalyptic visions continued almost to the end of his long life. Looking at inner city disturbances in 1985 he pronounced on the future of the country: "It will be a Britain unimaginably wracked by dissension and violent disorder, not recognisable as the nation it has been, or perhaps a nation at all."

Yet a quarter of a century on and Britain remains recognisably what it was then and what it was fifteen years before that, when Powell was making the most famous speech of his life at the Midland Hotel, Birmingham. The Tiber has not yet foamed with much blood.

Enoch was about as British as you can get and Enoch was wrong.

Bibliography

Bower, Tom: *Fayed: The Unauthorised Biography* (Macmillan 1998)

Burt, John: *The Harder Path* (Macmillan 1998)

Campbell, Alistair: *The Blair Years* (Hutchinson 2007)

Cannadine, David: *Making History Now and Then: Discoveries, Controversies and Explorations* (Palgrave Macmillan 2008)

Colley, Linda: *Britons* (Yale University Press 2008)

Crick, Bernard: *George Orwell, A Life* (Secker & Warburg 1980)

Davies, Norman: *The Isles* (Macmillan 1999)

Foster, R.F: *Luck and the Irish* (Allen Lane 2007)

Greenslade, Roy: *Press Gang* (Macmillan 2003)

Hain, Peter: *Changing Wales: Changing Welsh Labour* (Progress 2008)

Hazell, Robert (editor): *The English Question* (Manchester University Press 2006)

Heffer, Simon: *Like the Roman: The Life of Enoch Powell* (Weidenfeld & Nicolson 1998)

Hendy, David: *Life on Air: A History of Radio Four* (OUP 2007)

Hitchens, Peter: *The Abolition of Britain* (Quartet Books 1999)

King, Anthony: *The British Constitution* (OUP 2007)

Lee, J.J: *Ireland 1912-1985* (Cambridge University Press 1989)

Marquand, David: *Britain Since 1918* (Weidenfeld & Nicolson 2008)

Marr, Andrew: *The Day Britain Died* (Profile Books 2000)

Marr, Andrew: *A History of Modern Britain* (Macmillan 2007)

Mount, Ferdinand: *Cold Cream* (Bloomsbury 2008)

Mount, Ferdinand: *Mind the Gap* (Short Books 2004)

Murkens, Jo Eric, with Peter Jones and Michael Keating: *Scottish Independence: A Practical Guide* (Edinburgh University Press 2007)

Oborne, Peter: *The Triumph of the Political Class* (Simon & Schuster 2007)

Redwood, John: *The Death of Britain?* (Macmillan 1999)

Sampson, Anthony: *Who Runs This Place?* (John Murray 2004)

Wilson, A.N: *Our Times* (Hutchinson 2008)

Index

The Author

Patrick Hannan's career as a writer, journalist and broadcaster includes periods as a newspaper reporter, an industrial correspondent, 13 years as the BBC's Welsh political correspondent, a television producer and a radio presenter. He has been a regular contributor to Radio 4 for well over twenty years and since 1998 has been half the Welsh team on the *Round Britain Quiz*. He has also been a newspaper columnist and has contributed to a wide variety of UK newspapers and magazines.

His other books published by Seren are *The Welsh Illusion, Wales Off Message, 2001 A Year In Wales*, and *When Arthur Met Maggie*.